First published in 1989 by William Collins Pty Ltd

Published in 2013 by Craig Johnston & Neil Jameson
Copyright ^c Craig Johnston & Neil Jameson 2013

ISBN 978-0-646-90548-8

Revised layout by Chris Totterman

Printed and bound in Australia by Lightning Source

WALK ALONE

IN MEMORY OF THE VICTIMS
OF HEYSEL AND HILLSBOROUGH

CONTENTS

HOME WITH **THE CUP**

CHAPTER 1

S aturday, 10 May 1986, 8.47 p.m. The elevator slumped to an unscheduled halt. A glowing fault light stated the obvious. We were stuck between floors. Downstairs, the champagne was on ice and a party awaited. The celebration was primed to uncork, but two of Liverpool's party boys were going nowhere.

Just four hours earlier we'd been parading the FA Cup around Wembley Stadium. Swept along by our supporters' rapturous acclaim, Liverpool had luxuriated in the honour of being only the third team in the past century to win the League Championship and FA Cup Double. Think about it. That meant being one of a mere thirty-six footballers in almost one hundred years to touch this peak.

From the trophy presentation and the victory circuit it was on into the dressing room media crush and an onslaught of interviews. There was more back-slapping in the champagne shower under the sponsor's marquee. Then we'd roller-coastered into the heart of London where we were to celebrate over an official dinner before painting the West End red.

In the four crowded hours since the ref had blown full time on a gloriously tension-charged season, it had been impossible to grab a minute's peace in which to reflect on events. But now a malfunctioning elevator had provided an unexpected refuge amid the madness, at least for two of us. How did I feel? Ecstatic? Sort of, but more a satisfying sense of relief — relief that the job was done.

I imagined the scene downstairs. Centrepiece of the sumptuous spread in the hotel dining area would be the object of the afternoon's contest — the Football Association Cup, its handles tied with red and white ribbons, the prized piece of silverware afire in the reflected orange glow of the candlelit table settings. The Cup's presence and the colour of the ribbons would say it all: 'We've won it!'

My mind ran over the events of the previous ten months. A decade after making my way from Australia to chase a professional contract in England, 1985–86 had looked like the vintage season, the year when all the elements would coincide to yield something special. I had not been disappointed.

Of the thousands of players employed in English football, few of even the most deserving pros ever get within cooee of the silverware. Nestling in my jacket pocket were League Championship and FA Cup medals - the magical Double. Unlike those other pros, I had two things on my side: luck and Liverpool. One was about being in the right place at the right time, the other was about being in first place just about every time. Yet, for all our trophy-winning ways, until today Liverpool had never won the Double. This was history and the stuff of which dreams are made. No footballer could want for more.

Yet, on top of all this, I'd been more blessed than most — *I'd scored in the Cup Final!* As an Aussie kid I'd fantasised long and hard about such a day, being romantic enough to believe it would all happen. If your dream is powerful and you chase it hard enough, it can come true . . .

I was roused from my reverie by Kenny Dalglish, who seemed almost to be thinking aloud.

'What was that, Boss?' I said to the Liverpool player-manager.

'Enjoy it, son.' My fellow detainee, hands in pockets, was staring absently at the far wall, but he might well have been reading my mind. 'This is as good as it gets.'

Coming from a man who had won just about everything football rates as important, the advice was one of those gems you shouldn't discount, but privately, I thought this day wad just the start of my real career. I'd played in a history-making match and made a contribution to the outcome. This was the realisation of not just a football dream, but virtually everything I'd aspired to in life. No matter what happened from here on, nobody could ever take this away from me. Whenever you reach the top of that personal mountain you must pause to enjoy the view. It is a different place, a warm plateau of intense satisfaction. Nothing can beat that sensation.

Surely, if I died now in this elevator I'd go a happy man.

So this is success? This is what it is all about? I mentally sampled it as you might a vintage champagne. It tasted pretty good.

It was the second time that day I'd had cause to appreciate Dalglish's advice. I thought about the first, uttered amid the intensity of the afternoon's all-Merseyside Cup Final against our great rivals Everton.

'Don't blow it now, son,' he'd said. 'You've worked too hard to let it slip away in just one game!'

Only those closest to the Liverpool dressing room could have known what it meant to Kenny to win that elusive Cup-winners' medal in what would be his first year as a manager and his last full season as a player. I felt I wasn't helping the cause. To the 100 000 fans at Wembley it might have looked like Craig Johnston was out there, but my mind was in another place. The atmosphere and the pressure of the Wembley build-up had got to me. The rough-nut Aussie who supposedly held the game's lore and traditions in little regard had fallen under the Wembley spell. His mind had gone walkabout.

I can recall, before the match, standing in the gloom of the players' tunnel. I was thinking of two things only: the glory of the dream come true, and the agony and humiliation of defeat. What if? An official gestured and the line in front of me started towards the light and the din. I felt like somebody taking a first ride on a rollercoaster. 'It's too late now, we're bolted in for the ride.' A team-mate's hand in my back prodded me forward. *'This is it!'*

I had long suffered from pre-match nerves but had developed psychological ploys to use them to my advantage. The ploys didn't work this time. Of all the hundreds of football matches I'd played, this was far and away the most monumental. The occasion was simply too big.

This was no ordinary match nor was it an ordinary Cup Final. This one was the scriptwriter's dream - the unprecedented clash between the two teams representing the city of Liverpool - a showdown between football's greatest rivals and the two most powerful club sides in the land. In the sudden-death nature of the FA Cup format, the chance of a final featuring Merseyside's mighty football institutions almost defied the laws of probability.

When the British Empire was at the height of its power, Liverpool had been one of the nation's great ports, receiving the wealth of the world at its door. Although the Empire was long gone, the famous pride of economically depressed Merseyside was still intact. Football was now the city's finest commodity. Those of us who traded in this most universal of products were considered the best in the business. All season long these deadliest of rivals had staged a ding-dong battle for honours with the Reds emerging with the League Championship. The Cup Final was Everton's chance to get even.

In the week before the match the build-up had turned Liverpool into a nuclear reactor undergoing meltdown. It was a city about to boil over and it did just that on Cup Final eve, sending its soccer faithful streaming down the motorways towards London. Those without the cash hitched. With or without tickets they arrived by every conceivable means and from every outpost of the football empire. After the match I would meet one Scouser who left his desk job with an airline in Detroit, flew to London, paid a scalper a couple of hundred quid and joined the supporters standing on the terraces behind the goals. There was no way he was going to miss this one. Amid the desperate scramble for tickets, his story wasn't unusual. With a 10-pound ticket fetching 100 quid and a 35-pound seat selling for almost 500 quid, I was relieved to know that four of my match tickets had been well allocated. Safely seated in the stand with the players' families were my Liverpool next-door neighbour Colin Bridge, two of my best mates, Neil Jameson and Chris Watson, both journalists from the *Newcastle Herald* in Australia, and my young cousin Margo Levinspiel, who was over on holiday. Absent was my wife Jenny who had just given birth to our second child.

Throngs of fans, unable to secure tickets, also made the pilgrimage, wanting to be near the scene of the action. In cheerful legions of red and blue they deployed themselves around the stadium, giving it the appearance of a fortress under siege. One ticketless Scouser, dressed as a nun, got through the first three security stages before a sharp-eyed gatekeeper spotted a beard under the habit. Another desperate fan seriously injured himself attempting to scale the outer wall of the Wembley compound.

The opening ceremony was a blur. A friend who watched the game from the stand told me later that I'd looked dazed when I'd entered the stadium and that, instead of strolling along in line, I'd marched numbly like a clockwork doll to the beat of the combined bands of the Grenadier, Coldstream, Scots and Irish Guards. Along with the others, I was formally introduced to the Duchess of Kent, but I have no recollection of the event. I knew that a world-wide audience of 500 million was watching us, and that among those glued to their television screens would be my family and mates back home in Australia. The thought of letting anybody down almost paralysed me with pure dread.

At last it began. Before long Everton were trampling all over Liverpool's reputation. They made us look like a bunch of schoolboys. They were doing a Liverpool on us! They won the crucial tackles, they had more options when in possession, they closed us down and put in the crunching tackles. Psychologically, we were well and truly rattled, knocked out of our stride. Where was our famous elegance? Where was our famous composure? Above all else, where was our famous commitment?

Our first half effort was a shambles. Piecing it together much later, I could see what had happened. Everton had worn our early barrage, then thrown on a defensive grid-lock that denied us space and made it difficult to play the ball out of our own half. Meanwhile, they were dictating the attacking terms and possibly deserved a penalty in the twentieth minute. Gary Stevens overlapped down the right flank and looped in a cross for Graeme Sharp. Steve Nichol had just one chance to clear the ball, but did he foul Sharp in the process? Everton, thought so, the referee didn't.

They were. outplaying us so comprehensively that their reward was bound to arrive. It did, in the twenty-eighth minute via the telepathy of Peter Reid and Gary Lineker. Reid's radar picked out the channel for a perfect through-ball that put the gazelle-like Lineker clear of the defence with, only our keeper, Bruce Grobbelaar, to beat. My acrobatic roommate parried the left-foot attempt but the Blues' scoring machine latched onto the loose ball and smacked it into the back of the net. 1–0.

What I had thought would be a dream day had turned into a nightmare. Playing wide on the right, I was doing a hell of a lot of running for no return, ploughing back and forth between defence and attack without receiving the ball or being involved in play. Players feed on possession, If you do nothing but run without actually playing, your energy and confidence are quickly sapped. One look at the scoreboard confirmed that, yes, this was Wembley, Everton were all over us, and, indeed, the score was 1–0. How could the script have gone so disastrously wrong? Why today? Why Everton? My mind was gone. I was in never-never land.

Dalglish read my thoughts. Running past me to take up a defensive position, he had enough presence of mind to recognise a case of Wembley walkabout when he saw it.

'Don't blow it now, son,' he snapped. 'You've worked too hard to let it slip away in just one game.'

His words jolted me. Too bloody right I'd worked hard! And I knew that even harder work was the only way out of this nightmare.

Half-time and the refuge of the dressing room could not have come quickly enough for us. It was a dejected mob that slumped down, backs to the wall. It was a warm spring day outside so the first thing we did was gulp down gallons of cool water and change into fresh playing strip. Coach Ronnie Moran instructed us to calm down while he slowly and deliberately stated the facts. We were not playing like Liverpool Football Club, he said. Dalglish took up the thread and reiterated what he'd said to me earlier: 'You've all worked too hard to let it go in one game.' Both Moran and Dalglish reminded us of how good we really were rather than the fact that

Jumping for joy -- FA Cup Final, 1986

we were being outplayed. After addressing us collectively, the Boss spoke to certain players individually, as did Moran, offering the objective and higher experienced voice of someone from the sideline. When Dalglish reached me, the nightmare was still unfolding in my head. I was a schoolboy again in the middle of his final exam. All the hours of study, preparation and good reports meant nothing. This was the acid test and I was failing. Dalglish took one look at my face and then rammed home the point again. 'You've worked too hard to blow it now!' This time it sunk in.

Now my mind was totally focused on what had to be done. This time when I walked up that long corridor towards the light, there were no nerves, no crowds, no distractions — just one clear thought: 'Nothing but hard work.'

Everton's half-time strategy was simple: do what they did to us in the first half. And it worked. Our fans might have been excused for thinking that instead of pulling up our socks at half-time, we had tied our bootlaces together. Players of quality who had barely put a foot wrong all season were committing the most elementary mistakes. Nobody could believe their eyes when our frustration led to Bruce and full-back Jim Beglin almost having a stand-up stoush in our penalty area. This couldn't be Liverpool! Where was the discipline, the sense of tradition, the mistake-proof professionalism? You could guess what everybody, from the hard-bitten types in the media box to the ball boys, was saying: 'They're gone!' I glanced at the bench. Ronnie Moran had his head in his hands.

But the Reds are never gone. It was football caller John Motson who, on seeing the opposition score during a previous trophy decider, had remarked: 'Liverpool — never more dangerous than when they're behind.' On this day his words were to prove more accurate than ever. Twelve minutes into the second half Gary Stevens made a basic error due to what I feel was Everton's over-confidence. He attempted to play a ball out of the right back position only to see Ronnie Whelan intercept the pass. It was immediately relayed to Molby who swept it onto Rush and the genius striker rounded the goalkeeper to score. Quick and clinical, the Liverpool way. We were back in the match.

The media and Everton boss Howard Kendall later crucified Stevens for what they saw as a wayward pass. But having seen Ronnie Whelan pull off similar intercepts so many times before, I know who deserved credit. Ronnie had the uncanny knack of appearing to be out of the play and then, before the opposition can react, he'd nip into the space to claim possession. Ronnie Moran had taught us to walk away and look as though we weren't interested. I've seen it done a hundred times.

The sight of Liverpool celebrating another Ian Rush goal had a crushing effect on Everton. For the previous week every soccer critic had dissected Rushie's goalscoring genius and concluded with the awesome statistic that the Reds had never lost a game in which he had scored. It was an omen imprinted on the mind of everybody jammed into Wembley that day. We knew it and, more importantly, so did Everton.

Desperate to disprove the Rush prophecy, they raided our goalmouth only to see the power of the omen reinforced when Everton failed to knock home a gift chance. Under pressure from Lineker, our skipper Alan Hansen momentarily forgot his rating as one of the world's coolest defenders by ballooning his attempted back pass not into the grasp of the advancing Grobbelaar but straight into the path of the rampaging Graeme Sharp. Liverpool hearts leapt into mouths as the Everton striker arched his back and crashed his header goalwards. Committed to receiving the ball directly from Jockie Hansen, Bruce was stranded. But the player we called Jungle Man can perform more miracles than a witch doctor. He shot up and backwards to flick the ball over the bar. Everton could only look on in disbelief. Now it was Sharp's turn to bury his head in his hands.

Lubricated by Rush-inspired confidence, vital cogs in the big red machine clicked into gear. Molby, the great Dane, strode through the Everton defence like one of his forebears might have done in their pillage and plunder period. Shaking off a final tackle, he squirted his pass across the box where red shirts were arriving in force.

Let's just hit the pause button there. I was in one of those red shirts. I thought, this is me, back stick, without the blue shirt that has been shadowing me all afternoon. Hard work, sheer hard work alone had got me there. For the umpteenth time that day I'd busted my guts to support the attack. Bursting from a deep midfield position on the right I'd clapped on the pace, leaving my marker behind.

Hit the play button. Molby's pass somehow evaded a cluster of legs, clipped the Boss's heel and ran on right into my path.

Pause.

That's how it seemed to me. One frozen frame. There was nothing else - no noise, no movement. The ball sat up perfectly for me. It seemed the simplest thing in the world to sidefoot this lovely football into the back of the net. And that's what I did. 2–1.

Hit the play button again. The sound returned as the Kop erupted I was overcome with a feeling of sheer relief. I jumped into the arms of Rushie and Ronnie Whelan. As they would often remind me later, I was shouting, 'I've done it, I've done it!' That goal meant my personal nightmare was over. The job now was to protect the lead. Every time the ball went near our goals I inwardly screamed, 'Get it out of there!' I had visions of another Everton goal ruining our Double dreams and turning my mates' beers sour back home in Australia.

I shouldn't have panicked. For the rest of the match we looked and played like any of the great Liverpool sides, authoritatively stroking the ball around and raiding away at a disjointed Everton defence. The coup de grace was delivered with a classic Liverpool touch. Beglin won it at the back and the ball was relayed to Whelan, on to Johnston, forward to Rush and then to the super-confident Molby who prodded his pass through a defender's legs to seek out Whelan on the left. Ronnie dipped a short lob right into the path of Rushie who finished with the precision of a trained assassin. 3–1. The final whistle was the sweetest sound I'd ever heard.

Ten minutes later, draped in the scarves of ecstatic fans, we were making that magical trip up the Wembley stairs to receive the Cup and our medals. Standing there on the dais, looking towards that heaving sea of red where the Liverpool loyalists sang an umpteenth round of 'You'll never walk alone', we felt like kings of the universe.

I was to learn later that my effort was the one hundredth FA Cup Final goal scored since the war. The official computer forecast not only tipped the right scoreline but also that Rushie would get two and Johnston one. These were a few of the trivial statistics among our record-breaking achievements. From a personal viewpoint I would have swapped any of my medals to have played better at Wembley on the day. I've always been self-critical when it comes to evaluating my performance and I had desperately wanted to pull out my best for the Final. I felt I hadn't done myself justice.

In his match analysis, the *Guardian*'s David Lacey wrote: 'Then there was Johnston's selfless performance for ninety minutes during which he often became more of a wing-half than a forward. But he still managed to follow in Rush's first goal and was perfectly positioned to give Liverpool the lead. With Rush, Johnston was Liverpool's most consistent player.'

Thanks for the plug, David, but the fact is I didn't play well in the Cup Final. Yet there is one redeeming aspect of which I can be proud. Because I worked so hard and busted my guts to get there, I was in the right place at the right time to make an impact on the outcome. As for the goal, I thought about all the times I'd played well for no reward. That goal wasn't merely for the ninety minutes at Wembley; it was my return on every drop of sweat, every bruise and every sacrifice I'd made chasing that dream.

There were plenty of hangovers the next day but I wasn't among the sufferers. You don't need a drink when you're drunk on life itself. My first impulse in the dressing room after the match had been to call Mum and Dad.

Ee-aye-addio, we won the Cup!

I grabbed an ITV cameraman's phone and made the call from the bath. I asked Dad had he watched the game and before he could reply told him not to swear because he was on television. He swore anyway. Then I placed a call to Liverpool to talk to my wife Jenny in hospital.

As for that elevator, the Boss and I did finally escape to enjoy our fair share of the celebrations. But I chose not to overdo it.

It was just as well because the Cup Final turned out to be but one part of what would be the most hectic week of my life. The two teams flew home to Merseyside together and took part in a cavalcade through the streets of our city. More than half a million people turned out to welcome us home. After all, Liverpool and Everton had finished first and second in both the Cup and the League to establish Merseyside as custodian of all that was great about the game in the country of its origin. As the showcase and climax of the English season, the first all-Merseyside FA Cup Final had been a monument to good sportsmanship and quality football. The city of Liverpool had a right to be proud.

I still couldn't explain what had happened to me during that first half of the Cup Final but I'm sure part of my system failure had something to do with events in the Oxford Street Maternity Hospital where Jenny had given birth to our second baby, Cassie, on 1 May. Such had been the madness on Merseyside prior to the Final that it was decided that Jenny should be induced rather than run the risk of missing out on Wembley. As it was, postnatal complications kept her in hospital, meaning that she would certainly miss the Final. You can imagine the scramble for Jenny's ticket among the hospital staff once it became apparent she wasn't going to Wembley. We suggested it be raffled to raise cash for the maternity wing.

Jenny had made a habit of attending every home match and one of my pre-match preparations was to look up into the stand to where she sat. She had become a shrewd student of the game and I had grown to value her dispassionate summaries of my performances above those of journalists or mates. I had definitely missed her presence at Wembley.

Cassie's birth was not without complications. Jenny had been in labour for ten hours when the doctor made a decision to deliver by caesarean section. I'd been by her side for the arrival of our first baby and, as on that occasion, I fainted. So much for tough footballers. I came around in time to witness the birth and to hold our new baby in my arms. The event was not without its humour. The anaesthetist had shown his colours by slapping an Everton sticker on Cassie's crib.

Having been closeted in the team hotel near London for most of the week before the match, hospital visits had been restricted, so I jokingly asked the driver of our open-top bus if he would make a detour via the hospital. As it was, the cavalcade could barely make it into the city centre, such was the pressure of the crowds turning out for a glimpse of the teams and trophies. Just near our home, my next-door neighbour, who had been minding our elder daughter Chelsea, appeared at the side of the bus holding her above his head. She had a huge Everton rosette covering half of her body. They both had ear-to-ear grins.

We were headed for a civic reception but I decided to postpone my partying until after I had a chance to see Jenny and Cassie. I had no way of knowing then that events in store would preclude me from enjoying a proper victory celebration. It was an absolute relief and joy to hold and admire my new baby at the tender age of ten days and a few hours. While Jen admired the medals, I admired the baby.

Jenny and Cassie had to spend a few more days in hospital. I headed home. After the madness and pressure of the previous week it was a relief to put my head down in my own bed for a few hours.

The sound of the telephone jerked me awake early on the Monday morning. My Cup Final performance had gone down a storm in sports-mad Australia and there was somebody on the telephone wanting to know whether I was willing to fly Down Under and promote the Aussie leg of Bob Geldof's Sport Aid campaign. My immediate reaction was that this was some kind of joke. Liverpool has more practical jokers to the square mile

Nursing the Cup and then off to nurse Cassie Lee Johnston

than anywhere else in the world except Australia. Was someone having a lend of a rather tired and somewhat confused footballer?

But this was fair dinkum, I was assured. If I was interested, I should immediately contact Sport Aid's London office. Curious, I dialed the number and spoke to a young woman who turned out to be personal assistant to Bob Geldof, scruffy Irish rock singer and architect of the international Band Aid extravaganzas to feed famine racked Ethiopia. Here was a man I admired, a non-conformist unwilling to take no for an answer, prepared to kick over convention and bore it up the bureaucrats and politicians who lacked the nerve to get the job done. I'd watched the Live Aid event and had been profoundly touched by its humanitarian overtones. When I went to church the following Sunday, I'd waited for the priest to praise the modern day miracle that had moved the world. He didn't rate it worth a mention. I felt like shouting, 'What about Geldof?' Maybe I should have walked out.

I rang Sport Aid and told them I was packing.

Not even a post-match football dressing room scene could have been any more chaotic than that which confronted me on strolling into the central London bunker that passed as Sport Aid's headquarters. Office workers, who looked as though they would have been more at home backstage at a Boomtown Rats concert, were madly piecing together the scraps of information that would form yet another international effort on behalf of the world's starving. Telex machines clattered incessantly while the phone system threatened to blow a fuse under the weight of incoming international calls. Telexes littering desktops and a much-scrutinised wall map gave an indication of the size of the undertaking. Through the chaos weaved a Japanese news crew trailing cables and apologising frequently as they inevitably got in the way of Geldof's busy troops. Amid this apparent disorder sat Saint Bob himself. For a bloke who always looks tired, he looked tired. Yet, ever the energised performer, he handled the succession of questions and calls that streamed across his desk. Geldof had his finger perfectly on the pulse.

There was no show-biz hype. With Geldof, what you see is what you get. He was comfortably familiar, like someone you've known for a long time. There were no formal greetings. He was glad to see me and I was glad to help. We both knew I was there for one reason — as another potential missionary to beat the drum in far-off Australia. Get him motivated, point him in the right direction and hopefully the good folks Down Under would open their hearts and wallets.

As he explained it, the Sport Aid project was taking shape but as far as its promotional impetus was concerned, it had no profile down in Australia. My job was to kick the publicity machine into gear, get down there, make a noise and encourage Aussies to contribute as well as take part in a simultaneous, world-wide fun run.

Is that all? I gulped and pondered the magnitude of the assignment. Australia is a big place, definitely not the sort of country you whip around in a day or two, rattle the collection tin and think that will do the trick. If what Bob said was true, Australia had already missed the start. For us to create any impact in time for the world-wide run on 25 May, I would need some pretty impressive help.

'Why don't we get the Cup?'

It was just one of those top-of-the-head ideas that trip off the tongue before they've been thought through, yet the minute I said it I realised we were on to something. The Aussies had seen me before and they'd see me again. But the Cup ...

I looked at Geldof. A roll of the eyes and the way he pushed his hand through his mop of hair indicated what he thought of the idea. 'We'd never get the Cup,' he said. 'Forget it.'

'You're Bob Geldof,' I said incredulously. 'You can do anything!'

He drummed his upper teeth with his fingernails and looked sideways at me. He was interested.

I continued: 'You've got to get hold of the Cup. If I go out there on my own, I'll just be another Aussie sportsman returning home for a break. But if I arrive with the Cup . . .'

I offered to phone Liverpool immediately, which I did. The answer was polite but definite: 'No way. The Cup is booked for public appearances in Liverpool after which it will be under lock and key in the Anfield trophy cabinet.'

Geldof took the phone but he got no further. Liverpool were not parting with their trophy. Not even for a few days. It had been too hard to come by.

But we weren't beaten. If the front door approach wouldn't work, perhaps a dose of creative blackmail might do the trick. We called British Airways. Yes, they would be only too happy to supply two first class seats for me and a security man to nurse the Cup. The next call was to the Securicor company which not only agreed to supply a guard to and from Australia, but offered to lay on the security van to transport the Cup from Anfield to Heathrow. We then called Football Association secretary Ted Croker who said that the FA would be willing to oblige, but permission would have to come from Liverpool Football Club as custodian of the Cup.

With those arrangements in place, Geldof's redoubtable personal secretary then placed a call to Liverpool. I wasn't privy to the conversation but I can only suspect that more than a little healthy arm twisting was brought to bear. I imagined Liverpool were reminded that, in light of the thirty-nine lives lost as a result of our fans' part in the Heysel Stadium disaster twelve months before, the club might be keen to show a humanitarian face. After all, an airline, a security company and even the FA were willing to come to the party; would it not be churlish for Liverpool to decline the invitation?

Take the Cup, they said.

As I hurried out of the Sport Aid office, Geldof shouted at my back: 'By the way, what was it like?'

'What was what like?'

'Scoring in the Final.'

I threw him the thumbs-up sign.

There wasn't a minute to lose. If the trophy were to arrive in London in time for us to make the flight booked for Wednesday, everything would have to go without a hitch. At one stage of the drama I found myself in my hotel room talking by phone to British Airways, the FA and Liverpool were hanging on the line and the switch

Take the Cup, they said

With Saint Bob

CRAIG JOHNSTON
"SPORT AID" AMBASSADOR
WANG RACE AGAINST TIME
The Domain 9am Sunday, 25th May

was waiting to clear traffic so it could place another call to Securicor. It was a question of synchronisation. Miraculously, all the pieces fell into place.

Roger Eales, the security professional chosen to mind the Cup, had just arrived home after a hard day taking care of the nation's assets when his office phoned to tell him they had another assignment for him.

'Is your passport valid? Then pack your bags,' he was directed, 'You'll be babysitting the FA Cup all the way to Australia and back!'

An hour later he was with me at Heathrow. We made the flight with nothing to spare. The Cup had been rushed down from Liverpool with the aid of a police escort. Then it was up to Roger and me to ferry it through the airport crowds and on into the departure lounge from where it would be carried on board as hand luggage. No problem. It was almost as if the mysterious wooden box encasing the Cup contained a magic of its own. Nobody, with the exception of the attendant press corps, could have known what the box contained, but one look at Roger and his burden, and the crowds simply parted before us. In no time at all we were relaxing in our first class seats with an ice bucket of champers at our side and a long flight in front of us. I thought of how incongruous it was — the highly paid footballer riding first class on a diet of champagne and caviar to save the world's starving.

In the hours after Wembley I'd had the odd chance to reflect on my good fortune. Nobody deserves that much luck in one lifetime. When the chance arose to put my blessings to work for those without hope, I'd leapt at the offer.

The flight put down in Perth but the Cup stayed under wraps. It was on to Sydney where the FA Cup would undergo its official Oz unveiling at a Sheraton Hotel function to launch the Down Under leg of Sport Aid.

By the time we winged over Sydney Harbour, Roger and I were about as fresh as last week's seafood salad. Once the other passengers plus captain and crew had learned the Cup was aboard, we'd played hosts to a constant chain of well-wishers all keen to have their photos taken with the trophy. The result was barely a minute's sleep in thirty-six hours. Athletes are capable of coping with such physical demands but not so the Cup's minder who had already put in a full shift before learning he was off to Australia. It was to be the longest working day of his life.

They were ready for us in Oz. Among my final chores in those hectic few hours before clambering aboard the big bird were a couple of stand-up interviews with Australian television crews in London. The news items made much of my Wembley goal and the fact that the trophy was leaving British shores.

The enthusiasm of the Sydney welcome made us forget about the jet lag. After the speeches I was whipped through the radio and television chat circuit where I was given ample opportunity to rattle the tin on behalf of Sport Aid.

In the space of a few days this process was repeated in almost every state capital as we carted the Cup around the country. Wherever complacency was evident I had no qualms about letting them know that compared to Ethiopia, Australia was still the lucky country and therefore Aussies shouldn't think twice about helping those in genuine need. A few people told me I was coming on a bit strong, but I'd learned from Bob Geldof that Australia was still trailing the rest of the Western world in the generosity stakes and there was plenty of catching up to be done.

My feelings at the time were that Australia was a sports-mad and wealthy country, but compared to everybody else, it was doing the least for Sport Aid. By contrast, New Zealand, with a quarter of the population, had raised as much as Australia. By nature Aussies are generous people. They wanted to contribute but the problem was that the administrative component didn't want to know.

Our priority was to extract as much mileage as possible from the Cup for the few brief days it was in our keep. The trophy was due back in England by the end of the week and it was imperative we maximise its potential.

Brisbane was planned as the final stop on the tour and our departure point for England. Then we had a brainstorm. Why not take the trophy to Perth and put it on display with the America's Cup? We could then fly out of Perth. Within twelve hours we were in the Western Australian capital via Melbourne and Adelaide. With minimal notice the Royal Perth Yacht Club had ferried sailing's greatest prize to the Merlin Hotel where it stood awaiting the arrival of the FA Cup. Word had got around. The unique display lasted less than an hour but more than 2000 people crammed into the vast expanse of the foyer to view it. It was pandemonium.

We were desperately short on sleep, jet-lagged and never sure from one day to the next what city we were in. But it was all worth it. With the licence at large to act on behalf of Sport Aid came the distinction of being named an honorary United Nations ambassador. I still have the certificate tucked away with my trophies and medals and it is something I cherish more than many of the awards won throughout my career.

One of the by-products of the exercise was that it illustrated the tremendous respect Australians have for English soccer and such institutions as the FA Cup. It was feted everywhere it went. At a packed Sydney Cricket Ground where the Sydney Swans were about to play Hawthorn in an Aussie Rules premiership match, the Cup received a standing ovation when paraded around the field.

Alan Bond, the Perth-based tycoon who had stormed the citadel of the New York Yacht Club and snatched the America's Cup, was at that match, and he'd also been at Wembley the week before. We were introduced. I didn't know it then, but two years later I would be working for his television network.

There is one very special memory from that whirlwind week. I was aboard a television news chopper flying from Sydney to Newcastle, New South Wales, where I was to show the trophy and kick off the annual City versus Country representative rugby league match. Coming in low over the outer suburbs of my old home town, I could see below us a junior soccer field and twenty-two young kids in the thick of a game. I was struck by the poignancy of it. Here was I nursing one of soccer's greatest prizes when a mere ten years earlier I'd been on the same field with the same dreams and ambitions as those kids. I felt like brandishing the trophy out of the window for their benefit. We landed and there, striding towards the chopper in his best and only suit was my dad. We were both in tears as we hugged each other.

From Perth, it was back to England to return the Cup to the Anfield trophy room where, we learned, there had been a break-in. Somebody had tried to steal the Cup not realising it was on the other side of the world. My plan was to head off to join my team-mates in the exclusive Spanish resort of Porta Banus. Club chairman John Smith, normally an undemonstrative man, had described the double-winning effort as the finest achievement in the club's history. A grateful board of directors had shouted the squad an all-expenses paid victory bash in Spain. It was also billed as a belated wet-the-baby's-head for a certain squad member.

I never did make it to Spain nor have that party with my team-mates. I regret that now. We'd just come through six months of intense pressure together. Not making it to Spain with the boys was like having experienced the battle but missing the homecoming. The post-war celebration is vital. It's part of the shared experience, the last act that cements the bonds of team spirit. I've heard the stories since and wish I'd been there. The standing rule was that anybody who went to the bar had to shout the order loud for everyone to hear: 'Make that a *Double*!'

During the around-Australia jaunt it had occurred to me that I could hardly expect people to take part in the international fun run unless I was prepared to run myself. So, when a journalist popped the question, 'Will you be running in Brisbane, Craig?', I said, 'Sure.' There would be no Spanish holiday.

This meant I had barely enough time in England to kiss Jenny and the girls, and turn around and catch a flight back to Australia. By the time I finished that Brisbane 10-kilometre Sport Aid run, I would have travelled three times between London and Oz and around the country in the space of a week for a total of about 85 010 kilometres. The last 10 kilometres were the toughest I'd ever gone in my life. Coming from a bloke whose fitness is his livelihood, that's saying something.

To coincide with the rest of the world, the Brisbane race was timed to start at the unholy hour of 1 a.m.! Sports celebrities and dignitaries were on hand. People were emptying out of nightclubs to run in the race or, at least, to watch the start. The live television feed was beaming in from countries all around the world direct onto a huge screen in the downtown shopping area. It might have been one o'clock in Brisbane but we were part of a global event.

Standing at the start I felt fine although, after the biggest week of my life, I could have slept forever. A gunshot heard around the world set us running off into the night. By fun running standards this was a hot field. My inexperience showed when I bolted out in front. In no time at all I was back in the bunch and feeling knackered. The hot shots started to pull away and I tried to go with them. For me, it was a matter of pride. Fifteen people had already gone past me. That was enough. Two-thirds of the way through the race the pain was unbearable. This was the biggest physical test I'd ever encountered. I tried to push the pain out of my mind by focusing on the previous week's events. 'You've worked too hard. Don't let it slip now.' I couldn't quit. My goal now was to finish. I crossed the line in sixteenth place.

It was over, not just the race, not just the week, not just the dream. My personal ambitions had been more than fulfilled at Wembley, and I'd been able to use this good fortune to help somebody else. This generated a feeling every bit as powerful as the emotion I'd sampled in that elevator on Cup Final night.

The next morning the owner of the *Kookaburra Queen* cruising restaurant threw a party for the United Nations crew who had handled the Sport Aid project in Australia. We celebrated the spontaneous effort which had raised more than a quarter of a million dollars for famine relief. Later that night, I returned to my hotel room high above the Gold Coast. Fresh from the shower, I poured myself a beer. It was only a few hours before dawn. I was exhausted but too wired to sleep. This was my celebration. Cheers. I opened the balcony doors and from my vantage point high above the Surfers Paradise beachfront, gazed at the lights and the coastline stretching away to the north and south. Alone there, with Australia sleeping below, I thought about fate and the course of events that had brought me to the here and now. I was a month off my twenty-sixth birthday. What a life!

'Enjoy it, son. This is as good as it gets.'

Within two years I would turn my back on football and trophies forever.

The greatest physical test I'd ever endured – the Brisbane Sport Aid run

IN THE GENES CHAPTER 2

My name is Craig Peter Johnston. On the day I was born, my dad made the sort of prophecy only a new dad would make. Planting a kiss on my mum's cheek he declared with genuine pride: 'Didn't you do well! This little bloke will be a footballer. One day he'll go to England to play.'

He wouldn't have been the first father to forecast such a fortune for an infant. How many proud fathers have idly fantasised that their offspring might be the next world-beater? I've already entertained the notion of my daughters strolling out together on a July afternoon to win a Wimbledon doubles final for Australia. It is the great extension-of-ego fantasy. Parents are suckers for it.

In the case of my folks, there was much more to it than passing fantasy. Let's say it was in the genes. What my parents bestowed upon me was something far more important than the aptitude for kicking a ball around a park. From Mum came the philosophy that you can achieve whatever you put your mind to, if you apply yourself. From Dad came that innate Aussie aggression that most people where I come from call 'having a go'. When the time comes to turn my toes up I wouldn't mind if these words were scratched on my tombstone: 'He had a go.'

From both my folks I absorbed the philosophy that conformity is a value best practised by others. They took the view that conformity and convention were two breeds of sheep, which is fine if you simply want to be one of the mob. There are the conformists and there are those who listen to a different drummer. These are the ones who walk alone. There would be times when this philosophy would run me into trouble, especially with those in authority, but more often than not it served me well.

It is fair to say that Mum and Dad shared a different outlook on the world than most. And it was the world they wanted to see when, aboard the Otranto, they sailed out of Sydney Harbour on Australia Day 1955, bound for the United Kingdom. Neither Colin Johnston nor Dorothy Cornish had met the other before boarding ship. Yet, they would return to Australia within ten years as husband and wife with three children to their name. As two young adventurers going abroad for the first time, they had much in common. Both just out of their teens, they struck up a shipboard friendship and discovered they hailed from the same neck of the woods, on the shores of Lake Macquarie, near the New South Wales industrial city of Newcastle.

Dorothy was a pretty young schoolteacher intent on broadening her horizons with work experience in England, motherland of Australia's white culture. Colin was an ambitious, semi-professional soccer player who had grown up on the northern New South Wales coalfields, considered in those days to be the nursery of the round ball code in Australia. Imbued with the traditions of the British game as fostered by immigrant miners, Col took the attitude that anyone serious about his soccer should endeavour to play at the highest attainable standard. Winter woollies and boots duly packed, he was off to convince British scouts that the missionary work done by those who first preached the football gospel in the Antipodes was about to bear fruit.

Not long after stepping ashore to seek their respective fortunes, the two young adventurers were obliged to go their separate ways. While Col humped his football swag through a succession of clubs in search of a contract, Dot had no trouble securing teaching positions. When it came to imparting knowledge she had a true gift passed on from her father, himself a teacher, and her paternal grandfather. My grandfather was a teacher based in Dorrigo, New South Wales, when Mum was born. Since she was a little girl she never wanted to be anything but a teacher.

Coming from the quiet of near-country New South Wales, the young Dot Cornish found the grim winter schoolyards of urban London quite a change. But she revelled in her work, finding a particular affinity with the so-called 'lost causes' among her pre-adolescent charges. On her days off she walked London discovering its museums and galleries and wondering at the history to be found at every corner. While appreciative of Australia's rugged, untrammelled beauty, her Anglo-Saxon heritage drew her strongly to Britain's rich culture. Intelligent and well read, Dot had a heightened appreciation of the country and its culture. At nights the Australian teacher warmed herself by a small heater in a fine Maida Vale house she was lucky to share with two friends, and wondered how Colin was faring on his football quest.

Colin had looked for a town that offered few distractions to his single-minded purpose of making it in the English professional ranks. The football culture runs strongest in the industrial cities dotting the Midlands and the North. Art galleries and museums aren't thick on the ground. Colin Johnston found exactly what he was looking for when Preston North End accepted his application to trial with the club.

At that stage Preston had a good crop of talent in its squad and opportunities for a mature trialist were few. He should have landed in England when he was fifteen, not twenty. Now I can understand how hard it must have been coming from Australia in those days to compete in an environment where football is much more than something you do with your mates on Saturday afternoons. My dad was a hard case who could give as good as he got, but nobody had warned him of the mental toughness of the average English pro. Years later, I would learn that this mental toughness was really a shell hiding genuine fear. With the exception of the truly talented, many pros live in fear of being ousted by a new arrival. From the dizzy heights of football stardom, it's a sudden and humiliating drop back to the dole queues. To protect his ego and livelihood, the insecure pro adopts a hard-man image that serves to intimidate aspirants to his job and his wage packet. This mental toughness can manifest itself in very ugly ways. A generation later it would provide a fresh set of challenges for another Johnston.

From Preston, Colin moved on to Dundee United, partly in the hope that the Scottish League might provide a more amenable introduction to full-time football. My dad's father had left his home near Edinburgh to emigrate to Australia. Perhaps there was something in Colin's belief that his Scottish heritage would help him find a soccer home north of the border,

But it didn't work out that way. After a succession of appearances in the lower ranks he was compelled to admit that he had left his tilt at the big time too late. For the first time in his life he had to concede personal defeat. Having been there and almost conceded defeat a thousand times myself, I can understand what a bitter pill that was for him. His bedside wish on the day of my birth was an unashamed expression of hope that his son might fulfil his dream. Knowing how much he had wanted to make it would later inspire me to tough it out through some of the bumpier passages of my own apprenticeship.

Colin returned to London, not to play football but to team up again with Dot. In his bleak British sojourn she had definitely been the brightest ray of sunshine. They would rendezvous at the Eagle pub in Maida Vale and share each other's dreams. It was a great romance.

With a group of fellow Australians they tripped off for a North American adventure. Dorothy, the cultivated schoolteacher and Colin, a real Ned Kelly — a rough diamond but an innocent abroad. They were married in Toronto where Dad played for Ulster, obviously the local Irish side. Continuing their tour they wound up in Miami where Dorothy gave birth to a daughter they would call Cindy Louise. On the day mother and baby were due home from hospital, the nursing staff told them there were complications. The baby died of a hole in the heart later that day.

Dad had a job as a diesel mechanic at the Miami base of the West India Shipping Company. His American workmates were so touched by the young Aussie couple's tragic loss that they rallied to support them. A whip around at work raised a sizeable amount of cash to help the Johnstons on their way. Their visas had expired so they made a beeline for the nearest British colony — Nassau in the Bahamas — where the West India Shipping Company had an office.

Mum opened up a nursery school while Dad worked for West India and played tennis in his spare time. Few local whites could match it on the court with my old man so he went looking for competition among the blacks. This was frowned upon by the whites. As a result, the Johnstons discovered that the hospitality they had encountered in Miami didn't extend to Nassau. It's worth saying that this all happened well before the jet age revolution created an era of cheap travel. In the conservative mid-1950s it wasn't the accepted thing for young couples to blaze their own trail of international travel and high drama.

They returned to Florida to find that the arrangements they'd made to have their car repayments met had not been fulfilled. Somebody had simply pocketed their cash. With no money and a 'hot' car they headed back to Canada. Mum was pregnant again but this time there was no cash, no job prospects and a lethal winter looming. They knew that they couldn't afford the hospital bills for the birth. Wisely, they pooled what little money they had left and took the cheapest flight back to Britain and its national health system.

Arriving in Scotland in the winter of 1956, wife eight months pregnant and 20 quid left in the kitty, what does Colin Johnston do? He backs a double on the results of Glasgow Rangers' and Celtic's home matches — 20 pound to collect 16. Rangers beat Hearts and Celtic knocked over Stirling Albion. To increase the odds, the old man had taken the option that both home teams would be in front at half-time. His collect bought a decent meal and the train fare to London where my elder sister Charmaine was born.

Dad picked up a job washing taxi cabs and pulled in extra cash playing for the police, the fire brigade and whoever else would meet his 3 quid a match appearance money. No sooner was the cash in his hand than he'd be off to Stamford Bridge, Wandsworth or White City dog tracks to do battle with the bookies.

While Mum and Charmaine went to church on Sunday, Dad strutted his stuff in the Fulham junior league. From what I've heard, he had natural ability to burn and had he been more single-minded would have been a far better footballer than me. Even now, after a few beers, he is not frightened to say so. By this stage his professional aspirations had been reduced to attending local first division matches — as a spectator. When they could find a babysitter, Col would drag Dorothy off to Stamford Bridge to watch Chelsea at home or, his favourites, Fulham at their picturesque Craven Cottage ground overlooking the Thames. Although they could not know it, my mother and father were forging the link of destiny that would one day cast their yet-to-be-born son into his own footballing future. This is how Mum relates the story:

> 'We always stood on the terraces at the football and one of my most vivid memories is of how cold it was. Fulham were a top side then and had plenty of support. I can recall how much Col used to admire them. We'd arrange a babysitter for Charmaine and then bundle ourselves up in our warmest clothes to shiver for a couple of hours at the football. It was our last winter in England as we were heading for South Africa where Colin had an opportunity to sign with a club. I think he wanted to watch as much football as possible before we left in June, 1960.
>
> I was pregnant again and, although the weather was not so cold late in the season, I would still wrap myself up in my favourite overcoat to keep me and my unborn son warm. I never gave it any thought then, but perhaps Craig was already soaking up some of the atmosphere of English football.'

And so it was that I received a prenatal introduction to English soccer. You might say I was on the scene before I was born.

The Johnston family flew out of England that summer on what would be the first leg of a rather protracted home trip. With the winnings from a Stamford Bridge dogs plunge, Dad put down cash on a pay-half-now-half-later immigrant air fare to South Africa. To save on baggage fees, the Johnstons were wearing all their clothes on their backs. When they saw the ancient prop-driven aircraft that was to take them to South Africa, they realised their down payment could have bought the airline.

Taking off after a scheduled stop in Lisbon, my diesel mechanic dad noticed oil streaming from one of the four engines. The take-off was aborted at the last moment and the passengers spent the night in a Portuguese hotel. The next day's leg was to Agadir in southern Morocco. The aircraft was on its descent when the flight control tower informed the pilot that due to a severe earthquake, the airport was not only inoperable but there were no fuel supplies. The only option was to try for nearby Marrakesh. By now the flight had turned into a chapter from one of those B-grade cinematic air dramas. From Marrakesh they were bound for Leopoldsville when a severe electrical storm shook the daylights out of the aircraft causing further damage and an unscheduled stop at Kano in darkest Africa. With no mechanics and no service facilities the two pilots had to fix the aircraft themselves. By day four of the enforced stopover, the strain was beginning to show among the passengers. It was 40 degrees in the shade. There was Col wearing his entire English winter wardrobe, Mum eight and a half months pregnant and now feeling it, and toddler Charmaine hot and exhausted as only kids that age can get.

They made it to Leopoldsville but the drama was far from over. At Leopoldsville the captain told his charges that the malfunctioning fourth engine would have to be 'kick-started' on take-off. That meant gathering enough speed for the air flow to rotate the prop blades to fire the cylinders. Fortunately it worked.

In Lourenco Marques, Mozambique, eight days after setting out from London, the exhausted passengers stumbled off the plane. Colin Johnston slumped to his knees and kissed the ground. There was no way the family was getting back on that flight. Train, coach or horseback, it didn't matter, they were travelling overland to Johannesburg.

I was born in Queen Victoria Hospital, Johannesburg, on 25 June 1960. Later, during my football career, there existed a fair bit of confusion about my nationality and antecedents. I can understand why. I was conceived in England, born in South Africa, but, as far as I am concerned, I will always be an Australian. Both my parents were born in Australia and we travelled on Australian passports.

It might have been otherwise. Dad almost took up a job offer in the United States and it looked like the globetrotting family, expanded to five with the birth of my younger sister Faye, would depart South Africa for America. Instead, my parents decided they would rather go home so the tribe sailed to Australia where we received quite a welcome from both my folks' families. They had not seen their children for ten years, and on top of that, there were three grandchildren they had never met. At the quayside reunion everybody was crying. We kids couldn't work it out. It his was supposed to be a joyous occasion.

Our choice of a home base in Australia would be one of the most crucial factors in determining my footballing future. As true internationals my parents might have happily settled down anywhere in the vast land of Oz. Instead, they returned to the shores of Lake Macquarie. At that stage the townships and suburbs around the northern end of the lake contributed nobly to the powerful heritage of soccer in the Newcastle-Northern New South Wales Coalfields region. One of the greatest disadvantages for Australian kids learning the game today is that, unlike their overseas counterparts, they do not grow up in a strong football environment. There are simply too many distractions. The game in Australia lacks the glamour of the overseas product. Australian soccer trails Aussie Rules and rugby league in spectator popularity and funding. Ask an Australian what soccer team he supports, and he is likely to name an English or European club. Ironically, there are more kids playing soccer in Australia than either of the other games.

I was lucky. By settling down at Speers Point on the northern shores of the lake, our tribe was camped virtually on the fringe of Australia's greatest soccer nursery. The lush Hunter Valley area of New South Wales, with Newcastle as its regional capital, is one of Australia's largest coal producing regions. Coal can take the

credit for the region's rich soccer heritage. When miners from all over Britain set sail for a new life in the Great South Land, it was for the Northern New South Wales Coalfields that many headed. With them they brought their favourite leisure pursuit: soccer, or Association Football as it was then known. How ironic it should be that these folk, who eked hand-to-mouth existences from such a dangerous and dirty endeavour, should select as their weekend distraction the code Pele would call 'the beautiful game'.

It was said on the Northern Coalfields that you could pick a man's place of work by his accent. The Welsh gravitated to certain pits, the Geordies stuck together as did the Scots, the native born Aussies, the Lancashire and Yorkshire lads and so on. Most migrants hailed from Britain. Nearly all were steeped in the twin traditions of mining and football. With them they brought the concept of collective bargaining as their only weapon against ruthless and autocratic mine owners. Australian school children learn about the heroics of the gold miners who rebelled against authoritarian excesses at the Eureka Stockade. Compared with the protracted and bitter industrial warfare on the northern coalfields, Eureka was but a brief skirmish. The Rothbury riot of 1929 was the bloodiest and most dramatic chapter in the cruel history of the Northern New South Wales Coalfields. The Battle of Rothbury was fought at a pithead just outside the town of Cessnock in what is now one of Australia's finest wine growing areas. The events which triggered the violence started on 2 March 1929 when employers locked out 10 000 northern miners who by that stage were producing two-thirds of the country's coal. The proprietors had demanded the miners accept a 12.5 per cent cut in pay. The miners refused to budge.

The pits remained idle for nine months during which time the miners and their families suffered terrible hardship. On 14 December the state government delivered the ultimatum that either the miners return to work or, outside labour would be used to man the Rothbury colliery. In retaliation, the Miners' Federation called for a mass demonstration outside the pit on the following Monday. At dawn on that day, 6000 men marched to the pipes of the Richmond Main band to the Rothbury gates. In the ensuing hours one of the bloodiest civil disturbances in Australian history took place culminating in the police opening fire on the miners. There were many casualties and one miner was killed by police bullets. In the end, the employers' lockout succeeded. Five months after the riot the miners accepted the cut in pay. They returned to work in June 1930. None had been paid for fifteen months. There are old-timers in our district today who can recall going down the pits at the age of twelve. With memories of the Battle of Rothbury still vivid in their minds, the suspicion of authority is as ingrained as the coal dust on the faces of those who extract a living from below ground. The mine owners included among their number some of the richest men in the colony and their power was absolute. Should a miner run foul of a mine owner and cop the sack, then it often followed that all his relatives would be laid off too. Depending on the circumstances, the proprietors would blacklist the entire family. No mine would employ them. Victimisation and lockouts were the strategies used by the owners to keep the miners in line. Hunger and deprivation were common. The only options for a banned family were to hit the road or prevail upon the kindness of the community. In this harsh environment, the intrinsic Aussie traits of mateship and suspicion of authority flourished and became the values by which people were judged. It was this history and these values that set Newcastle and the coalfields apart.

Safety standards were scandalous, deaths common. The miners fought for better conditions and buried the victims of cave-ins, gas and dramatic explosions. In the Dudley disaster of 1898 the pit atop the seaside cliffs blew its head off claiming fifteen lives. Today a soccer pitch exists on the spot where the men once went below ground with their lanterns and picks. Where I come from the histories of soccer and mining are inseparably linked.

When they weren't working, drinking or attending union rallies, football was the miners' great diversion. They hacked playing fields out of the bush using the gum trees to make slab huts that passed as change rooms. On wintry weekend afternoons they would emerge from the pits with the coal dust still on their faces and tramp down to the local ground to boot the leather ball around. They formed clubs like Minmi Rangers, Wallsend, West Wallsend, Cardiff and Cessnock and soon were taking on the fledgling teams from small townships closer to Newcastle. Most of these clubs are still in existence today, some of them being more than one hundred years old which means they pre-date most British clubs. Lake Macquarie became the southern border of this soccer cradle. Many of those who settled by the lake had come from around the nearby colliery towns looking for a bit of bluewater serenity.

Mum was a country girl who had taught at the lakeside Eraring school, whereas Dad had been reared in Cardiff, a colliery suburb, just a few kilometres from Speers Point. From our home it was only a couple of drop kicks to Macquarie Field, home ground of Lake Macquarie Soccer Club, a member of the league known as the Northern New South Wales Federation. During the first half of the century Northern New South Wales supplied the backbone for successive Australian national sides. Players who had represented Australia from our neck of the woods became legends in their own right. It was this league which launched my father's football career. From here he went on to play for the top Sydney club Auburn and later represented New South Wales.

It seemed that Colin, or Bruno as he was known, was everybody's mate. A genial bloke with a crop of curly fair hair, he enjoyed a beer and the company of his former footballing colleagues. Many was the time he would stop in the high street to introduce his toddler son to one of soccer's local legends. As we'd move on, my dad would deliver a eulogy on the fellow's talents usually concluding with, 'Jeez, he could play.'

Dad in his prime

Reaching for the stars

My first coach

Dad taught me how to play and how to pose ...
I had to figure the camera out for myself

I noted the respect my father afforded these men and vice versa. I hoped that one day I too would be worthy of such regard. In time I would meet men like Pippy Wilkinson, a genuine local hero and the publican of the Speers Point pub overlooking the lake. He is dead now but to the locals the landmark is still known as Pippy's. Moving on to nearby suburbs, there were blokes like Alf Quill, a goalscoring freak who hit more than 600 during his senior career and would have been a sensation had he tried his luck abroad. Then there was the legendary Reg Date who blew fullbacks away with his sheer pace and had dynamite in either foot. My father's nickname for me was Reg — he still calls me that today. I can't ever remember Dad calling me Craig. Later, when Celtic won the 1967 European Cup, he wanted to call me Jimmy after Jimmy Johnstone, the great Celtic winger. Mum wouldn't let him. But she couldn't stop him calling me Reg.

'When Datey stepped up to take a penalty,' Bruno used to say, 'the goalkeeper never had a clue which foot Reg would hit it with.'

I'd listen in awe.

'If the goalie was lucky,' my dad would continue, 'he dived the wrong way. The unlucky ones were those who got in the way of the shot. Datey could just about put the ball and the keeper in the back of the net together!'

What a pity television wasn't around in those days. Datey was a larrikin and a larger than life character. Those who saw him play for club and country are in no doubt that he would have been a sensation in England or anywhere else.

I soaked up these yarns, part of a soccer education identical in most ways to that which a lad in northern England or any industrialised European community might have received. My childhood had all the ingredients of a complete football education: breeding, legends, the culture, respect and peer group competition. I cannot remember when there wasn't a soccer ball in our house. My dad rarely thought twice about what he'd buy me for Christmas or my birthday. I rarely thought twice about what I wanted. He'd stand there proudly in the living room with the new ball balanced on his palm. Then he'd drop it and juggle it from foot to knee to head and back to his foot again. I'd gape in wonder not sure whether the magic stemmed from my dad or the ball. When I'd have a go, the ball would bounce frustratingly away, inevitably knocking over Christmas decorations, endangering my sisters' presents and sending the house into uproar. I'd be banished to the yard to practise. The antidote to my frustrations could be found in my father's words: 'Get to know the ball — make it talk to you.'

I would take it outside and practise until the smooth leather wore away to suede. Bruno would look on approvingly and, at the first opportunity, buy me a new ball. If he came home and caught me playing with a cricket bat, he would take it, deliver a swift swipe to my rear, and then toss the soccer ball at me. Football was one of the cornerstones of my relationship with my father. I saw it as the men standing together. It was Mum who helped us with homework, hobbies and general needs. But when it came to soccer, there was the old man polishing my boots until they shone, pressing my playing strip. He'd had dodgy ankles as a player, and he wasn't going to let it happen to me. Before every game he'd spend ages bandaging my ankles for added support. During this ritual he would utter the magic phrases he'd learned as the keys to success. '*It's a cardinal sin to pass to the opposition . . . pace, pace, pace is everything . . . when ya gonna hit it, hit it! . . . get to the byline and cut it back, Reggie.*' I was quite overwhelmed by it all. Did it really mean this much? Of course it did.

We start our athletes young in Australia. Perhaps too young. I've seen kids, barely out of nappies, all tricked up in football strip and boots attempting to make sense of the intricacies of team sport. They're so young that when they get tired they sit down and cry or simply wander off looking for their mums. By the time they are sixteen they have had up to twelve years of competitive sport and are sick of it. They drop out of the game, buy a surfboard and go chasing waves far from the fields where grown men stalk the sidelines and bellow at young kids.

But nobody had to dragoon me into my first competition year. I was rearing to go. I can remember pulling on those thick woollen socks and then the boots. We ran out in our blue and gold quartered shirts with big red numbers on the back. The uniform of heroes. I virtually sprinted to the middle of the field where the tiny, orange ball sat in the centre circle. Nineteen kilograms of pure adrenalin, all I wanted to do was lay boot on that undersized bit of leather. The coaches ranged us out into some sort of formation but that was the closest we got to looking anything like a real soccer team. As soon as the whistle went the twenty-two players swarmed after the ball like bees, most of us uncertain in which direction we were supposed to be running.

It didn't matter. I had waited for this day and I was going to get in as many kicks as possible. I wasn't sure how you earned a penalty but if I got the chance I'd put the ball and goalie in the back of the net — just like Reg Date. It mattered little that Lake Macquarie Junior Soccer Club's humble budget didn't run to affording nets for the five-year-olds.

We switched ends at half-time, but I didn't notice. I was so full of energy I swooped on the ball from the re-start and took it right to our goalmouth until the screams of the frantic parents stopped me just short of smashing a shot past our own keeper. Despite all my old man's tutelage, there was plenty I didn't know about this game.

Nonetheless I was hooked. At school I couldn't wait until the recess bell rang so I could get out into the playground to kick the ball. These schoolyard games were all-ins with up to a hundred kids trying to lay boot on leather. You had to be pretty damn quick, strong or just plain lucky to get more than one contact with the ball. I got my share. On two afternoons a week I trained with Lake Macquarie's coaching class side and we played a game each Saturday morning. The rest of the time I spent practising in our yard, or with the kids next door. The Baldwins were English immigrants and the entire family was crazy about soccer. Every day we would play the backyard games as if our lives depended on it. It wasn't a five-a-side pitch, more of an urban backyard complete with chicken run. It improved our skill to have to dribble the ball through the frightened chooks. Later at Liverpool they would call me 'the headless chicken'. I wonder where I picked it up.

During these backyard games I was aware that the old man was sneaking looks out the window, monitoring my progress. He would come and watch me on Saturdays. Unlike those parents who bellowed from the sidelines, he said nothing. Yet I could always tell when he was pleased or upset with my performance. Dad tells the story against himself of how he and one other lone adult were watching us play in an under-fourteen game at West Wallsend.

'That kid can play a bit, can't he?' said the bloke pointing me out, 'Look, he's got two good feet, tons of pace and isn't frightened to have a go.' The old man was almost bursting with self-gratification.

'However,' the chap continued, 'they say his old man is a big-headed bastard!'

Bruno reckons he quietly excused himself and headed for the sanctuary of the gents toilet.

Whether it was Dad's influence or not, I couldn't get enough football. In our neighbourhood it meant something to be a good player and that's what I wanted to be. When I ran out in that blue and gold shirt I felt important. I was a soccer player. Years later, when pulling on the red shirt of Middlesbrough or Liverpool I would experience a similar sensation of belonging and respect for what the club and its colours represented.

Those early, carefree school days were not totally devoted to football. On those days when nobody brought a ball to school we'd play British Bulldog, a game known by various names to kids all over the world. One or two players are selected to be 'in' and their job is to enlist recruits to their side by tackling other players intent on charging through the middle to reach the safety zone beyond. It's a bit like rugby without the ball or the Charge of the Light Brigade minus the horses. In many ways it embraces all of rugby's essential skills: tackling and the ability to beat the man with a sidestep, swerve or change of pace. If those tricks fail, then you attempt to run right over the top of the would-be tackler. But for soccer's position as the premier code in our neighbourhood,

First day at school

My first team picture – Faye, me and Charmaine

I'm certain the better British Bulldog talents would have stepped happily into rugby league ranks. Being fortunate enough to be nippier than most of my mates, I revelled in the game. No quarter was asked nor given. Injuries were frequent and often serious. Bloody noses went unreported but when a spate of broken collar bones, cracked ribs and the odd broken leg came to the teachers' attention, our headmaster intervened. British Bulldog was swiftly and irrevocably added to the school's list of banned activities.

When summer made it too hot to career around the schoolyard at speed, we switched to cricket. My junior school days coincided with the onset of the Chappell era and we had no shortage of Australian Test heroes to emulate. Almost twenty years later Ian Chappell and I would wind up on the same team in television land.

When the sound of the 3 p.m. bell emptied the school of its hordes, we'd head home where our mothers would shake their heads and wonder aloud how our school uniforms would ever tolerate the wear and tear. Whenever it became too hot to ride bikes, boot the ball or organise an adventure in the nearby bush, our gang would head for the local pool or lake to cool off. Our neck of the woods was a great place for kids. We fished, sailed, swam and ran wild in the scrub. We made our own fun, took the natural amenities for granted and slept well at night. In the guileless innocence of my boyhood, I never imagined anything could spoil this idyllic existence.

I must have been no more than six at the time it made its appearance. At first it was a barely pronounceable medical term but all too soon it became chillingly familiar as my recurring childhood nightmare. Osteomyelitis. To this day the word fills me with dread. Osteomyelitis is an inflammation that attacks the bone marrow. It is not dissimilar to poliomyelitis. If not detected early and nipped in the bud it can destroy young limbs, cripple children, ruin lives. For an active kid who loved games and the great outdoors, it seemed like a life sentence.

One day I was the most active, precocious kid on the block, the next I was laid up in hospital wondering whether I'd ever run again. During a backyard fight I received an eye-wateringly painful kick on my leg. Within twenty-four hours I began to experience constant pain in my left thigh. When the pain became almost unbearable the family doctor was called. Tests revealed that the Johnston tearaway had osteomyelitis. My parents must have been worried sick. My father vividly remembers a crucial hospital visit:

'They took him into hospital for more tests and to decide whether an operation would clear up the osteo. Dot and I went in and saw Craig. After a while, he went to sleep. A doctor told us there was little chance of stopping the spread of the inflammation. He said the best chance was to amputate the leg at the thigh. I couldn't believe what l was hearing. Both Dot and I were crying. The doctor said there was a slight chance that by scraping the bone, they might get all the infection and thereby save the leg. The chances weren't good but it was our decision: to amputate or not. I guess, when it came down to it, neither of us could face the prospect of our son waking up in that hospital to a life with only one leg. There would have been no more running around, no more football. We were both very frightened but we wanted them to save that leg. They drilled twice to locate the infection, missing both times, if they missed the third time, the leg was coming off.'

Thankfully, they located the root of the problem. The next step was to scrape the bone of every scrap of infected marrow. It was a long and laborious operation, but thanks to the wonders of anaesthetic, I was out of it. I came to in the recovery ward to find a massive strapping covering the surgical wound. The long convalescence was to prove a trial in itself. As the wound began to heal it started to itch like crazy. The doctor said it was a sure sign I was on the mend. For a bored boy stuck in a hospital bed, the itch was too great to ignore. I reached down inside the dressing and scratched at the wound. When the nurse came to change the dressing she went through the roof. I had unpicked each of the stitches leaving the wound gaping. It meant my convalescence would take longer than expected.

I spent seven months in hospital, missed one football season and most of the next. I was frantic with worry that the other kids would be light years in front of me. There was no way of knowing then that my enforced lay-off would actually be a godsend. Much later, illness would again upset my junior career but sidelining only increased my enthusiasm. Later, when my mates had grown tired of the soccer grind, I was still rearing to go. They were dropping out at sixteen while I was chasing a pro contract in England.

I left hospital with a warning that I was to avoid robust sports. Football, the doctors cautioned, was definitely off the menu. Try swimming, they prescribed. I listened to what they said and promptly ignored their advice. When I felt strong enough I resumed training with Lake Macquarie, still mindful of the scar on my leg. As the excitement of being able to play again returned, thoughts of the operation receded. The following Saturday, my name was back on the team sheet. With plenty of fresh air, lots of exercise and self-belief, I was back as good as ever.

It was a bonus that I happened to be reasonably athletic and possess the priceless gift of good balance. I could beat most kids my age in the sprints and nobody could match me for sheer stamina. This all might have meant little to me had I not made a very important discovery at a tender age. Sport was a legitimate way to get out of school. A couple of selections in school representative teams and then graduation to regional teams provided momentary celebrity status and pleasant bus trips to playing fields in Newcastle and later in Sydney. There were interstate trips, too. One soccer tour took us to Tasmania on what was my first 'overseas' trip. For an eleven-year-old, this was a big deal.

'This beats school,' I thought, and promptly put my name down for every sporting activity imaginable. It wasn't that I was hopeless at scholastic pursuits — in fact, I was regularly top of the class — but I had a poor attention span and possessed a level of restlessness that could only be cured by lots of exercise. I figured that rather than remain in class and make a nuisance of myself, I would be better off charging around a playing field. With hindsight, the desire to dodge school became one of my greatest motivations. It would not only vault me into interstate trips but also, finally, aboard a jet bound for a trial with a professional club. If I had been older and wiser I would have looked at my dad's example and spent a bit more time in class. He was the perfect case study of a gifted athlete who had plunged heavily on a full-time career. When the gamble didn't pay off, he had no great qualifications to fall back on and was compelled to take a sound but modest job as a diesel mechanic with the local council.

Mum never reprimanded her kids for being headstrong. Privately, the schoolteacher in her must have wanted us to do better at our studies. Wisely, she would later use my ambition to play in England as an incentive to do better at school. 'Top the class and we'll pay your fare to England,' she said. We had a deal. Education is fine, providing you never lose sight of the fact that there is nothing worth knowing that can be taught. You learn by your mistakes.

Whenever there was a regional athletics team off to Sydney for the New South Wales schools championships, you can bet I was aboard the bus. I ran in everything from the sprints to 800 metres and even had a crack at the long and high jumps. Had I been better at athletics I might have ended up in a track and field outfit rather than a football club. Nonetheless, I did well enough as a junior all-rounder to receive some flattering press coverage. Also I had figured out while still in primary school that speed and stamina do not often come in the one package and that the combination was very handy in team sports. In addition, I was afraid of nothing. With a bit of skill and control thrown in, I just might make a reasonable footballer. The sort of player my dad would respect.

When it came to soccer and learning the basics, Dad was a perfectionist. Praise did not spill easily from his lips. I craved his approval but I had to earn it the hard way. I wasn't naturally skilled, a failing which must have caused Colin Johnston a degree of private grief. On the uneven playing surfaces common to junior soccer,

I like this winning business –
New South Wales Schoolboys

I managed to compensate for my lack of skill with sheer effort and aggression. With his expert eye, however, my father wasn't fooled. In the long run, nothing can substitute for skill. I practised harder than any of my mates, but I obviously didn't practise as much as I should. In time my lack of preparation and skill deficiencies would be exposed in the most humiliating manner.

In the brashness of my soccer adolescence, I mistakenly assumed that my ball control was passable. Whatever deficiencies I might have had, I more than compensated for them with sheer enthusiasm. People ask me what position I played when I was a kid. The question always stumps me. I don't know. I'd often run out in the number 10 shirt but would play all over the park. I figured I had the stamina and speed to be where my team needed me most. Our coach must have agreed because he never changed the strategy.

We weren't aware of it at the time but we Lake Macquarie lads were fledglings in what would become recognised as the most productive nursery in Australian junior soccer of the early 1970s. From my close circle of mates who kicked a ball around together after school, five went on to play national league soccer and represent their country at youth level. Peter Tredinnick, one of my closest lifelong friends, would follow me to England and later play for Australia's Socceroos at senior level. As kids raised on the exploits of Australia's sporting superstars of the 1950s and 1960s, we fantasised about wearing the green and gold. For a bunch of raggedy boys in short pants the first step on that road was the juniors' field at the bottom of the hill.

One of the parents, Lennie Lawrence, played Pied Piper to our soccer ambitions. Most of the hotshots who graduated from the Lake Macquarie nursery during the 1960s and 1970s came under Lennie Lawrence's influence at one stage or another. The trademark of his sides was a maturity that belied their tender years. For example, we had a plan for free kicks taken wide outside the penalty box. Nobody expected kids under thirteen to be really able to blast a ball, but we had a couple of belters in our side. A young keeper trying to defend a full-sized goalmouth had no chance. When the opposition would stack the goalmouth to counter the ploy, we would switch to plan B. Instead of taking a shot, our player would cross the ball into the space just outside the penalty spot where I'd arrive late and at speed to crash a header goalwards. That was another thing youngsters aren't good at: power heading. A few of the Lennie Lawrence kids, however, could really head a ball.

Lennie's strength was as an organiser whereas Bernie McKinnon was a coaching specialist. Bernie was another fatherly figure who guided us in those formative years. He knew the game and imparted knowledge. Of course, we thought we knew it all then. I can remember an instance when he was attempting to explain something to me and I looked at him and said with conviction, 'But I'm going to be the best footballer in the world one day!' At the time I really believed it.

At eleven I was given the opportunity of regularly playing a year above my own age group. The promotion came about by my regular appearance on the sidelines after my own age game had finished. The older team was short of a player one day and I was invited to fill the position. There were many Saturdays when I played in both age teams.

Just when our local soccer push might have started running out of inspiration, along came another motivational tool. ABC Television began telecasting the weekly 'Match of the Day' soccer program from the United Kingdom. It was compulsory viewing. The day after each show my mates would be abuzz with the action they'd witnessed on the box. To us kids used to playing on bumpy, gum tree-lined fields 20 000 kilometres from where soccer's laws were first drawn up, this glimpse of gifted players parading their skills before huge crowds put the game on a glamorous pedestal. We promptly dropped the local senior players as our heroes and began worshipping the stars of the English first division. An excerpt from the running commentary which accompanied our pick-up games after school might have gone something like: 'And Lorimer [me] glides past his man [in reality, a squawking chook] and lets fly with a brilliant left foot shot which Banks [David Baldwin] tips over the bar!'

My favourite book was an English publication chock full of action shots of the stars and diagrams of match strategies and how great goals were scored. I loved that book. We also devoured English soccer magazines and debated the merits of the great teams of the day. Manchester United, Arsenal, Liverpool, Spurs and even Chelsea had their supporters, but most of us agreed that Don Revie's Leeds United was the stand-out. What a side — Clarke, Bremner, Hunter, Sprake, Cooper, Mick Jones, Frank and Eddie Gray and company. And in the middle of their defence was Jack Charlton, a man who would later perform a pivotal role in my career. But all that was light years ahead. Meanwhile, there was a different superstar to discover each week: Mullery, Peters, Moore, Law, Hurst and Hunt. As the seasons unfolded they were replaced by Charlie George, Lou Macari, Rodney Marsh, Peter Shilton and the emerging push of the early 1970s. On Saturdays we consciously attempted to duplicate their artistry. Privately, we dreamed our adolescent dreams about playing at places like Elland Road, Highbury, Stamford Bridge and Old Trafford.

My father's dreams were far behind him. When it came to my career, he was ever the hard-headed realist. His creed was that the ambitious player should always play at the best level possible. In Australia, where you always stick close by your mates, this can cut against the grain. But I was certain that Dad knew best.

'How do you know if you're any good if you're not prepared to have a go against better players?' he would often ask.

In those days the neighbouring Newcastle Junior Soccer Association had greater depth than our Lake Macquarie Association and usually provided the bulk of players for the Northern New South Wales representative teams. By using my grandmother's address as a home base, I was able to leap boundaries and play with Lambton in the Newcastle Association. I wasn't happy about leaving my mates but immediately noticed the difference in standard. Instead of running into a competitive side once every three weeks, each Saturday was an all-out battle. In a matter of matches I noticed my game had taken on a tougher, more competitive edge. There was more bite in the challenge, more snap in the sprints and my concentration had to be much more intense. Once again, my old man was right. From then on I embraced his creed of playing at the highest level. By the time I returned to Lake Macquarie I was a better player able to command an automatic berth in my age representative teams. I looked forward to the trips, especially with the school teams. It meant being applauded rather than punished for skipping class.

From primary school I made the journey around the northern end of the lake to attend Booragul High School. I've already mentioned how the random twist of fate invariably worked to further my soccer ambitions. The choice of Booragul for my secondary education was one of the most crucial decisions of them all.

Perched on a grassy expanse running dawn to the lake's north-western shore, Booragul was a relatively small school dwarfed by the reputations and enrolments of its neighbours. Except for one peculiarity, it would have gone almost unnoticed in the great scheme of the New South Wales public education system: by school standards, little Booragul was a soccer colossus.

In those days the Tasman Cup was a statewide competition run along knockout lines. With more than 200 teams entered, and driven by student enthusiasm and school pride, it was the pinnacle of many a youthful sports career. By the time I landed at Booragul the school had already earned quite a reputation. With no more than 300 boys in its coeducational ranks, tiny Booragul had already won the trophy once and had enough talent in the feeder teams to do again. It did.

At Booragul High we had rugby league players, basketballers and sailors, surfers and cricketers. But to be somebody, you had to be a member of that Tasman Cup side, or at least on your way to being one. They were the clique, the elite, the in-crowd and the guys with almost half of the female student body chasing them.

There was only one girl I wanted chasing me. Her name was Jenny Jones. We were married almost ten years later. Like true childhood sweethearts, we shared secrets. I entrusted Jenny with mine. I told her that the boy she had teamed up with was bound for England to become a professional soccer player. She believed me. We were both thirteen.

CHASING THE **DREAM** CHAPTER 3

Inspiration comes from the most unlikely quarters. For some, it's a positive word or a timely reward. In my case, nothing motivated me more than somebody telling me that I wasn't good enough.

In high school there was one particular teacher who was convinced I'd amount to nothing. On the evidence he had a strong case. My hair was long and unruly, my school shirt refused to stay tucked in and the toes of my shoes were forever running to ruin from the playground soccer games. Despite the fact that I was a straight-A student, he was convinced I was too distracted to secure a successful future. A class debate on career prospects, held when I was away on a soccer trip, came to the conclusion that Johnno, or Scruff as I was nicknamed, would become either a barrister or a failed sportsman.

'What are you going to do with your life, son?' our teacher asked me one day.

'As soon as I can I'm off to England to become a professional soccer player,' I replied.

From that point on the boy with the inflated football ambitions became the butt of this particular teacher's jokes. He thought it was a real hoot and had plenty of laughs at my expense. But his jibes merely added steel to my ambitions.

I was such a skinny kid that the old man embarked on a radical plan to put some weight on me. Every morning at six o'clock he'd appear at my bedroom door and thrust a giant plate of T-bone steak, eggs, mushrooms and tomatoes under my nose. 'Here Reg, get this into ya,' he'd say. 'Build yaself up.'

I could barely stomach it but forced it down assuming it was part of some master plan he had. I'd then grab a ride with him on his way to work and, with the burden of breakfast lying heavily in my guts, land in the playground just before seven each day ready for the wall-ball battle.

Unlike our nearest neighbours whose favourite playground game was handball — something like tennis without the racquets — Booragul High's game was wall-ball. It was like a giant game of squash played with the feet and a tennis ball. Instead of just two players, we had a dozen or more, each occupying a square facing the wall. When the ball rebounded into your court, you could let it bounce no more than once before hammering it against the wall from where it would rebound into someone else's square. If you muffed your attempt, you went all the way back to square one and the fellow in the next square moved up to your space. The object of the exercise was to work your way up to the top square and stay there. Then you were king and everybody would try to dethrone you. Right of service went with the top square and that meant being able to pinpoint those you wanted to eliminate. The strategy was to knock out those players who posed the greatest threat to your chances of becoming king. The more skilled players could juggle the ball in their square before picking out which player they wished to eliminate. With sights set, they would play an unstoppable volley off the wall to send the hapless recipient back to the start. It became acutely competitive and conducive to nurturing advanced ball skills.

We'd play until the toes were kicked out of our school shoes. The damaged shoes were a statement about our soccer stature. We were the in crowd. Brett (Cowbie) Cowburn was brilliant at the game as was my mate Peter (Tred) Tredinnick, his younger brother, Howard, Michael Boogaard and Malcolm McClelland. Five of us would later try our luck at real soccer in England and all six would graduate from Booragul to at least Aussie national league level.

One of the highlights of my school years was representing Northern New South Wales in the Australian schoolboys interstate series against Victoria, New South Wales and the other states which had large populations from which to choose their sides. Because of its long soccer history, Northern New South Wales is seen as a separate soccer 'state' within the Australian system. Most players picked for the tournament were seventeen or eighteen while I was only fifteen. The nucleus of our side was the Booragul wall-ball boys — Cowburn, Peter Tredinnick, Boogaard, McClelland and Johnston. We were unstoppable, winning with an unbeaten record. That competition was just about the final encore for the Booragul clique. Never again would we play together for the sheer joy of it. From that point on our football would become increasingly controlled by the power of the pay packet.

When I think of football in its purest form, it is to those junior teenage years that my mind wanders. Then it was a beautiful game, free of cynicism, an expression of youth and athleticism. If I'm driving by a junior ground today and see kids in action I slam on the brakes and watch it as though I am viewing a first division game. But rather than tactics or technique, I look for the smiles on the kids' faces. That's the buzz. In one way, those years were the real pinnacle of my career. That's when the game was simple and sweet. The only financial concern was scraping up the 20 cents to pay the referee.

Life and football were pure adventure. Interstate trips meant you were away from home, school and authority in the company of your mates. I can vividly remember one trip north to sunny Queensland where we were billeted with soccer families. I was staying with the Parry family and therein lies a story. Over the evening meal the father told us stories from the English first division of his day when giants like Stanley Matthews, Nat Lofthouse, Jackie Milburn and Len Shackleton filled soccer's greatest stadiums. We listened in awe. Then our host told us about his brush with fame. Stanley Matthews was appearing in a match at Brisbane's Perry Park when play came to a halt after a lone parrot wandered onto the pitch. Nobody made a move to evict the parrot so our host leaped the fence, sprinted past Sir Stan and grabbed the errant bird. The action was recorded by the press photographers and the next day's newspaper carried a photo captioned: 'Mr Parry, the Perry Park parrot pincher!' What ensued was a round-table discussion of what we kids wanted to do with our lives. When it got to me, I said, 'I want to play for Leeds United.' This statement elicited even greater hilarity than the parrot yarn.

The next day, while the other kids went on a day trip to the beach, I stayed behind to practise my soccer skills in the Parrys' backyard. I sweated so much in the humid Queensland weather that the stench of my training shoes became unbearable. Mr Parry wouldn't let me in the house. So, while he was eating his dinner in front of the television, I put my shoes on my skateboard and shunted it into the living room just behind his chair. The other kids nearly died laughing as he sniffed the air. Seeing me playing outside he couldn't figure what was causing the stench. By the time he found the cause he was well and truly off his dinner.

It wasn't all laughs on that trip. A kid's holiday diet of soft drink and confectionery and not using a prescribed soap resulted in an abscess appearing on my old osteo scar. My leg was swollen and throbbing with pain. The osteo was back. The next thing I remember is being on an operating table at Royal Newcastle Hospital with Dad and a nurse by my side. This couldn't be happening — not now when I was playing the best football of my life. I looked at my old man and said, 'Tell her I'm going to England to play soccer, Dad.'

They reopened the old scar which was almost 30 centimetres long and two finger--widths wide running the length of my left thigh. This time the specialist was definite: 'He'll never play football again,' he told my parents. 'He should think about something else — like surfing.'

That stay in hospital was to prove a watershed in my young life. Middlesbrough Football Club, fresh from winning the 1974–75 English second division championship, had chosen Australia as the destination for their end-of-season tour. And they were to play a match against a Northern New South Wales select in Newcastle. I watched the televised match from my hospital bed as a talented and relaxed Boro blitzed the ill-prepared local lads. Even the manager, Jack Charlton, came on late in the game to complete the rout with a headed goal. But the real artistry flowed from Graeme Souness, a confident Scot who strode around the midfield like Errol Flynn around a Hollywood set. I was impressed. It wouldn't be the last I saw of Souness. We would develop a close association during the next decade or so.

The next day the local newspaper reported that Boro had agreed to grant a trial to Joe Senkalski, an immensely gifted teenager playing with Adamstown Rosebud in the Northern New South Wales first division. I was green with envy. Hey, I thought, this was supposed to be my dream. The next time my father visited the hospital, I told him I wanted him to write to English clubs and ask for a trial. He agreed. What harm could come of it? Mum and Dad wrote to Chelsea, Manchester United and Bruno's old favourites, Fulham and Middlesbrough. Only one club replied: Middlesbrough. It was decided that the Johnston boy would head for the UK at the end of the Australian school year in October. By then I would have turned fifteen. There was only one problem. How were we going to finance this long-shot venture?

For most of my life both of my parents had been in steady employment. Mum taught at local schools and Dad worked for the council. With their savings they had bought a small waterfront cottage at Fishing Point, then a secluded backwater on the western side of the lake. This little cottage provided the key to my soccer future.

'We're selling the Speers Point family home and moving into Fishing Point,' Mum announced. 'The money we save will be used for your England trip.'

I couldn't believe it. The England venture was the most hare-brained scheme you could ever prescribe for a kid, let alone one warned by doctors to give the game away. My dad, better than anyone, must have known that the odds were almost infinitely stacked against me making the grade over there. But when it came to soccer and his own flesh and blood, he was prepared to plunge almost everything on a squillion to one shot. As for me, I was under the impression that I was one helluva footballer. I'd show those Poms something. Boy, was I in for a shock!

For the four months of my convalescence there was no competitive soccer, as I couldn't afford to receive a direct blow on the injury. So Dad welded a set of goals out of pipe and set them up in the yard at Fishing Point, and here I practised endlessly by myself. The months dragged by. I kept up my studies to meet my end of the bargain in exchange for the fare to England. At school, when I wasn't watching my mates play wall-ball, I talked to Jenny Jones. She was my confidante. With her I shared not only the doubts raised by my post-operative scars, but the details of my plan to take the English soccer scene by storm.

Out of deference to the doctor's surfing prescription, my parents bought me a board and I went chasing waves along the coastal strip near Newcastle. I loved it. There is nothing to compare with locking into the raw energy of a wave. It gets into your system and keeps you coming back for more. It also gets you tanned and fit. The surf is a great leveller. Just when you think you've got the better of it, along comes a clean-up set of waves which dump a couple of tonnes of water on your head and leave you feeling rather inconsequential — like you've been dragged backwards through a wash cycle. After a couple of bad wipeouts, I thought, 'If my leg can cop this sort of stick, it can't be too bad.'

Surfing can be addictive. After a few months it became apparent to me why so many of my mates had dropped out for the surfing lifestyle. If my plan for life hadn't been so clearly defined, I might have followed them. During the cold, low points of my soccer career I often wondered whether my choice had been the right one.

The surfing look in those days was to the far left of casual. Dead scruffy might be an appropriate description. Surfers spent most of their lives chasing waves. Some of them lived out of the back of camper vans. Summer wardrobe was a pair of boardshorts. For winter it was a sweatshirt and a pair of Levis. The sun bleached the hair and the last thing you did was get it cut.

This then was the boy who stepped off an Australian beach and aboard a jet bound for England. The flight set down at Heathrow. Talk about an innocent abroad. My first glimpse of Britain was a sea of black faces at the immigration counter. Had I got off at the wrong stop? They must have been equally curious at the sight of

CHAMPION IN THE MAKING

Craig Johnston, 11, of Speers Point, is one of the most promising junior sportsmen in Lake Macquarie Shire.

He has just completed an outstanding season in junior Soccer and athletics.

He is one of the top players with Lake Macquarie under-12 first division Soccer team — the 1972 major and minor premiers.

Craig, who scored more than 30 goals this season, plays inside left for his club.

State player

This year he represented Macquarie Association, Northern NSW and NSW Schoolboys in representative football.

He played inside-right for NSW in the three games won against South Australia.

He played for Northern NSW against Manly and played inside-left and right.

He played for Macquarie Association against Coalfield teams.

Club officials say he has tremendous potential and, with ordinary luck and the correct approach to the game, should reach international standard.

The officials believe that it will be youngsters like Craig who will provide a

new standard of Soccer in Australia in the next six or more years.

Craig, who attends Speers Point East Primary School, won a pennant as senior boy champion at the Cross Road Zone athletic carnival.

The school team won the RSL Pointscore Trophy.

Craig will represent the

school at the area athletics carnival in Newcastle tomorrow.

His versatility is shown by his competition in five events, including the senior champion and relay for the 12 years age group.

His father is a keen Soccer follower, having played for West Wallsend. He also had one season in Scotland.

An early entry in my parents' scrapbook.

this kid under a shock of bleached curly hair, skateboard under arm, struggling with a bulging suitcase. They'd have been even more curious had they known I'd spent the last hour explaining to a customs officer that the year's supply of Rexona soap my mum had so dutifully packed was meant to keep my osteo scar clean.

A friendly face at the information counter told me how to catch the bus to Kings Cross Station from where I would connect with the Flying Scotsman train to Middlesbrough. He asked what I was doing alone in Britain and I told him I was going to play for Middlesbrough in the first division. He grinned and said, 'Good luck!'

The northbound train swept by countless soccer fields where local teams were training and playing. The sight heartened me. I closed my eyes and thought, 'This is where I want to be.'

'What the hell's this? It's the Wild Man from Borneo!'

The twenty or so apprentice professional footballers and triallists lodging at the Medhurst Hotel in Middlesbrough couldn't believe their eyes. I extended my hand. 'G'day, I'm Craig Johnston.'

They cracked up. These slick, fashion-conscious young professionals had never seen a beach let alone a beach bum.

'Is that your didgeridoo?' said the slickest of the bunch.

'No, it's my skateboard.'

They forgot about the television they had been watching and started asking me questions about where I was from, who I'd played for and what was I doing in Middlesbrough. They seemed genuinely interested but found it all a bit hard to believe.

Even the original Wild Man from Borneo could not have experienced a more profound cultural shock than that which hit me on my arrival on Teesside. Save for the fact this city provided the engineering skills to build the Sydney Harbour Bridge, Australia has little in common with Middlesbrough. For starters, I had stepped straight out of an Aussie spring into the depths of winter in north-east England. It was so cold that when I opened my wardrobe door I half expected to see my sweater wearing my overcoat. It rained on my first night and in the

The Wild Man from Borneo

morning I couldn't figure out why the water hadn't drained from the streets. Stepping outside for a closer look, I realised that the rainwater had frozen solid before it had had a chance to drain away. This was all a bit mind-numbing to a teenager who, just four days earlier, had been catching waves at Nobbys Beach.

Mum had lovingly prepared my wardrobe for an English winter but, unfortunately, her fashion ideas were locked in a 1955 time warp. My drainpipe trousers and track shoes were totally out of place amid the fashion-conscious Boro youths. The Medhurst gang rocked with laughter when they spotted me wrapped in my ancient red tartan dressing gown with its gold rope tie.

'Where the hell did you get that?' someone shouted.

'St Vincent de Paul,' I said with pride.

'Is he like Yves Saint Laurent or Pierre Cardin?'

'Probably.'

Craig Johnston's idea of fashion was something you skipped over while thumbing through the women's magazines in the dentist's waiting room. My roommate, David, was a bit of a spiv. He took one look at my clobber and said: 'You can't walk around in that' and promptly sold me some of his cast-offs. To compound my discomfort, I was having difficulty coming to grips with all the different accents of these youths from all parts of Britain. For some reason I'd thought that everybody would speak like me.

The only thing that got me through this initial embarrassment was the conviction that when it came to playing, I would be the equal of any of them. Out there on the park, fashion or funny accents would mean nothing. It would simply be a matter of who could play the best. Then I'll show 'em, I told myself.

It took less than half a training session for the awful truth to be revealed. The idiot from Australia couldn't play. He was an absolute joke. Moreover, what was he doing here in the first place? Didn't he understand that this was more than sport — it was a cut-throat business. The boys who made it into the bottom drawer of a professional club were the products of a vast sifting system that recruited the best from all over Britain. If there are 30 million blokes in Britain, 29 million want to be a professional footballer. Who was this Australian who thought he could jump the queue?

I can see it now, me with my harum-scarum tactics chasing expensive, cultured apprentice professional footballers around the pitch as if they were the Baldwins' chooks. It must have been a sight. My brand new Adidas boots were two sizes too big — Mum had bought them thinking I'd grow into them. There I was all boots, hair, arms and legs. One dip of the shoulder or sway of the hips was all they needed to send me sprawling into the mud.

In my brief life I had been ridiculed many times for my shortcomings, but none of it really sunk home. I told myself that whatever anybody said, I had one great gift working in my favour: I was pretty damn good at playing soccer. This belief had sustained me through many a bruising — until that first training session at Middlesbrough. It was so humiliating it felt as if somebody had ripped out my soul and used it as a football. Whatever had given me the impression that I could play? At home I was a member of a Tasman Cup side, a somebody. But compared to the Boro triallists and apprentices, I couldn't play to save my life. The more I tried to adjust, the worse I got. My head was gone. I'd kick the ball anywhere and they'd really crunch me in the tackles. It hurt and I wasn't smart enough to know what to do about it.

John Coddington was one of the club coaches and he took an instant dislike to this impostor from Australia. As far as Coddie was concerned this kid had no right to a trial at Boro. There were countless British kids out there who could really play, and none of them would ever set foot inside a first division club's door. What right did this Australian have to jump the queue especially when he had no talent whatsoever? In my narrow experience I'd never struck anyone like Coddington. I guess the ex-Huddersfield centre-half came from a different school. He was a sergeant major type. A lot of bluff and bluster. I was totally intimidated by him. Later, that fear would turn to disrespect.

By lunchtime I was out of the training session altogether. The others were having shots at goal. Guess who was fetching the ball? That's right — the Wild Man from Borneo. That's all he was good for. That night I slunk home to my bed at the Medhurst and cried bitter tears of shame and homesickness until finally I fell asleep.

The next day I was so sick at heart that I couldn't eat my breakfast. Even if I had wanted to turn to somebody for support, I couldn't. Home and hearth were 20 000 kilometres away. It was my own fault. What right did I have to be here, anyway? There were better kids at home who should have been here before me. Both Tred and Cowbie were playing first grade for Lake Macquarie seniors and they were only sixteen years of age. As for me, I hadn't made it beyond the club's juniors.

At Middlesbrough my torment was only just beginning. Staying at the Medhurst along with the apprentices were a few young professionals who'd already signed contracts with the club. They were about to teach me the English art of taking the piss. At first I was happy that they were talking to me. It took a couple of months for the naive Aussie to fathom that they were really having a protracted joke at his expense. When I finally realised that they weren't merely laughing at me but were actually degrading me as a human being, my spirit sank to an all-time low. How could I have been so ignorant?

In the meantime, I was prepared to do anything to be included in the crowd. At first it started with fetching the balls. They'd be sipping tea and I'd be running around stuffing twenty balls into the bag. It didn't take them long to start loading all their chores onto the eager Aussie. I was glad to do it. At least it gave me a role to play. The apprentices would head off for lunch and I'd stay behind to collect the kit and load it into the washing machines. Lunch was always rushed so that I could return and get stuck into jobs like helping to scrub the floors, cleaning out the players' bath, getting the referees' room in order and preparing the kit for the next day. Then the pros' boots had to be wiped off and left to dry so I could polish them the following morning.

By the time my chores were done it would be after six in the evening. When I would finally make it back to the Medhurst my dinner would be cold and the landlady would be angry because I was late. I'd arrive with my hair soaking wet and clomp around in my strange clothes while my mates would have a bit of fun at my expense. By now, I was learning to give them some back. One of my keepsakes from that period is a photograph of my fellow triallists and apprentices. Unfortunately, most of them didn't make the grade as professionals. I wonder what they're doing now.

A desperate man is likely to make the best of any situation and I was willing to try anything to improve my lot. Staying behind to do the extra chores gave me a glimpse of the young pros warming up beside the pitch and I'd watch them endlessly which helped me identify my deficiencies. Most of it was basic skills such as hitting an accurate pass, every time, or killing a ball stone dead with your first touch. In almost every aspect of the game's vital ingredients, I was grossly inferior to the other boys. To me it had been a game, but to them it was a culture and a profession. Most young players in Australia assume they're already proficient in all football techniques. The fact is they're not, as I found out when I went to Middlesbrough.

It came down to a simple choice: either learn to play properly, or get on the next flight home. What did I want most in the world? The answer was to be able to kick straight, just like those young professionals. The problem was how to learn. I didn't have a training partner so I used a brick wall. Out on the training field to get three kicks you have to run 6 kilometres. You soon get bored. The wall was different — the ball would come straight back.

But after a while banging a ball against a wall without purpose can become pretty boring too. I drew a cross on the wall to give me a goal to hit. It now became interesting because I had to concentrate hard to hit the cross. But how many times? My favourite number was three so I worked in multiples of three. I kicked the ball three times. Three times three equals nine. My next goal was twenty-seven times and the one after that eighty-one. Kicking the ball at the brick wall eighty-one times from close range meant it flew back at me eighty-one times. Therefore, I had to control it eighty-one times. Okay, that took care of the right foot, now the left. Three times three equals nine . . .

The entire exercise for right and left feet took about an hour. When it was done I experienced a sense of achievement. The next day I couldn't wait for my chores to be out of the way so I could get stuck into my new hobby. Over the course of the next few months I developed a series of ball exercises designed to improve my basic footballing techniques. My favourite wall, which adjoined the carpark at the Holgate end of Ayresome Park, Middlesbrough's home ground, was actually the rear of the local mortuary. This wall became my training partner and friend. I put another cross on the wall as a target and worked my way up to twenty-seven headers without losing control of the ball. Where the wall met an adjoining wall at right angles I could use the two for volleying practice — I'd belt the ball off one and then turn through 90 degrees and hammer it off the other. Borrowing some paint from the groundsmen I daubed a goalmouth on the wall and a stick figure goalkeeper so I could practise penalties.

Another control exercise was to volley the ball with the inside of the foot twenty-seven times without error. If I dropped it at twenty, I'd start the exercise again. This was great for my concentration. The incentive was the sooner I notched twenty-seven, the sooner I moved onto the next exercise and the sooner I knocked off for the day.

Exercise by exercise I worked through all the fundamental footballing skills: passing, shooting, heading, trapping, volleying, ball control and dribbling. The exercise I loved the most was the dribbling game. For this, I had to abandon the wall and set up a 50-metre-long slalom course of garbage cans in the carpark. The idea was to zigzag as fast as I could through the line of cans with the ball at my feet and without touching the cans or losing control. With the object being to complete the course twenty-seven times, this was physically and mentally a very demanding exercise. The rules were the same as for the other exercises. If you got halfway through and blew it, you went back to the start. Three runs using both feet; three runs using just the left; three with just the right; three with the inside of the feet only, and three with the outside of the feet only. And so on until twenty-seven perfect runs were complete. Then I'd stagger home.

There were times when I hated it, when it was freezing and it hurt to think that I could have been indoors with my feet up in front of the Medhurst's big fire. My goals were now clearly defined and I hated myself when I didn't reach them. I'd get so angry that at times I'd call the ball names. This made me laugh because it reminded me of how my old man used to say: 'Make the ball talk to you.' Well, I was talking to it, but it wasn't saying much to me, yet. I also remembered times when he had come home with a few beers in him, booted me up the backside and said, 'Practise, practise, practise. Practice makes perfect.' Slowly, I was beginning to understand the wisdom of these words and that maybe this practice thing was the key to unlocking all my dreams. A football is a beautiful thing simply because it is round. Perfect. Any mistakes aren't due to the imperfections of the ball but the inability of the player.

Every night I'd collapse into bed exhausted from the extra workload. Next day, my hamstrings, calves and abdominal muscles would ache. The discomfort was an inconvenience at first but in time I would realise it was building important muscle fibre and strength. I told my parents on one of my fortnightly reverse charge phone calls that Bruno's diet was out the window but the alternative wasn't much better. I'd graduated from T-bone steak for breakfast to Yorkshire pud and mushie peas for dinner. And, yes Mum, I was still washing my osteo scar with Rexona soap.

My training investment slowly started to show a profit. In the pick-up games I was still the last player selected, which indicated what the others thought of me. But I was no longer intimidated. The odd pass went astray but not by so much. At least I was contributing. And nobody could catch me for sheer speed or mobility.

Beach boy at Middlesbrough

They couldn't fathom how someone with so little football ability could still contribute something by getting in more tackles than anyone else. And I had another ace in my limited clutch of tricks. Part of my training routine included throw-ins. At the first opportunity in a pick-up game, I would pick up the ball over the sideline and throw it into the penalty area. The others were amazed. They had never seen a fifteen-year-old kid throw the ball that far.

My improvement was not significant but it wasn't entirely unnoticed. The apprentices and triallists were to play a trial game against a neighbouring club. I couldn't believe it when my name appeared on the team sheet. And it wasn't 'Craig Johnston' that was pencilled in, but 'Roo', my nickname. I had lost the Wild Man from Borneo tag and had gained acceptance on the field as well as off.

Boro Youths won the game and the Roo didn't disgrace himself. It didn't matter. A few weeks later I received a message from the club management. 'Your six-month visa has expired and the government is on our backs about it. You'll have to go.'

From a footballing point of view, the timing couldn't have been worse. For the first time during my short stay I had felt that I was finally getting somewhere. On top of that I'd grown to respect some of the club's senior players, not only as footballers, but as people. Men like Willie Maddren, Graeme Souness and Terry Cooper had a bit of time for struggling triallists. I admired them and my long-term goal was to be like them.

However, I wasn't unhappy to return home. Although there had been some genuinely warm people at the club, my six months had been a lonely, largely degrading ordeal during which I had battled constant homesickness. If I hadn't been so afraid of seeing the disappointment on my dad's face, I would have been home months earlier. But now I had an almost legitimate reason to quit: my visa had run out. I felt like a soldier with a self-inflicted wound.

Australia was much as I had left it — beautiful. Dad still wanted me to make it as a pro footballer, Mum was keen that I extract something tangible from my schooling, and Jenny Jones still carried a torch for me. No doubt her folks, at least, would have hoped she had gotten me out of her system. Her dad, Peter Jones, was a self-employed builder and a no-nonsense realist. I was sure that he considered me something of a juvenile Don Quixote tilting at windmills.

A good slice of the school year had already gone but I returned to Booragul High for the purpose of at least passing my Lower School Certificate. Dad still insisted that I play at the highest level possible where I was likely to learn more. Sadly, that meant by-passing Lake Macquarie seniors and my mates and playing in Sydney with Hakoah-Eastern Suburbs. The club was backed by members of Sydney's wealthy Jewish community and, although short on supporters, always had a bit of quality in its playing ranks. Later, as Sydney City, it would win a record number of national league titles before tragically folding through lack of support.

I turned sixteen in June of 1976, which made me the youngest player in Hakoah's senior ranks. This semi-professional club's home ground was in Sydney, 160 kilometres from my parents' place. In normal circumstances anyone playing in the reserves would be obliged to train with the side on at least two or three evenings a week. But I was excused. Instead, I caught the train down on match days with my football kit slung over my shoulder and a skateboard under my arm. The train terminated at Sydney's Central Station and I'd ride my skateboard out to the ground via every hot skateboard slope downtown Sydney had to offer. If the coach had known about my pre-match preparation he would have killed me. It never showed in my game. I had stamina and energy to burn. When the match was finished I'd click-clack and hot dog my way back to Central and do my schoolwork on the train home. In my spare time I worked hard using my own training system and still had enough enthusiasm left to train and play with the Booragul High team. One of the highlights of that year was playing in Northern New South Wales' national schools championship side. Neil Jameson was there and this is how he remembers it:

'This is as good as it gets!' FA Cup Final, 1986

Catch me if you can – against Manchester United at Anfield

Most you win, some you lose, but all great memories

The interstate championship series was played at Austral Park in suburban Newcastle and Northern New South Wales' first appearance was in the second match of the evening. By the time the players involved in the first game had showered and changed, word had gone around the ground that a slightly-built kid, not yet turned sixteen, was taking the opposition apart. Who the hell was he? The visiting players, most of them seventeen or eighteen, gathered at one end of the ground and swapped opinions. At that age most of the nation's outstanding teenage players were well known, but this kid was a bit of a mystery.

As soccer scribe for the Newcastle Morning Herald I was obliged to cover the championships both for my paper and Australian Associated Press. What I had taken to be a routine and unglamorous assignment had suddenly been transformed by one player in particular. This kid lit up the night. He buzzed around the field like a bee in a bottle. His brand of football was something akin to guerilla warfare. No reputation was safe. He literally terrorised any opponent who afforded himself the luxury of dwelling on the ball. His speed around the park was devastating, his acceleration left defenders foundering and he appeared totally fearless. He gave them no peace and appeared to have enough stamina to run all night.

I can recall one instance when a Northern attack broke down as the opposition's right fullback retrieved the ball near the corner flag The defender had bags of time to either knock the ball downfield, back to his keeper or even out of play. With his back to the opposition, he was attempting to shield the ball when this whirlwind swept out of the dark. He shouldered the defender out of the way and in the one motion hammered a left-foot cross towards the penalty spot. Brett Cowburn, anticipating what was on, arrived on cue to hammer a perfect volley past a stunned goalie.

By half-time everybody knew the kid's name. The next day I made the journey from Newcastle to Fishing Point to interview Craig Johnston. He hasn't been out of the news since that day.

It was a golden period full of fun times with my mates surfing, riding skateboards and playing football. After six months away, I saw and appreciated my home life in a different light. And I grew closer to Jenny Jones. But a disquiet gnawed at my soul. In my short life I had never let any challenge get the better of me. The tirne at Middlesbrough had created an itch that I needed to scratch. I couldn't help thinking about it. I felt like the mountaineer who had slogged his way alone into the Himalayan foothills only to be turned back by his own lack of preparation. But just before he retreated, the clouds momentarily parted and he caught a brief glimpse of the summit of Everest. He knew there and then that he had to return for another crack at the peak.

My parents knew too. Mum outlined the deal to me. If I put my head down and completed my School Certificate, they would come up with the money to send me back to Middlesbrough, providing the club would keep a place for me. We contacted Boro and were told that if I was willing to pay my own way and could afford the 8 quid a week for food and lodgings, they would give me a trial.

I had my hair cut and bought a new suit for my return. I wasn't about to be humiliated again. The first words that greeted me on setting foot back in the Medhurst were 'Oh no, not you again!' It was November, three months into the new season. I had missed pre-season which meant, fitness-wise, everybody had the jump on me. To make matters worse, it was a particularly bitter winter and I was instantly homesick. Back in Australia they were entering summer. I went upstairs to bed and shed a few tears. The next morning I woke and realised that it was going to be the same sketch all over again unless I pulled myself together and got on with the job.

After training and all the chores were out of the way, I took a ball to the carpark to work at my system. It was there and then that I realised my dreams weren't that easily crushed but were just as strong as ever. In my mind it wasn't a carpark but a football stadium and we were playing Leeds United. Every pass meant something.

George Wardle discovers the best way to give a team talk to an Aussie player

When I trapped a ball and pivoted to pass, I fantasised I was setting up a winning goal. In my mind I could hear the roar of the crowd, the shouts of my team-mates and I could see the opposition's goal as I hammered a drive fair into the top left corner.

A few of the young pros would come by and laugh at the daft Aussie playing by himself, but it didn't worry me. Each day I would rise at seven before everybody else and run the few kilometres to the training ground. It would still be pitch black and the place would be locked up but I'd scale the gate. By the time the others arrived in the van I would already have done a couple of hours training. When I'd give a wayward pass in a practice game I'd say, 'You bloody idiot. You did a hundred of those perfectly yesterday!'

By this stage Joe Senkalski and David Kamasz, another young prospect from Northern New South Wales, had come and gone. The good news was that some of my Booragul mates were going to try their luck in the UK. Brett Cowburn and Malcolm McClelland were headed for Manchester City or Aston Villa. Peter Tredinnick was bound for Middlesbrough.

Although I hadn't realised it at the time, what I was missing most was a mentor, somebody to look up to. Back home there had been my father and coaches like Bernie McKinnon and Wayne Leary to offer inspiration and guidance. At Middlesbrough there was no guiding light, nobody who believed in me. That is until George Wardle strolled into my life.

George was to become a very positive influence in my life. I was going about my chores one Thursday morning when he sauntered in, beaming under a thatch of grey hair. He had a spring in his step and exuded goodwill and an enthusiasm that belied his sixty years. Later that day I learned he would make the trip down from Durham each Thursday to coach the Boro kids. He was a man in love with the game and in love with life. I would learn later that as well as being a topline footballer (he'd played for Queens Park Rangers) and coach, he spent countless hours organising sport for disadvantaged and disabled kids. Unlike others I had encountered during my short stint at Boro, there was not a fibre of cynicism in George's body. Nothing gave him greater pleasure than to see the boys who had come under his tutelage go on to fulfil their potential.

I knew straightaway that George Wardle and I would get on. He was taken by my enthusiasm and the fact that I was fitter than anybody in the club. Plus there was my long throw and the fact that I was brave almost to the point of being suicidal, particularly in the opposition's penalty area. George knew he could make something of me. Unfortunately, not everybody agreed with him.

With George Wardle in charge of the under-nineteens I began to win selection for the odd trial match. The scheme was to throw the triallists in with the apprentices and those who hadn't yet made reserve grade. In reality it was part of the club's cleaning out process. If you didn't produce the goods at this level, you were usually invited to leave. As luck would have it we played Jack Charlton's old club Leeds United, and the great man took a special interest. We were deplorable and he appeared on the scene within minutes of the final whistle to give us the greatest tongue-lashing of our young lives. When it was my turn he said: 'As for you, you'll never be a footballer while your arse points to the ground!' I was devastated but I was desperate to prove him wrong. There was no time to lose. No club carries players and I knew I was that close to being sent packing.

I stepped up the private training. I rose even earlier and ran the 3 kilometres to the Hutton Road training ground to arrive well before the rest of the squad. When the other boys would be heading off later for a drink or a game of snooker, I'd take the ball into the carpark and practise some more. They were so good they didn't need the practice. I did. I had no energy left to join the boys later when they went out at night. Besides, I was still a virginal sixteen and neither drank nor smoked. Mine was a monk-like existence with but one objective: to play first division football. I had no time for anyone who didn't respect my ambitions. When the apprentices demanded that I do their chores, I politely told them that I wasn't working for them any more. A year older and wiser, I had my own ideas of what needed to be done.

I got on well with most of the young pros with one notable exception — Tony McAndrew, a sarcastic Scot who had taken a real dislike to me. It was the start of a simmering animosity which would prevail right up until 1980 when I finally left the club to join Liverpool. I was becoming totally single-minded about my ambitions and it was plain that a few of the others didn't appreciate the change. To guys like McAndrew I was no longer the affable idiot but 'that cheeky Aussie bastard'. Also, I had a knack of rubbing a few people up the wrong way. For example, I had no money to speak of and would ask the senior players if I could borrow their old boots to train in. Then I made the mistake of borrowing boots without asking. They noticed that the studs were worn down and knew who was responsible. It didn't make me too popular.

It's worth remembering at this stage that I was still paying for the privilege of trying out with Boro. The man who turned my fortunes around was Graeme Souness. I was cleaning his boots one night when he came back for a sauna and asked what I was doing.

'I'm cleaning everybody's boots,' I replied.

'How much are they paying you for this?' he queried.

'They're not paying me — I pay them.'

'Bullshit!' he exploded, 'We'll see about this,' and he turned on his heel and swept out of the room.

The next day I was practising in the carpark when the assistant manager Harold Shepherdson came storming up to me.

'What have you been telling people?' he demanded.

'Nothing,' I said, 'Only that I've been paying you 8 pound a week for me to stay here.'

'You what?' he thundered.

'Well, haven't I been paying you 8 pound a week?' I asked him.

'Yes, you have,' he said, looking somewhat flustered, 'but don't go telling people. From now on you're not paying any money. And here's 5 quid to go on with.'

From that date on until I became an apprentice, Middlesbrough paid me exactly the same expenses as the other triallists. Things were looking up, but not everybody was going to do me favours — least of all the man who counted most, Jack Charlton OBE.

I was in the change room scrubbing out the sauna when I overheard a conversation between two people in the bath. It was Big Jack handing out instructions to Harold Shepherdson. 'Oh, by the way,' the former England and Leeds star said almost as an afterthought, 'when you see that Roo, tell him to pack his bags — he's wasting his time here.'

My heart must have stopped. I could hardly breathe. They were sacking me! For the next couple of days I avoided everybody. My only hope was to keep my head low until I had a chance to do something on the playing field that might give them reason to change their minds.

The chance came one day when the reserves were short and I was picked in the squad for a North Riding Senior Cup match against Whitby Town. My hopes weren't high when I saw that I was merely the substitute but I vowed I'd give it everything if given a run. The newspapers gave a glowing report of Boro's easy victory. They made special mention of a sixteen-year-old Australian called Craig Johnston who scored a hat-trick after coming on as sub. A few more reports like that, I thought, and they'll forget all about sending me home. My position was still tenuous. After all, I was only a triallist which meant they didn't think I was ready to be offered an apprenticeship. But there was no doubt in my mind that I was worthy. Circumstances contrived to force the issue.

It was Christmas and Brett Cowburn was in the UK knocking on club doors. He had come across from Manchester City to visit and I asked if he could accompany us on an away trip to Sheffield to watch me play in Middlesbrough's youth team. It was chucking down rain and when we stopped at a motorway cafe the news came through that our match had been called off. Brett decided that he would journey on to Manchester. I didn't fancy the idea of returning to Middlesbrough without a match to play, so I told the coaching staff I was heading for London to see some cousins. Instead, I travelled to Manchester with Cowbie.

We headed straight for City's Maine Road ground. It was a Sunday and their manager Tony Book and his assistant Ken Barnes were putting England international midfielder Colin Bell through a fitness test. I was introduced and, as there was nobody else about, Book put me through a test as well. He was amazed at my fitness and immediately offered me a trial match. I did brilliantly. The reserves had a match scheduled and he found a place in the side for me. Again, I played out of my skin.

Before I had time to catch my breath I was in the manager's office being offered a contract. City wanted to include me in the A youth team for Saturday's derby match against Manchester United. I wasn't ready for this. At Middlesbrough they were talking about sacking me. Here at Maine Road they were offering me the world. In football, as in so many other endeavours, it is a fine line between glory and garbage.

'I can't sign,' I spluttered.

'Why not?' asked Tony Book. 'You're not contracted to Middlesbrough.'

'I have to play an important FA Youth Cup match next Saturday and I couldn't let George Wardle down.'

My plan was to return to Middlesbrough, play what would be my last game in their red and white shirt, say goodbye to George Wardle, then beat a trail back to Manchester and accept the offer. Things didn't quite work out that way.

We murdered Seaton Delaval, a famous northern pit-town side. I was in cracking form and scored with a sweet volley. No sooner was the match over than I found myself on the mat in Harold Shepherdson's office.

'How are your cousins in London?' he asked.

'Fine,' I lied.

Polishing skills

'You didn't visit them at all,' he said. 'Our information is that you were somewhere else altogether.' With that he thrust a contract under my nose and said: 'Sign this.'

I didn't want to sign. As far as I was concerned I owed Middlesbrough nothing. But I was indebted to George Wardle. It was for George that I reluctantly took up that pen and applied my name to the contract. I was a Middlesbrough apprentice at last and I should have been leaping for joy. Instead, I was thinking about Manchester City and how gracious they had been in offering me an opportunity. I was in no doubt that if I hadn't made that trip to Manchester, Middlesbrough would have been in no hurry to chase my signature. Had I known that Middlesbrough were about to dispense with George Wardle, I wouldn't have signed. We had some real talent in our youth ranks and were progressing well under the Wardle influence. I knew he had a high regard for me but I was desperate to know just what sort of reports were finishing up on the manager's desk. George kept a match analysis of each player's performance with a score out of ten plus comments in the next column. Every now and then he'd call a player in and say, 'Look, you've scored an eight, two fives and a nine in your last four games. What do you think about that?' The player would add his two bob's worth and then George would disclose what he had written down against each score. He'd say something like: 'You're a good strong tackler but you're not using your brains off the ball.' Then he'd explain what the player was doing wrong and how it could be fixed.

One of the turning points of my apprenticeship came after we had played Doncaster away from home. Total exhaustion and a sense of satisfaction made me think that my effort hadn't gone unnoticed. I was dying to know what George had entered in his log book. As soon as the chance presented itself I took a peek and was stunned to see he had a ten against my name. This was all the endorsement I needed. This was my reward for all the extra training. Inspired, I decided to step up my private practice sessions. The problem was that I had to fight for space in the carpark. Instead of laughing at the Aussie, the other apprentices had started taking a leaf out of his book. Now I had some practice mates — the makings of a daily carpark five-a-side game. It was the era of David Hodgson, Stan Cummins, Mark Proctor, Craig Johnston and Peter Tredinnick.

The big news was that Middlesbrough were again heading Down Under for an end of season tour. Great, I thought, this is my chance to return to Australia as part of the club. I had my bags packed when at the last minute I received word that the wife of a club director wanted to go. I was out of the tour. It seemed there would be no trip home for me that year. I was so upset I told them that if they didn't let me go home, I would leave the club. It was a ludicrous threat for a mere apprentice to make, and they knew it. They calmly pointed to the door. That's when George Wardle stepped in again. He prevented the club from releasing me. I wasn't allowed to travel with the team but the club provided the air fare to and from Australia. This all coincided with a crucial period in the club's history as Jack Charlton was moving on and John Neal was joining from Wrexham as manager. When Boro played in Sydney I went to watch them and meet John Neal for the first time.

'Hello,' he said, 'I've heard about you. I'll see you next season.'

I was happy with that.

Seeing that I wasn't on the end-of-season tour, I signed on with Lake Macquarie as a guest player. What a mistake! The side comprised one or two older hands and a bunch of my teenage mates. After my experiences in England I had become much harder in my attitude to life. Nobody, I had resolved, would ever take advantage of me. I had taken on this outlook like a second skin and it was about to land me in deep trouble. We were playing our neighbours Cardiff and, as often happens in derby games, it became pretty physical. From my position it seemed our kids were coming off the worse, chiefly from the attentions of one guy. He was kicking everybody but when he hacked Peter Tredinnick down from behind, I saw red. Tapping him on the shoulder I waited until he turned to lay a Liverpool kiss fair on his face. There was nothing subtle about it. He went down bleeding. The result was a sending off for me and more than a thousand dollars worth of dental work for my victim. I wasn't proud of what I'd done but I thought he deserved it.

As the snow falls, I get an early Christmas present – I become a real apprentice

The Northern Federation met the following week and deliberated whether to put me out of the game for a long stretch. That would have been fair punishment. After all, the Cardiff fans were ready to lynch me. I didn't have the money to pay for the damage. The Northern directors decided to ban me from their competition until I settled the debt. I got off lightly. They could easily have imposed an international ban which would have put an end to my professional aspirations. That was my final appearance for Lake Macquarie. I didn't dare show my face around Cardiff. At the time I blamed the referee for letting the situation get out of hand. Now, I can see how stupid and impulsive I had been. When July came I was happy to slip quietly out of the country back to Teesside for the start of the 1977–78 season.

THE DEBUT CHAPTER 4

O n returning to Middlesbrough I was disappointed to learn that George Wardle was no longer youth coach. The political guard had changed and George had been shuffled out of the frame. Later, when the club reappraised its youth policy, George would be reinstated. Meanwhile, Bobby Murdoch, who had won a European Cup medal as a member of Celtic's famous 'Lisbon Lions' side of 1967 and had seen out his playing career at Middlesbrough, moved into the youth coaching job.

I was back in the carpark hammering the ball at the wall when he stepped out of a meeting and asked me what the hell I thought I was doing. Rather than tearing strips off me, he tossed me a tennis ball and said: 'Here son, use this wee one. Do it with that, you can do it with anything!' My mind turned instantly to the Booragul wall game and I decided that Bobby Murdoch was a kindred spirit. In the ensuing months I would learn much from this warm, affable Scot.

Years later, when I went to Liverpool, they equated my playing style to the antics of a headless chicken. I wonder what they would have thought if they had seen me before Bobby Murdoch arrived on the scene. Revved up with sheer enthusiasm, my game plan was to attempt to be everywhere at once. It was Murdoch, the man who had run the Glasgow Celtic engine room and had put the finishing touches on Graeme Souness's midfield education, who taught me something about tactics. He made me use my brains, not just my heart. Murdoch, winner of everything worth winning with the all-conquering Celtic, was a big, gentle, beer-barrel of a man. In his prime he was known as the finest passer of the ball and one of the game's great on-field schemers. His vision was out of this world. With the ball at his feet Murdoch could see something that didn't exist and then provide the pass that turned it into reality. He was a genius who in the ensuing twelve months would cultivate one of the finest crop of youth graduates ever to wear the Boro strip.

We loved and respected Bobby Murdoch. Unlike clod-hopping centre-halves-turned-coaches who barked at our every error, Bobby praised and encouraged our youthful creativity and taught us how to learn from our mistakes. I can still hear him now calling 'R-r-r-oo, R-r-r-oo' in his high-pitched Glaswegian accent. It was a compliment to hear him call your name.

Under Bobby's encouragement, my appetite for self-improvement was insatiable. The opportunity to play against seniors showed me just how easy it was for a lightly framed player to get knocked off the ball and hurt. At Bobby Murdoch's suggestion, I hit the gym with a vengeance and started pumping iron until my body ached from exhaustion. Then I went back for more. Over the ensuing year the improvement was dramatic. My weight shot up, I added centimetres to my upper torso and put on muscle in the vital areas of my thighs and lower abdomen. This meant I had extra strength to go with my speed. The benefits became obvious. I could hold my ground in a tackle and, when two of us would jump to head the ball, it was my opponent who was nudged off balance, not me. And I noticed my club-mates were handling me with a lot more respect. Overjoyed at the improvement, I took heart from the realisation that I was on the right track. It encouraged me to work harder than ever.

All the elements were coming together. Almost without realising it, I had dropped into a routine of self-improvement. As I mastered each task, I would set myself a new challenge. It became a game and a reward in itself.

Bobby Murdoch had told me to have more shots at goal. For my next carpark session I practised eighty-one volleys, the same number of attempts where I would chip an imaginary goalkeeper, and eighty-one sweet, accurate drives. The following afternoon we met a local school team, St Mary's College, in a trial game.

The day after the game, Harold Shepherdson called a special meeting and described our performance as the worst youth team showing he had ever seen from a Boro side.

'If it wasn't for the Roo's three goals,' he said, 'you'd all be getting your wages docked this week.'

Bobby Murdoch winked at me. We'd won 3–2. The match report read: 'Johnston hat-trick — chip, volley and drive.' My head was in the clouds but I could see the steam coming out of the other lads' ears.

Prior to the countless kicks against the carpark wall, the probability of the Aussie impostor one day playing in the first team would have been nil. Now it didn't appear so far fetched. I lived and breathed soccer and studied it obsessively. Whenever it was on television I'd be glued to the box watching how such great players as Manchester United winger Gordon Hill would beat a defender. The next day I'd be down at training by myself imitating how Hill dropped his left shoulder to send the defender the wrong way. Gordon Hill, Peter Barnes, Kevin Keegan, Trevor Brooking, Liam Brady . . . whoever was the player of the week, I'd study his good points and try to steal his tricks.

I bought George Best films, particularly Manchester United versus Benfica in the 1968 European Cup Final, and showed them on a projector in my room, charging the other apprentices admission. With the proceeds I'd buy more films until I'd saved up enough cash for a tiny camera. In those pre-video days we would capture ourselves messing about at Ayresome Park. When we weren't watching films, we were playing impromptu skills games on the landing outside my room. Our laughter would ring down the stairwell to those watching 'Coronation Street' in the recreation room below. In time my top-floor room became the focus of a new commitment and fun element among the apprentices and triallists.

Billy Askew was a ginger-haired Geordie lad with a pit-town background. Girls, drinking and gambling held no fascination for Billy. He had one thing on his mind: to rise above his origins by making it as a pro footballer. We became soul mates and training partners. From disparate backgrounds, we lived for the common obsession to be better footballers. He envied my athleticism and I was equally jealous of his ingrained natural ability. Billy Askew had the sweetest left foot you could ever wish to see. He became a fixture in the film sessions.

Along with George Best, my other hero was Pele. Ever since I'd been old enough to get a grasp on international football, he had been my idol. Watching films of him in World Cup action for Brazil, I suspected even then that we'd never see his like again. It wasn't just his football that lit up people's lives, it was the way he deported himself, attributing his genius to God and his family. He really impressed me.

The first division games at Ayresome Park were a fertile source of ideas. Not only was there plenty to be learned from watching the Boro stars in action, there was also the chance to study the quality players from visiting clubs. Yet, as far as midfielders were concerned, few shone brighter than Souness. He was as tough as he was gifted. In an FA Cup-tie against Liverpool at Anfield, the home side's midfield had not only taken control but were taking a few liberties. Souness, however, illustrated that nobody took the piss out of him. At one stage he pinned Liverpool hard man Jimmy Case to the turf by the throat and, with clenched fist, indicated that the midfielder's afternoon might end there and then. He was a bruiser but, when it came to pure skill, he had the touch of a maestro.

In my private games I would imagine myself in Souey's boots, dragging the ball back under my foot to fool a defender or delivering game-breaking passes. Amongst the players he was my role model and in many ways I would follow in his steps, although never reaching the career heights he would later enjoy. Little did I know that 1977–78 would be the Scottish international's last season with Boro. I would never play alongside him in a Middlesbrough shirt. In January 1978 they would sell him to Liverpool for 352 000 pounds. Yet, even after his departure I could not dislodge the impression that he hadn't seen the last of me.

Another off-field mentor was Graham Hedley, a Geordie and the most naturally gifted human being

I've met. He could do anything. I've no doubt he could have played soccer or cricket for England. He was a born entertainer who could sing, dance or hold an audience rapt for hours. Good-looking and intelligent, his one problem was that he had too much talent. While others could focus entirely on one discipline, Graham's light would shine far and wide. Nonetheless, he still had time for a sixteen year-old foreigner. One evening I was watching him splashing on the aftershave before heading out into the night. 'Where are you going?' I asked.

'Out to chase women,' he said grinning.

'What do you do when you get them?'

He then proceeded to deliver a very humorous but for me, embarrassing account of the facts of life. 'Like football,' he said, 'it's the international language. They're the opposition and you have to break down their defences. You start up front with the boobies and gradually work your way down to midfield . . .'

The student was burning red with embarrassment. Graham was almost in tears as he tried not to laugh openly at my discomfort.

Graham Hedley never really fulfilled his sporting potential. But, in my eyes, that didn't diminish him as a man. He was his own person, a bit of a rebel with a generous streak. By watching Graham and Graeme, I recognised two footballers whose personalities dictated that they would make it on their own terms or not at all. They contrasted sharply with those who compensated for their lack of ability by creeping and crawling their way into favour.

Meanwhile, my own footballing obsession was paying off in the shape of goals and man-of-the-match awards as a regular member of the reserves. On a couple of occasions Souness stood down from first team trial matches to rest an ankle injury and John Neal shoved me in for a run. The ankle had been worrying Graeme for some time and he was particularly intolerant of anybody who gave it a nudge, especially during training. One of the coaches committed the sin once and Souness gave him a warning. We all winced when the transgression was repeated. Souness shaped to clout him with the heftiest elbow you've ever seen but at the precise moment of impact, the transgressor slipped and thereby missed having his head knocked clean off his shoulders.

Graeme was the sort of player who commanded respect. Inordinately skilled, he could be as tough and physical as the game required. At Boro he was an institution. Always immaculately dressed, he drove around town in a silver Mercedes sports and squired women who could have stepped out of the pages of *Vogue*. One of the most famous photos ever taken of Souey was after Liverpool had beaten FC Bruges 1–0 at Wembley to win the European Cup. There was the Liverpool star, right arm around the trophy and left arm encircling the waist of Miss World, Mary Stavin. Part of the Souness folklore was that, as captain, he would stride into the centre circle before kick-off and toss his gold American Express card rather than a coin. Describing a drama-filled European Cup-tie behind the Iron Curtain, one match report said that the difference between the two sides was this bear of a man with the touch of a violinist. Souey had an aura, a genuine star quality. All this and a football genius as well! His departure left a void at Boro. When he left, he thought enough of me to ask his landlady if she needed a new lodger. I thereby inherited his digs and the motherly Phoebe Haigh, a delightful lady of whom Graeme thought the world. Maybe there is something in her cooking, I thought, only half-jokingly. The move got me out of the Medhurst and created another source of jealousy among the lads. But at least I had my independence within a family environment.

If the club was missing Souness in January 1978, the coaching staff had other things to worry about. The first team was enjoying a whiff of FA Cup magic, and there is nothing like it to stir the imagination and the loyalty of the average English fan. A run in the Cup means brimful attendances, money in the bank and a chance for the average supporter to dream about seeing his side at Wembley. On 28 January Boro were drawn to play Everton at Ayresome Park in the fourth round. The Boss had a real selection dilemma on his hands. Souness had gone and, in the subsequent reshuffle to fill the gap, McAndrew had been dragged into a defensive midfield position. The problem was he had a suspension hanging over him and it was likely to coincide with the Cup-tie.

With the pressure building, John Neal carted the side off to Jersey to prepare for the game away from the public gaze and distractions. Nobody was more surprised than me when I was invited along for the trip. It meant nothing, I told myself. Clubs regularly included apprentices on away trips if only to expose them to the rarefied atmosphere enjoyed by the first-teamers.

Jersey was noticeably warmer than the North-East and as soon as we were granted free time I took myself off across the sandspit to explore the nearby island fortifications of Elizabeth Castle. Feeling a bit run down after, a recent cold, I parked myself out of the breeze behind the castle wall and began to soak up the rays of the weak winter sun. It was so pleasant there on the soft grass that I dozed off. I awoke with a start, alarmed to note that night had fallen. Retracing my steps I came to where the causeway should have been and was panic-stricken when I saw that the infamous tide had turned the strip to a kilometre of open channel. I was cut off from the main island by a vast expanse of water. The thought of being the centre of a general alarm and resultant search parties filled me with dread. There was no option. I had to make it back to St Helier. Discarding my shoes, I plunged into the icy waters and started wading. Soon the water was up to my neck. I had to swim for it. The current was strong and I couldn't afford to think what the water temperature might be in late January. In my surfing days I had been forced to take a few swims through ugly surf, but not at night, nor fully clothed. If I kept my head and reminded myself that I was fit and a sound swimmer, I knew I should make it.

A freezing eternity later, I struggled ashore on the beach near the lights of our hotel. Sloshing through the foyer, dripping wet and covered in seaweed, I must have presented a rare sight as I asked for my key at the desk. The first-teamers were incredulous, the hotel staff were overcome with laughter. I was simply angry that nobody had told me about the damn tides. My swim created an urban myth. It was said that as I emerged from the sea, a startled local was heard to say, 'Where in the hell have you come from?' According to the story, I replied, 'Australia!'

My club-mates shook their heads in disbelief and dubbed me Dawn Fraser. John Neal took a boat ride the next day and noted the distance of the swim. He subsequently told the press, 'I think we've got something special here.' But that wasn't the end of it. When the Boss informed the media that his surprise midfield replacement for the vital Cup-tie would be the Aussie Channel swimmer, the scribes had a field day.

Still trying to get a hold on the sudden turn of events — I had stood open mouthed in disbelief when the Boss pulled me aside to tell me the news — I phoned my folks back home in Australia.

'Guess what, Dad? I'm playing in the first team on Saturday!'

I pictured Colin Johnston standing there in the living room of the tiny waterfront cottage. It was late at night and he would have been in his pyjamas, bleary-eyed. I wondered what went through his mind when I told him the news. He didn't speak.

He simply handed the receiver to Mum. 'Congratulations,' she said in her beautifully understated way. 'That's wonderful news. When are you coming home?'

Middlesbrough versus Everton, FA Cup fourth round, 28 January 1978. How could I forget it. At seventeen I was the youngest player in Middlesbrough's 102-year history to play in an FA Cup tie.

The stories about the Channel-swimming Australian who had paid his own way to trial with Boro had tweaked the fans' imagination. Counting those who had travelled over from Merseyside to support Everton, there were 33 692 in attendance. This was my first taste of big match atmosphere from the inside. A swarm of butterflies performed aerobatics in my tummy as I waited anxiously in the dressing room. I had been all right until the moment I took the red and white number 10 shirt off the hanger and pulled it over my head. I looked at the others in the room. I was the same as them — a first-teamer. At that moment I entered another world. I had set foot on my personal Everest. Now I was one of an elite — a first division footballer. The realisation hit with the

Boro Cup boy in sea drama

Young Boro star goes in at the deep end

BORO BOY'S SEA SCARE

A happier splash . . . as young Johnston enjoys the water during the Jersey break

Stranded Cup hope survives 90-minute swim ordeal

CRAIG Johnston, a 17-year-old Australian who travelled 12,000 miles in search of football fame with Middlesbrough, is lucky to be alive. A half mile stretch of icy sea nearly cost him his life.

Johnston could make a dramatic first team debut against Everton in the FA Cup on Saturday. But that ordeal would not c ompare with the one he faced during Middlesbrough's four-day break in Jersey.

impact of a dumping wave.

There is no turning back now, I told myself. This is why you travelled 20 000 kilometres, tolerated the homesickness, the hard work and humiliation. This is why you scrubbed toilets. By the time we ran onto the field, every nerve in my body was tingling with excitement and anticipation. The noise and colour of the crowd made me think of a carnival. The only difference was that instead of watching the show, I was part of it. I felt alert and confident.

My assignment was fairly simple: 'When Everton are in possession, destroy the man on the ball. When we've got it, get forward and lend support.' That's precisely what I was doing when I found space on the left for Ian Bailey to lob his throw-in at my feet. It was my first touch, and as any footballer knows, your first touch can often determine how you will play for the rest of the match. I had the Holgate End behind me, packed to the rafters with Boro fans. For most of them this was the first time they had seen me touch a football. What would the kangaroo do? I dragged it back under my foot, Souness style, and then drilled a 25-metre crossfield pass with the outside of my right boot straight to John Craggs in the right back position. The crowd heaved and roared in approval. Their response set me up for the rest of the game.

The Everton side included their prolific striker Bob Latchford, midfield maestro Martin Dobson and the lion-hearted skipper Mick Lyons. They were on their way to finishing third in the championship during the season when Latchford would top the first division scoring with thirty-two goals. For these reasons and more, I couldn't believe it when we went in two up at half-time and I'd had a hand in our first goal.

'We're beating Everton,' I was saying almost incredulously, 'We can win this. We can win this!'

A few of the older pros — blokes like Davey Armstrong who had been doing it for five years and would go on to play for England — laughed good-naturedly at my excitement.

Win it we did, 3–2. As we saluted the crowd, a few excited kids escaped the security cordon and ran onto the ground. One of them was a scruffy little lad who had sat on the carpark wall after school each day for the past three months and watched me train. He was more excited than anyone. I ruffled his hair as we walked off together and a press photographer snapped the shot. The next day I had to ask the first person I saw whether the events of the previous week had been a dream. It all seemed so incredible. Billy Askew and the landing lads found it all very hard to believe, but I knew they were delighted for me.

There was no time to dwell on the euphoria of the occasion. That same week I was picked to play against Birmingham in an away league game. Although I was replaced late in the match, I was more than happy with my form. This was where I belonged, I thought.

Then, would you believe it, they put McAndrew back in? Sure, I was young and would get my chance, but it wouldn't be the first time in my career that I would be dropped when in good form. It's like giving a starving man a taste of food and then taking it away from him.

When you are young, everything is black and white. Intangibles like team blend, politics and experience mean nothing when you are full of running and explosive energy. Youthful exuberance blinds you to the subtle considerations of the team effort. I was better than McAndrew and that was it as far as I was concerned. Nothing jacked me off more than warming the bench. I would rather play reserves and miss out on the first team money than be the one to wear the number 12 shirt. Yet, here was jack-in-the-box Johnno sitting on his rear end unable to do a thing about it. It didn't matter that the fans and the media were on my side. In fact, former England and Newcastle United great Jackie Milburn wrote in the local paper that by picking McAndrew, who was essentially a defender, instead of Johnston, Middlesbrough were severely limiting their options. By this stage I was keen to show John Neal that I was worthy of a regular spot. I made the reserves versus firsts practice games pretty hot for any first-teamers who came within my sights. The Boss eventually put me on the other side, swapping me for one of McAndrew's mates. At this McAndrew blew up and said, 'Stop the game.

British press fete Johnston

LONDON, Monday (AAP). — The debut of teenage Australian football starlet Craig Johnston in Middlesbrough's top side last Saturday was heralded today as "stunning."

Johnston, 17, was singled out by sections of the press for his part in first division Middlesbrough's impressive 3-2 FA Cup success over championship-chasers Everton at Ayresome Park.

"Johnston gave a display of almost unbelievable composure in midfield," said the Daily Express.

The Yorkshire Post chimed in: "Johnston, on his debut, showed all the stamina that he must have needed in that much-publicised hour-long sea swim after being marooned while the club were preparing for the cup tie at Jersey last week."

The newspaper was referring to the youngster's lack of knowledge of local tides when he went off to explore an island off Jersey only to become marooned during a swift tidal change.

When he tried to return he found the half-mile causeway had been enlarged to a swirling stretch of sea.

The Yorkshire Post said it was Johnston's clever touch on the right wing last Saturday that was crucial in the build-up of Middlesbrough's all important first goal.

Johnston seems certain to make his second appearance for the English first division club when the side plays Birmingham in a Football League match on Saturday.

He replaced 21-year-old Scot Tony McAndrew, who is serving a two-match disciplinary suspension, for the Everton game.

A close observer of Johnston's performance last Saturday was Scottish international midfielder Graham Souness.

It was Souness' high-fee transfer from Middlesbrough to Liverpool recently that created the space in midfield to permit Johnston to join the first squad.

Since arriving at Middlesbrough's Ayresome Park headquarters three years ago Johnston has learnt much from Souness and the Scot's attention has been partly responsible for the development of the youngster's midfield play.

Souness was one of the first to congratulate the young Australian after the match.

My first-team debut against Everton in the FA Cup fourth round

First division footballer complete with scars

There's no greater feeling than scoring at Old Trafford

Celebrating a win with Bruce Grobbelaar

I'm not playing with him,' and stormed off. His inference was that my rawness and unbridled enthusiasm were a hindrance rather than a help to the team. Looking back on it now, I can understand his attitude. I was still naive and undisciplined. Moreover, as far as McAndrew was concerned, I was a threat, not just to his place in the team, but to his very livelihood. In ensuing seasons, the situation would continue to deteriorate, particularly when the Boss went looking for a new club captain and ended up giving the job to Tony McAndrew.

By contrast, a man who gave me every encouragement was Middlesbrough's World Cup veteran defender Terry Cooper, one of the game's real gentlemen. The year before, in a typically generous gesture, he had invited a lonely Aussie kid to join his family for Christmas. Now, after my first senior game, Terry pulled me aside to say, 'If I'd played like that, I wouldn't be cleaning anyone's boots.' Bolstered by those words from Boro's most distinguished pro, I promptly fronted the management and asked for and was granted a professional contract.

My new weekly basic wage was 35 pounds. After the poverty of my apprenticeship, I felt like a millionaire. I'd never really considered that money went with the job. Technically, I was still an apprentice when I received my first big pay packet. It was the week following my debut and, with appearance, win and crowd bonuses from three matches, my total pay came to 420 pounds. They've made a mistake, I thought, this is embarrassing! They'd given me an extra 385! My first impulse was to take the money back. I didn't. Instead, I went out and bought a new sound system with my windfall. In the remaining few weeks before I moved from the Medhurst to Phoebe's, the sound system became the landing lads' icon to what could be achieved in this football business.

Between 28 January and May, I played five first-team games for Boro, scoring my first goal for the club in a home match against West Ham United. The football scribes predicted a golden future for Boro's newest professional. Their crystal balls must have been on the blink that year. In reality, the worst was yet to come.

Fame and fortune can turn a young man's head. And other parts of his anatomy too. Reporters would phone me up and invite me out to dinner so they could conduct an interview. At first I was flattered, but later I realised it was another distraction and cut into my training time. At about this time I became dynamically aware of the opposite sex and their attraction to professional footballers. There had been a couple of well-meaning attempts by local people to match the lonely Aussie with one of their daughters. Seeing I was still carrying a torch for Jenny, I wasn't particularly interested, and as far as girls were concerned I was pretty naive. That innocence was to disappear in a flash one evening when I arrived back at my digs in time to receive a phone call. A woman I had met during the course of my association with the club, and had assumed to be happily married, was on the other end. What she was proposing would have made a hot plot for the raunchiest of blue movies. For a sexually naive colonial boy a long way from home, it merely made him blush to the roots of his hair. I dropped the receiver in fright. For the next few weeks, I kept my head low dreading the prospect of encountering the woman -with or without her husband. It would take a few more years of living in the public eye before I would cease to be amazed by the forthright nature of some folk.

In that same season I received a letter from Australia with a clipping from a hometown paper. It was a month or so after my debut game and there was the photo of a footballer ruffling the hair of a young admirer at the end of a game. Pictured were me and my little mate from the carpark coming off the pitch after the Everton match. It was an almost mystical experience gazing at that photo. Suddenly, I was a boy again looking from the outside at the magic and mystique of first division football. Then, it hit me. The photo was of Craig Johnston. Me. The boy from Lake Macquarie. The headline read: 'Crippled Aussie — Now FA Cup Hero,' Was it possible? Only then did I realise how far I had come and what had been achieved in the past two and half years. It had been a case of crash through or crash. By instinct rather than design I had made most of the right choices.

Now I made a serious mistake. Against my father's advice I accepted an invitation to appear as guest

CRIPPLED AUSSIE KID NOW FA CUP HERO

When the doctors said he must never play Soccer again, Craig Johnston went to bed with his football and refused to get up for two weeks.

"He wouldn't let the football go," said his mother, Dorothy Johnston, a teacher at Booragul Public School at Newcastle.

"Craig's whole world had crashed ... he was shattered."

In fact, there was a good chance Craig would never walk again due to a crippling osteomyelitis.

Yet last Saturday, at the age of 17, this once heartbroken boy became an FA Cup hero with first division Middlesbrough in England.

Johnston's clever touch on the right wing set up the all important first goal in a 3-2 victory over championship chasers Everton

The Daily Express trumpeted: "The young Aussie gave a display of almost unbelievable composure in his first team debut."

Johnston set himself the goal of playin...

brough when he saw the famous English club on TV three years ago during one of his many bouts in hospital.

Continuing to ignore his doctor's advice to take up golf, he wrote to the club and asked for a trial.

When Middlesbrough offered young Johnston a chance providing he paid his own fare to England, the doctor realised the youngster's determination could not be shaken, and cleared him.

Mrs Johnston says: "Some people criticised us for allowing a 15-year-old to give up a promising academic career.

"But my husband (C. Johnston, the former Aubu. and NSW player) didn't wa. Craig to make the same m take he did.

"Colin was 23 when went to Scotland ...

Playing football for a living – what a job!

player with my hometown club, Newcastle KB United, in the Australian national league. In retrospect, I should have put my feet up and had a damned good rest. I needed it. One of the by-products of all my extra training was a slight groin strain which I had ignored for fear John Neal would drop me. Ironically, the real damage was probably done while training on the unforgiving carpark surface where I had worked so hard at improving my skills. The guest appearances on the harder Australian grounds really aggravated the problem. By the time I returned to Middlesborough for the new season, the injury had become something more than a mere strain. Try as I might to put it out of my mind, the pain was constantly there. And it showed. My old zip had disappeared and I was loath to commit myself when challenging for the ball. When the first team squad was named, Craig Johnston wasn't included. I was bitterly disappointed. It was then that my instinct betrayed me again. Rather than admitting I had developed a serious injury and seeking immediate attention, I attempted to work my way out of trouble. Resorting to my old formula, I stepped up my training and vowed to work harder during the reserve games. I was patently fooling myself. Eventually, Harold Shepherdson, who had been on the staff for England's 1966 World Cup squad and knew a thing or two about players, pulled me aside.

'What's the matter with you, son?' he asked. 'You've lost your speed, you're not winning the ball any more . . .'

'There's nothing wrong,' I said, cutting him short.

A fortnight later I was compelled to admit that my groin was giving me hell. The club trainer had a look at me but could detect no problem. Meanwhile, I battled on futilely in the reserves. By this stage I was on cortisone and painkillers just to get me onto the field. Little did I know that in this state I had no chance of making it back to the first team. But while I was there on the fringe, I could at least put some pressure on others to perform. As diminishing and demoralising as it was, I still had a role to perform. The grim reality was that I was plummeting towards the football scrap heap with every step I took. I was about to be washed up at the grand old age of eighteen.

I was in so much pain after a game that I had to taker sedatives to sleep at night. The next morning I couldn't walk. The training staff were under the impression there was nothing wrong with me but they eventually sent me to hospital for tests. When the results came to hand, the specialist was flabbergasted. 'How did you get here?' he asked.

'I caught a cab and walked from the corner.'

'Then you'd best go home in an ambulance. You're not to walk for at least a fortnight and you can forget about running for at least a month.'

'What about football?'

'You can forget about that for the time being,' he said. 'You won't be playing again this season.'

This was disastrous news. My contract was based on the understanding that I'd be making plenty of first team appearances. It was bad enough playing in reserves. But not playing at all - that was unthinkable! Without the bonuses my basic was a mere 35 quid a week. I had just bought my first car and a small terrace house in Middlesbrough. How was I going to make the repayments? On top of all this Jenny was about to land on my doorstep. Throughout her final year at school she had worked part time in a supermarket to save the fare, and she was on her way. It would be impossible to support the pair of us plus pay the bills on my meagre allowance.

Jenny's folks must have been frantic with worry but they didn't stand in her way. Middlesborough was one helluva culture shock for her and my sorry plight wouldn't have helped. It was during this period that I discovered her real strength of character. Barely out of school uniform and to all intents unworldly, Jenny sized up the situation in a flash and went looking for work. And found it. As she recalls:

I scored a job in a pub. What a shock. Here I was, seventeen, fresh out of Booragul High School. I'd never been in a pub before, let alone an English one. I didn't have a clue what to do. My dad would have died if he'd known I'd gone to England to be a barmaid. You had to feel sorry for the customers. Not only did I not know how to serve a beer or what a pint of bitter was, I couldn't even understand what they were saying! Their accent made them sound like they were talking a foreign language. But I was lucky. Most of the people were wonderful to me and only too willing to be patient. It was a crash introduction to Mliddlesbrough social life. Before long I had dropped into the pub routine. The pay wasn't great but we needed every penny if only to cover the heating bills.

In retrospect, it must have been very much like the early days of Mum and Dad's courtship. The woman worked to help keep the football dream alive. Jenny worked an awful lot of double shifts for the extra cash and my contribution would be to drop by around midnight to drive her home. It upset me to see her working in a pub, especially when drunks would take the piss because of her accent.

'When you jump for joy, beware that no one moves the ground from beneath your feet.' Whoever coined that quote had aptly described my predicament. My injury was much worse than a mere groin strain. By exposing the original damage to persistent work, I had wrecked my pelvis. Muscles had torn away from bone, not just in the groin area but right down the thigh almost to my knee. The wear on my pelvic structure had created irreparable damage. The club sought one expert opinion after another from specialists all over the county. John Neal even took me to a Harley Street specialist in London but no matter where we went or who examined me, the verdict was the same: 'He's finished.'

Harold Shepherdson took me aside: 'Look, I know it's hard to accept, son, but you're not the first promising young player who has had to give it away because of injury. You've worked hard but look on the bright side — football is not the only thing in life. You're young enough to finish your education and get a job.'

Looking back on that period, I now appreciate how invaluable it was as a learning experience. The day after my debut against Everton Souness had returned from Liverpool to throw his official leaving party at Phoebe's place. I'd been invited and had been overwhelmed by the attention and flattery afforded me as the latest Boro star. People I'd never met suddenly wanted to be my best friends. Six months later, with my star extinguished, my fair-weather friends were nowhere to be found. They'd discovered new 'best friends' in Mark Proctor and David Hodgson who, under Bobby Murdoch's tutelage, had made the leap to first team status. Out of Souey's departure party, however, emerged two or three mates whose friendship has endured to this day. One was Davey Rea, a distant relative of Chris. Davey would become a father figure to me and would eventually emigrate to Australia.

Modern medicine and cortisone cures have their place. What I needed to resurrect my career was a magician. I found one, thanks to George Wardle. He was no longer on staff but he still had some say. Just about everyone else had given me away as a flash in the pan. McAndrew was ensconced as captain and John Neal had paid big money to Newcastle United for midfielder Irving Nattrass. Craig Johnston was superfluous to needs. Worse than that, I was a troublemaker. During an exploratory session, the club's appointed specialist had put me out under general anaesthetic so that he could manipulate the injury. I awoke in terrible pain convinced the session had exacerbated the damage. I let them know exactly what I thought of their treatment. On top of that, I refused to submit myself to more cortisone injections rightly believing they were doing me more harm than good. And I said so, which caused dreadful political ructions within the club management.

It was George Wardle who introduced me to the man who resurrected my career. Bob Farrelly was no white-coated physician, but he knew footballers. And he knew injuries. The wise old man with the magic

Two goals at Goodison on the way home

Reaping the rewards – receiving the Young Player of the Month award

hands prescribed rest, rest and more rest. Time, he said, is what it needs. Time and his magic fingers. He literally massaged the damage out of my body, kneading away with his fingers to work nourishing blood back into those ruptured cells. In spite of the logic of modern medicine, there are healers with the ability to work absolute wonders with their hands. Bob Farrelly was such a man. Bob's therapy was alternative medicine rather than the mainstream kind prescribed by the club's experts. Middlesbrough did not approve. I couldn't have cared less about their feelings.

The months and long sessions of therapy rolled on but I could feel myself responding.

It was late in winter when I returned to training. Season 1979–80 had been pretty much a write-off and a damned expensive one at that. But, as with the osteo, the long lay-off only served to fuel my enthusiasm. I resolved to be back better and wiser for the new season. And the time spent convalescing hadn't been a total waste. As an insurance against early retirement I had completed a coaching course. Also I discovered photography, a pursuit which has continued to bring me much satisfaction.

One thing was certain — there would be no more groin injuries for this boy. To this end I embarked on a program to strengthen my lower abdomen and pelvic area. While the rest of the squad spent the close season in Majorca, I stayed behind on Teesside and worked on my fitness, because Jenny and I couldn't scrape up the cash to return to Australia. The thought of the other young professionals hitting the nightclubs and the beaches of the Mediterranean made me more determined than ever as I burned up a deserted Ayresome Park. By the time John Neal took the Boro squad to Wales for pre-season, I was fitter and hungrier than ever. Just how fit and hungry was evident in a postcard I sent to Neil Jameson.

Dear Jamo,

Hi, how are ya? As you might have gathered I'm in Wales at the moment. Pre-season has been dead easy this year. I keep on waiting for something hard. I haven't even been sick yet. We've done a few five-mile runs at full speed and a few sand dune sprints. We're playing Shrewsbury Town in a trial tomorrow and Aberystwyth on Friday. Then it's straight to Casablanca for a couple of games and a suntan then back to Middlesbrough to play a Yugoslav side before flying out to Athens to play AEK and Olympiakos. Better than playing the reserves in the carpark I suppose! Shit, I nearly missed the plane. By all reports back here, Manchester City and Everton were two clubs interested in me during the off season. I'll stick my head down this year and work hard. Hope everything is okay at your end . . . Craig.

John Neal couldn't believe my fitness level. There was no mucking about this time. I marched straight into the team as a central midfielder and picked up a string of man-of-the-match awards in the first half of the season. Then there was a BBC monthly award for the best young player in Britain. My most memorable goal of the season came late in our away game against early pacesetters Manchester United. I had the ball in centrefield from where I knocked it out to Terry Cochrane on our left wing. Throwing the rejuvenated legs into turbo drive I sprinted for the penalty area and arrived in time to meet the cross with a diving header past goalkeeper Gary Bailey. The Sunday papers had a few nice words to say about that one. In fact, they started to have a few nice words every week. I was firing on all cylinders, desperate to make up for lost time.

On the Thursday morning before we were due to play Everton at Goodison Park, I received a phone call from Mum. Her mother, whom I loved dearly, was dying of cancer. My family hadn't seen me for eighteen months and the thought of never seeing Nanna again was too much for me. I told Harold Shepherdson and the club executive that I was going home. They said: 'No, you're not — we're playing Everton on Saturday.'

'OK,' I said, 'I'll play against Everton and I'll leave for Australia on Sunday. If you don't want me when I come back, you can sell me.'

Let me at that ball!

MIDDLESBROUGH SCRAPBOOK

The carpark

The wild man from Borneo!

Souness (me)

The Landing Lads

Hodge and proc

Billy Askew and the rewards of this soccer business

John Neal hands me my first pro contract

Goal h ManCity

NICK - NAMES

Peter Tredinnick is called "Skippy" and Craig Johnston is called "Roo" and both have caught the eye of past world famous player Jackie Charlton as they train with his Middlesbrough Club. Charlton in a quoted comment in Barry Bridge's News of the World (London) football column is reported to have said of Craig Johnston. "He would be the most dedicated football player that I have ever seen. He trains before training starts, he trains during the break and he trains after training. That is a dedicated footballer."

Pete Tred
in the snow

First England Shirt

First Car

R. Chris Rea

I asked for financial help. They refused. That's when John Neal came to the party. He called me into his office and gave me the cash. En route to Australia, I picked up the Sunday papers and turned to the sports section. Everton 0, Middlesbrough 2. A week later in Australia, I watched myself scoring both goals on television. I was away for about ten days, missing one game. Most importantly, I saw Nanna and had a chance to say goodbye before she died.

Back in England, our first division neighbours, Sunderland, were celebrating their centenary year and were due to play an England selection in a celebration match at Roker Park before Christmas. In a squad with a large representation from the North-East, England manager Ron Greenwood sprang a bit of a surprise by including Boro's nineteen-year-old Aussie midfielder as replacement for the injured Brian Robson. I had a blinder.

Meanwhile, Bobby Murdoch was pushing my case for inclusion in Scotland's under-21 side. The late, great Jock Stein even came to Middlesbrough to watch me play against Manchester City. With Scottish and Irish forbears and English residency, I was eligible for any number of national teams — including Australia. After the match he asked me to throw in my lot with the Jocks. I'd phoned Dad and he suggested I take John Neal's advice. I had great respect for the Boro manager and so when he said, 'Your bread and butter is in England,' the die was cast.

The news came through that the newly appointed Australian national coach, West German Rudi Gutendorf, was on his way to England to see me play. I wished he had stayed at home and so did John Neal after I turned in a shocker against Arsenal at Highbury. Gutendorf was undeterred. He wanted me for Australia. When I was a kid I had dreamed about wearing the green and gold of my country. But could I accommodate national duty 20 000 kilometres away and still hold down my place in the English first division? After all I'd been through I decided against taking any course of action which might jeopardise my position at Boro.

A few weeks later, when names were posted for an England under-21 side to play Norway in a friendly international, Craig Johnston was included.

Throughout that season my form continued to attract rave reviews almost to the point of becoming embarrassing. I'd always been a highly energetic player and I could handle descriptions such as 'action man' or 'jack-in-the-box Johnston'. But then the scribes started making comparisons with two of the great high-energy players of the post-war period: Alan Ball and Kevin Keegan. 'Bullshit!' was the stock response from my team-mates.

What brought this fabulous season to a sudden halt was not so much a date but rather a painful collision with destiny. Manchester United might have set an early lead, but everybody knew Liverpool was the team to beat. We met them at Anfield. When I eventually became a Liverpool player I came to appreciate how the atmosphere of that famous ground could intimidate visiting teams. The last thing the players see before they run out onto the field is a sign above the tunnel. It carries the ominous words: 'This is Anfield!' It is the greatest understatement of all. One of the Liverpool rituals is to reach up and touch that sign as you run out.

Then there is the Kop, that vast red wall of heaving humanity rising from ground level to tower above the goalmouth. The Kop typifies the spirit of Liverpool. After the club had won its second League Championship in 1906, the board rewarded the fans' loyalty by building a steeply inclined banking at the Walton Breck Road end of the ground. The sports editor of the *Liverpool Post and Echo*, Ernest Jones, took one look at the banking and christened it Spion Kop. The name came from a hill in South Africa that had been the focus of a strategic battle between Boers and a Lancashire regiment in 1900. More than 300 Englishmen, many of them from Liverpool, died trying to take that hill. Over the years the Kop became something more than a vantage point for the low-income fan. It became a war memorial, a symbol of heroism, loyalty and sacrifice.

It was to the Kop that the diehard Liverpool fan came to worship up to thirty times a year. The sheer passion and volume of vocal support that emanated from the throats of those fans was enough to paralyse opposing teams. The English sides grew to accept it, but teams from the Continent were often blown away by the Kop's volume before the game had kicked off.

This Anfield aura blew me away too. In the build-up to the Liverpool game, the media made much of the kid who, on his flying visit to Australia, had swung by Merseyside to pinch the points off Everton. Would he do it again? Part of our strategy was to let them shuffle it along the back four but deny them an outlet via their fullbacks. Then, if central defender Alan Hansen tried to dribble through midfield, I was to hound him into error. I waited for the first opportunity and saw Hansen, ball at the feet, make his move. I pivoted instantly. My upper body moved but my legs didn't follow. With a snap the cruciate ligament in my left knee gave way.

So distracted had I been by the Anfield atmosphere, I had failed to take note of the state of the pitch. The prime purpose of the pre-match pitch inspection is for the professional to determine boot choice and stud length. I had trotted out wearing studs that were a centimetre too long. They had caught in the firm playing surface and stopped my legs from following the rest of my body. Five minutes into the match I was being assisted off with torn knee ligaments. The Scouse match steward who helped me to the sideline said: 'Never mind, mate, I've seen it happen to better players than you.'

Liverpool swamped us 4–0 with Souness playing a blinder. It didn't help to read the following snippet in the Sunday papers: 'Any hopes Middlesbrough held of taking anything away from Anfield were dashed in the fifth minute when their industrious Aussie midfielder Craig Johnston limped from the park.' The doctor's report was no better. I would be out for another three months.

By now I was an expert at keeping myself amused during enforced layoffs. Photography and music managed to keep me out of trouble. I'd crank up the sound system and disappear into the dark room for a few hours.

It was around about this time that I struck up a friendship with Chris Rea — Middlesbrough boy, brilliant singer-songwriter and football fan. I'd trade my spare match tickets for his concert passes. He'd pump me about what was happening at Boro while I'd ask him about the guitar which I was learning to play. In time we became good mates. It's a friendship that has lasted to this day.

As a young couple starting out in the world, Jenny and I were blissfully happy in our modest terrace nestled away in urban Middlesbrough. Whereas I'd been the lonely interloper convinced that the whole world was against him, Jenny's arrival opened up my life to new acquaintances and experiences. We forged a few binding friendships and discovered in the process that people the world over are pretty much the same.

Whenever I suffered an injury, I usually came back better and stronger than ever. The ligament healed and I started receiving rave reviews again. Just when I was wondering how my football progress was being monitored back home, I received a call from '60 Minutes', Australia's top-rating current affairs show. They were sending reporter George Negus over to the UK to do a feature piece on the only Australian playing in the first division. One thing was for certain — George was bound to ask me if I would make myself available for the Socceroos, Australia's national team. He did and I told him that playing soccer for Australia would be akin to surfing for England. It was a rather blunt put-down of Aussie soccer but it seemed the simplest way to alert everybody Down Under to what was at stake. I had come to England to play at the highest possible level — just like my old man had taught me. And, for the time being, that meant putting my patriotism on the back burner.

THE TRANSFER **HUNT** CHAPTER 5

Aussies couldn't give a XXXX about celebrity status. Perhaps something to do with the continent's wide open expanses encourages Australians to respect the personal space of others. It is not necessarily so elsewhere in the world — as I was about to learn.

Public recognition is one of professional sport's more seductive and dangerous by-products. For every favour it bestows, you get to pay double in loss of privacy. On one Saturday you're in the obscurity of the reserves and the next you're in the first team. Suddenly, everybody wants to know your business. It's all part of the package.

I ran into Michael Parkinson in Sydney once and he told me a story about Fred Trueman. The firebrand English fast bowler was enjoying a drink with friends when a bloke shoved a grubby piece of paper under his nose and said, 'Here, sign this.' Fred slowly lowered his pint glass and contemptuously looked the man up and down. The bloke soon got the messsage. 'Would you mind very much signing your autograph, please, Mr Trueman?' he asked. Sometimes I wished I could have been like Fred.

You don't know how precious anonymity is until you lose it. Initially, Jenny and I were very naive. When the papers wanted to do a story on us, we allowed a photo to be taken of us posing outside our Middlesbrough house. The picture duly appeared. During the team's next away trip, when I was playing down in Ipswich and Jenny was working, our house was burgled. Jenny rang me in tears. It was very traumatic for her considering Jenny was still only eighteen, a long way from home and I was hundreds of kilometres away in East Anglia. Once the game was out of the way, I hurried home to survey the damage. They had taken everything valuable including irreplaceable family heirlooms, all our household appliances and my England under-21 shirt. Three months later the police apprehended a young man wearing an England number eight shirt. He admitted everything and, although he had sold most of the electrical goods, we were able to recover all of the invaluable family heirlooms including an antique gold chain Mum had given me as a going away present. That away trip to Ipswich was the only time since arriving in England that I'd gone anywhere without the chain. I've never taken it off since. After a second robbery we began to learn about unlisted numbers and other ways to ensure a measure of privacy.

In 1980–81, however, I was merely a new noise on the professional scene. There was still much to learn. Football is a business and an intensely competitive one at that. The major component of that business is the club. There are a number of misconceptions about this business of football. The average fan who fronts up every week with the scarf around his throat and hope in his heart believes that those who really pull the strings feel as passionately about the product as he does. The fact is, they don't. Players, by and large, are there to feed their kids and it is a very fine line between feast and failure. Managers and coaches will leave the job tomorrow and take another one elsewhere. You can count on one hand the number of managers who actually hold down jobs in the town of their birth. As for directors, well, Len Shackleton said it all years ago when he devoted an entire page of his autobiography to the average club director's knowledge of football. The page was blank. Yet, the directors play a game of their own in which managers, coaches, players and fans are simply their pawns. Many directors, or football businessmen as I prefer to call them, couldn't give a stuff about players or managers — they're both expendable. Football is an entertainment business. At the bottom of the pyramid is the supporter, the little guy who has nothing to offer but his faith and the few quid for his entrance fee. To keep him happy, directors will readily cite the club's former greatness and traditions and promise that those days will return. The fan gets his hopes up only to read in the press a few days later that the club is already planning to sell off its latest crop of outstanding young players.

Like the fans, I was naive enough to believe that John Neal's young Middlesbrough lions were a side with a real future. That belief evaporated on the day Middlesbrough chairman Charlie Amer called me in and said; 'Leeds United have bid a million pounds for you; we want you to go. But first sign this contract.' My existing contract had almost expired. What Middlesbrough could reasonably expect for me in the market place was geared to what the club was paying me. A new contract meant the club would have a stronger bargaining tool in transfer negotiations. Who knows, it might compel a Leeds United or another prospective buyer to pay more than a million pounds. Of course, Boro could have dug in their heels and backed John Neal's bid to retain that talented side. But that wouldn't have been smart business, would it? I declined the offer to sign the new contract.

I was twenty, competing against older men for contracts and kudos. Without parents or somebody older to confide in, I had to go it alone in negotiating contracts and looking after our welfare. This responsibility hardened me, something I now regret. I was naturally suspicious of putting my signature to anything with the result that I later earned a reputation as a tough negotiator. Leeds said they'd make me their highest paid player and throw in a house and a car. I said no because I genuinely believed Middlesbrough had a brighter future than Leeds. I thought about that around-the-table chat when I had told Mr Parry — the parrot-pincher from Perry Park — that one day I'd play for Leeds. I had an impulse to ring him and say: 'Remember me, the kid with the smelly training shoes? I've just knocked back Leeds United!'

Soccer writers — not just those in the North-East but national journalists as well — were making flattering forecasts about Boro's Australian midfielder. They were intrigued by the story of the bloke who had paid his own fare twice from Australia. As a human interest story it was a headline writer's dream that generated coverage I didn't entirely deserve. It caused more resentment among the older pros.

I knew my contract was nothing flash compared to what most players were receiving and I knew that almost any club would pay more than Boro. On an away trip with the England under-21 squad I'd been amazed

Remi Moses, Gary Shaw, Steve McMahon, Craig Johnston and Dave Hodgson – what a brave lot!

to learn just what the other lads were earning. There were those who hadn't even made it beyond their club reserve ranks who were on a far better wage.

My initial hopes were that Boro would offer me enough inducement to stay. Despite my traumatic introduction, Middlesbrough had given a battling Aussie the chance to get his foot in the door. This industrial city had become our second home and life was good. Neither Jenny nor I wanted to move. All that was about to change, however.

We were visited by an Australian journalist who wanted the goods on his countryman playing in the top league. He was amazed by the tale but still couldn't understand why I had chosen to forsake the lucky country for a life in England's depressed North-East. Wiping a gap in the condensation on the window pane of our loungeroom which lacked the luxury of central heating, I pointed down the misty cobblestoned streets at a bunch of kids absorbed in a game of five-a-side, oblivious to the drizzle and their grey environment. The smiles on their faces and joy in their calls said it all.

'That's why!' I said.

'Yeah,' he said, 'but the weather is miserable and the place is a dump.' He'd missed the point.

'Well, maybe it is,' I replied, 'but football is a source of inspiration to me and these people and that's why I'm here.'

He ran the story in an Australian paper with that anecdote in context. A woman, who had migrated to Australia from Middlesbrough, also missed the point. She told the *Evening Gazette* that I had branded her town 'gloomy' and 'a dump'. I was driving home from training when I saw the banner headlines on the newsagent hoardings: 'BORO STAR BRANDS TOWN GLOOMY AND A DUMP.' I had no idea at the time that the story involved me. When I found out, I was mortified. Even though I tried to explain what happened, it was the beginning of the end of what had been a fabulous rapport between me and the Boro faithful. It seemed ludicrous that a simple anecdote to explain my presence in England had created a monster. People started shouting obscenities at me. 'If you don't like it why don't you sod off home?' they yelled.

If I thought that busting my guts on the park might provide an antidote for their venom, I was wrong. That Saturday I scored against Manchester United. When being interviewed by '60 Minutes' in a nightclub restaurant that evening, I looked up to see a pint glass smash into the middle of our table. I wondered if that woman enjoying the good life back in Australia realised that she had soured a relationship between me and the Boro supporters. That relationship had been part of the reason I was still with the club. I knew the real story would never be told. As far as everybody was concerned, I had insulted my hosts. All I could do was to pull on the colours of the city's football club and play like my life depended on it. The ironic twist to the tale was that my desire to do well was so strong that my form improved and attracted even more interest from other clubs, thereby fuelling the process that would ultimately lead me away from Teesside.

The transfer market is an intriguing, shadowy world peopled by football's more colourful characters. As with icebergs, the bulk of the activity lurks beneath the surface. It is here that scouts, journalists, coaches, agents and managers churn the waters until yet another major transfer story bobs to the surface.

And so it was with me. Any in-form player with youth and a nearly expired contract on his side is bound to become the centre of transfer speculation. Once the youngster is thrown aboard the transfer merry-go-round it becomes impossible to concentrate on the job at hand. He becomes dizzy with the hype and media coverage associated with glamour clubs. Aside from the Leeds United offer, most of the hype about me was pure press speculation. Nothing really serious emerged until the halfway mark of the season had been and gone. On the day before we were to play West Bromwich away from home, a report appeared in a national newspaper claiming that Tottenham Hotspur had jumped into the bidding with a bid of a million pounds for Boro's Aussie boy. The story was given credence by the fact that Spurs looked set to sell one or both of their two Argentine stars, Osvaldo Ardiles and Ricardo Villa, to Continental clubs at the end of the season. More by accident than good management, I had developed my own playing style based on sheer enthusiasm and a direct approach. John Neal recognised it and gave me a free rein. Rival managers couldn't put their finger on it, but whatever it was, they wanted it and were prepared to pay for it.

Until the trouble with the 'dump' story, life was good. I was in great form doing what I loved most — running my guts out for a manager I respected. The local car dealer had given me a sponsored car with 'Craig Johnston — Boro's action man' written on the side. With wheels, I was no longer confined to the carpark for my extra training sessions. I drove around until I found a wall abutting a grassed playing area where I could practise as hard as ever while protecting my old pelvic injury from excess wear and tear.

We played West Brom and the papers reported that the Midlands club had joined Spurs and other clubs in the transfer chase. The following week, after I had scored and won a man-of-the-match award against Aston Villa, a *Sunday Express* report appeared under the heading 'Battle for Boro's Action Man'. Below was a tagline which said: 'Johnston sinks Villa — and draws big money offers.' The list was mounting — Manchester City, Leeds, Arsenal, Tottenham, West Brom and Nottingham Forest were all said to be in the hunt.

Christmas-New Year came and went and we were into the toughest part of the season when playing conditions are at their worst and injuries are taking their toll. Boro were staging a great rearguard action against the financial tide with yet another run in the FA Cup. All the transfer speculation was a monumental distraction, not just for me and fellow midfielder Davey Armstrong who was also the focus of bids, but for the entire squad. John Neal was sensibly playing it as low-key as possible. 'I don't know anything about other clubs' interest,' he told the soccer scribes. 'I hope and imagine that Craig's future would be to continue playing for Middlesbrough.'

When I was sidelined with injury for two weeks, Neal wisely arranged time out of the pressure zone by sending me to the Algarve in southern Portugal to recover. Jenny came with me and we enjoyed a welcome dose of sunshine. At the time I was leading the side's goal-scoring with nine for the season. I returned from Portugal relaxed and ready for more football. Jenny and I had footed the bill for our sojourn in the sun but the impression within the side was that the club had paid. It was another thorn under the saddle of the senior players.

I'll never forget that moment when I first heard the news. We were about to step out for a social engagement when the familiar opening theme music to *Match of the Day* emanated from the living room. I paused for a moment to learn what games they would show. The news hit me like a bombshell: '. . . and it has been confirmed today that Liverpool have now joined the chase for Middlesbrough's Australian midfielder Craig Johnston.'

By the next morning it was being discussed in every pub and cafe where Boro fans met. Our phone was running hot with reporters wanting to know what I thought of a possible Anfield approach. In the wake of the departure of Souness to Liverpool, there was particular resentment on Teesside that the same club should be chasing yet another Middlesbrough player. In fact, it was Souey who had phoned me to confirm the report. It was the first word I'd heard from him in ages and he was short and to the point: 'Liverpool are in for you. They asked me for a character reference and I said you were okay and that you could play. But I must warn you — they're buying you to replace my best mate, Terry McDermott, so I can't do you too many favours.'

Liverpool boss Bob Paisley had already notified Boro that his outfit was interested in negotiating for my signature. By their usual excellent standards, Liverpool had lost their way that season. They had made an early exit from the FA Cup and would do no better than fifth in the League Championship. A few of their senior hands were moving on and the fans were calling for new blood. The side did rally at the end of 1980–81 to win both the League Cup and European Cup, but by then the Reds' refurbishing program was well under way. I was out practising against my new wall when Liverpool manager Bob Paisley phoned the house. Jenny answered and said that I was too busy to talk — I was out training. She hadn't realised it was *the* Bob Paisley.

TAKE YOUR PICK !

- LEEDS
- WEST BROM
- ARSENAL
- NOTTM F.
- TOTTENHAM
- MAN UNITED
- EVERTON
- VILLA
- LIVERPOOL
- IPSWICH
- Q.P.R

Boro to sell Johnston

SPURS CHASE £1M JOHNSTON

CRAIG QUITS!

CHASE FOR ACE

Boro poised for £750,000 deal on deadline day

Don't cry for Craig, Boro

By Peter Thomas

CRAIG JOHNSTON'S departure from Middlesbrough has caused some tears and not a little anger on Tesside. And the lad is getting it in the neck.

Those two little friends of mine, Yvonne Dale and Elizabeth Larkin — who between nursing shifts nurse the Boro in their deepest affection — write from Acklam, Middlesbrough.

The remarks Craig Johnston made last year that Middlesbrough is a dump really hurt.

From then on this lad, for whom we had the highest regard, both as a player and a person, has time and again opened his big mouth and put his equally big foot in it.

Surprising

"If it were not for the Boro, we ask ourselves — and Bobby Murdoch, the coach, in particular — where would the over-publicised, publicity-seeking little Johnston be now? Probably in the Australian outback."

The point is Craig Johnston would not have been in any such place. The only surprising thing about Boro's anger at Johnston's defection is that there is any surprise at all.

The nature of the lad is of the wanderer. A kid who was brought up in South Africa and travelled at the age of 14 from Australia to England to seek his fortune, must surely have suggested that he was of the wandering kind.

Not the kind to settle in a comfy little semi in Middlesbrough.

Once a wanderer, always a wanderer. The itchy feet of the outback kid will always be on the move. After Liverpool, who knows?

Hamburg? Rio? The world? Even, perhaps, America?

Stagnation

We Boro folk get very possessive, and we are hurt easily by such defections. But we mustn't ignore the facts of life.

Not everyone is a Tony McAndrew, and let us hope that a policy of stagnation (if there is, in fact, to be such a policy) at the Boro doesn't lose us more hope-loving lads.

Perhaps another ten thousand Yvonnes and Elizabeths each home match would go to making sure they stopped. That and a bit of adventurous expenditure.

The Boro needed the glamour and charisma of Johnston. It has always demanded the electricity of exciting talent.

But don't cry for Craig Johnston.

Let's hope a couple of fivers for the two girls will help to wipe away their tears at least!

Wonder-boy Craig set to wander again

Johnston says 'No' to new contract by Boro

Shock move by Johnston

TUG-O-CRAIG

Liverpool and Forest in deadline war for Boro star

WHY CRAIG HAS TO GO!

We want Craig – Liverpool

KOP COBBER!

THE NEW RED?

It's £1m Craig

MAGICAL MOVE!

Johnston for Anfield at end of season

After the first couple of stories and long before Liverpool's entrance, I had learned to take all this transfer speculation with a pinch of salt. After all, it gave the press something to write about. That was until Nottingham Forest cruised into the frame.

A couple of my better performances had come against Forest and I had a faint suspicion that the club's enigmatic manager Brian Clough had a certain regard for my contribution. This was confirmed when he phoned me out of the blue and said that he wanted to sign me. Unfortunately, he had to go abroad for a while but said he would secure the deal on his return. When Clough came on the phone with that typical north Yorkshire accent, I thought it was one of my mates winding me up.

'Okay, Keith,' I said, 'stop taking the piss.'

'I beg your pardon,' said a very serious Brian Clough. He left me with the clear impression that I would play for Forest the following season.

It's funny how you can remember snippets from games. In my first meeting with Forest I was mindful of the fact that they were one of the finest sides in Europe. Under pressure near the sideline in our half, I had turned and belted a 30-metre pass to put one of our forwards clear through the middle. As he ran past me, their veteran winger John Robertson said with a grin, 'That was a brilliant ball, son!' In reality, it was a fluke, but I appreciated his words. They said something about a side that still understood that the game was there to be enjoyed.

Clough had built a magnificent team around a few established stars, a couple of players nobody else wanted, and a crop of bright young talents who had come through under his tutelage. In 1978–79 and 1979–80 they won back-to-back European Cups. Clearly, they had developed that ingredient ambitious players seek: the ability to consistently get among the trophies. They may have lacked the traditions and buying power of the Liverpools, Manchester Uniteds or Tottenhams, but Forest and Clough were claiming their own kingdom by virtue of their winning ways.

I'd been a fan of Brian Clough ever since I'd attended a football dinner where he was the guest speaker. He was inspiring, intelligent and irreverent and came across as a man who knew exactly what players required to achieve their full potential. Playing under Cloughie, I thought, would be the right career move but, up to this point, I'd had no say in the transfer bidding. My main priority had been to focus on the next match and keep our Cup ambitions alive.

The prospects looked good. We were drawn at home to play Wolverhampton Wanderers in the sixth round. I was happy about that because I'd picked up a man-of-the-match award when we had knocked them over in our previous league encounter. But the Wolves were ready for us this time and left Ayresome with a draw. Boro would journey to their Molineux den on 10 March for the replay. We had given away the home advantage but, with a semi-finals spot at stake, we still had everything to play for.

The 10 March midweek contest was a night of tension and drama such as only the FA Cup can provide. We didn't play to our potential at all. The scores were still level at full time but two goals in extra time dumped us out of the Cup. It had been the Middlesbrough faithful's best ever chance of basking in the glory that for so long had eluded them, and we had let them down. They had travelled in hope only to see their dreams evaporate under Molineux's harsh lights. When we stopped at a motorway cafe on the way home our team bus became the target of the impromptu outrage of disillusioned Boro supporters. Their disappointment was palpable. I saw grown men with tears in their eyes singling out individual players for abuse. It was a pathetic scene. Despite their anger, I felt dreadfully sorry for them as I thought how different things might have been if we had won that night.

That Cup quarter-final had been the most important match of my life and I had never felt so depressed about losing a game. I arrived home after midnight and collapsed gratefully into bed after taking sleeping pills to shut out the nightmare.

One door closes and another opens. With the season's transfer deadline falling at 5 p.m. on 11 March, the clubs in the hunt for my signature had less than twenty-four hours to finalise their bids. Otherwise they would have to wait until the end of the season. While I slept off the aches and pains of the Wolves trip, football managers in different parts of the country were looking to sign players.

The office phone at Ayresome Park was already ringing when staff arrived for work that morning. It was Liverpool secretary Peter Robinson with the news that Bob Paisley was keen to meet with Craig Johnston to clinch a deal. My phone rang at 9.30 a.m. Would I be available to drive to Merseyside that day to talk terms with Bob Paisley? I wasn't ready for this. They had roused me out of a deep sleep to book me in for one of the most important days of my career, and now here I was being ushered off to Liverpool like a bit of livestock. It was flattering and degrading at the same time. Unbeknown to me, the plot had been hatched months before. Our Cup exit was the signal to throw the plan into motion. My understanding had been that I would almost definitely see the season out as a Middlesbrough player.

Harold Shepherdson accompanied me to Liverpool. Earlier that winter Shep had called me into his office and said, 'An admirer of yours was asking about you on the weekend.'

I took the bait. 'Yeah, who was that?'

'Bill Shankly,' he replied.

It was months later that I learned that Liverpool's greatest manager, then in retirement, had been recommending a few players for different clubs, including Everton. Until this point it was tipped that I'd start the new season in a Nottingham Forest shirt. Before I stepped out the door to make that trip to Merseyside, I phoned Cloughie to let him know what was happening. He made just one request — that I not commit myself to any Liverpool offer until he'd had a chance to talk to me again. I had read Clough's biography and thought I understood a little about the man who had taken a modest club straight from the second division to the top of the first and then on to Europe to win the European Cup at their first attempt. Then, lest anyone think that a fluke, Forest had collected Europe's greatest soccer prize a second time.

Clough was the kind of man who took great personal care of his players and he had little time for club directors who assumed that their cash input gave them a say in the running of the football operation. Forest's recent sale of Martin O'Neill and Larry Lloyd had been seen as part of the making room process for the arrival of new blood. I had no doubt that Clough wanted me in his squad. What would my decision be?

This was the dilemma I nursed all the way across the Pennines to Merseyside. Forest or the Kop? Liverpool didn't have Brian Clough who at that stage was arguably the greatest manager in the world. But take Cloughie away from Forest and what was left? Take Bob Paisley away from Liverpool and the base of the pyramid would be as solid as ever. Liverpool had a winning formula forged into the very foundation of Fortress Anfield. Winning had become the way of life at Anfield. It permeated every facet of the club structure from boardroom to bootroom. A Liverpool man is considered a breed apart. The greatest character reference a player can have on his curriculum vitae is to say that he played for Liverpool.

The architect of that success was Bill Shankly, the former Scottish international who had played for Preston North End. He had been raised in the mining village of Glenbuck near Ayr with coal and football in his blood. After an undistinguished spell in Carlisle's reserves, he was picked up by Preston whom he later captained. Perhaps because his career was interrupted by the war, he directed his football ambitions into coaching and management, first with Carlisle and later with Grimsby, Workington and Huddersfield. It was from Huddersfield that Liverpool secured his services in December 1960. The Reds were in the second division then. He said he wanted to build a bastion of invincibility. He did. When Shanks retired twenty years later the club's fortunes passed gently into the hands of his assistant, Bob Paisley. By then Liverpool were about to glide past Arsenal's record for the most League Championships.

We were ushered into Bob Paisley's office where we met the manager along with Peter Robinson and Liverpool chairman John Smith. They put their offer to me. It was a figure tens of thousands more than the modest yearly wage I'd been earning at Middlesbrough. The actual transfer fee Liverpool were prepared to pay Boro was 650 000 pounds of which I would receive 5 per cent. It would be a nice little nest egg for the impending wedding of Craig Johnston and Jenny Jones, I thought. And there would be enough for the down payment on a new house. Yet, I didn't sign. They'd made it clear I was wanted to replace an existing team member and I'd be called on for Saturday's derby game against Everton. That news threw me. I'd been hiding a knee injury for weeks in order to play in the Wolves replay and I knew it needed rest rather than an examination at the highest level football could offer. If I didn't handle this situation with the required delicacy, I could blow the lot.

'I need to make a couple of phone calls,' I told the Liverpool bosses. 'One to my dad and the other to Brian Clough.'

They could understand the former but the very mention of Cloughie's name set the alarm bells ringing.

'Why do you want to ring Cloughie?'

'Because I promised I would.'

I felt almost embarrassed as Bob Paisley, a kindly man who ran one of the world's great football outfits with the gentle care of a benevolent grandfather, eased himself out from behind the desk and led his delegation from the room.

Brian Clough was waiting for my call. He listened to what I had to say about the Liverpool offer and then offered to double the weekly wage as well as the signing-on fee.

'Two years with me and you'll be in the England squad,' he said. 'Two years with Liverpool and you'll still be in their reserves.'

He is a very persuasive man and said if I waited outside the gates for him he would jump in his car and belt across to Liverpool to sign me.

'Liverpool are holding an axe over your head, son,' he said. 'It's the transfer deadline today and they're just trying to pressure you into signing.'

I phoned my father in Australia, rousing him out of bed. He was even more nervous than me but he knew what was at stake. Colin Johnston said one word. 'Liverpool.'

A large media gathering was on hand awaiting my signature. We pushed our way through the throng and were about to drive off when the Liverpool manager came after us to say that there was an important telephone call for me in Peter Robinson's office.

'There is no call,' said Bob Paisley once we were inside. 'We just want to up our offer.'

I was astounded. They must have thought I was heading off to sign for Cloughie! In fact, I had no intention of signing for anyone but Liverpool. All I really wanted was a bit of time to take stock. Less than a day before my heart and hopes were in Boro's Cup bid, now I was being stampeded into the biggest career decision of my life.

'I give you my word I won't sign for anyone else,' I promised. We shook hands and walked back outside to meet the media. When Bob Paisley told them that he had secured Craig Johnston on a handshake, they looked at each other in disbelief. The Liverpool boss said that my word was enough for him.

On the way back to Middlesbrough we heard a radio news report claiming that Craig Johnston had failed to come to terms with Liverpool and was now on his way to Nottingham to sign for Brian Clough. After the tension of the past forty-eight hours, Shep and I permitted ourselves a good belly laugh. Another amusing sidelight to the day had come with the routine yet very exhaustive medical check that accompanies any transfer deal. Everything went all right until the doctor poked me in the lower midriff. I let out a howl of pain and he leapt back in alarm certain he had detected something seriously wrong with me. In fact, he had jabbed my swollen bladder which, due to my anxiety, I had not taken the time to empty. I went for a leak and duly passed the medical. Luckily my knee stood up to the test.

Much later that day Shep and I were both glad to get back to Teesside. With the transfer hassle out of the way, I had some unfinished business to complete.

In his post mortem on our exit from the Cup, our skipper Tony McAndrew had suggested via the press that certain Boro players had let the team down. 'I don't think some of them have their hearts in the club,' he had said. 'If they don't want to play for Middlesbrough, they should go.'

There was more, but I'd read enough. I jumped to the conclusion that McAndrew meant that players who were the subject of transfer interest had run dead so that Boro would lose. The crazy logic would be that we would want Boro out of the Cup so that our club would have no further call on us for that season and would willingly sell us to other clubs before the transfer deadline expired that same week. I was so furious that my immediate impulse was to drive around to McAndrew's place and perform grievous bodily harm upon his person. We had a long-running score to settle and after this latest insult I wished I'd taken care of it before.

The opportunity had presented itself much earlier that season during a practice game when I had shot for goal. McAndrew had passed a remark that I had missed but John Neal hadn't. 'Leave it out,' he said to McAndrew, 'I want to see him taking shots at goal.' I asked McAndrew what he'd said and within a flash we were glaring at each other. He dipped his head towards me and I flew straight into him. Our club-mates tried to separate us but two of them grabbed me before the others restrained McAndrew, which gave him the chance to get in a couple of free shots while my arms were pinned. I wanted to kill him. The game resumed but I was seething. There was a blur of red behind my eyes and all I could think about was getting hold of McAndrew and wiping that smirk off his face — for good. As soon as we arrived back at Ayresome Park I went looking for him.

'Let's have it out, right now,' I invited him. He was taller than me and outweighed me by more than half a stone. I didn't care, he either fought or I called his bluff. I was hoping he would fight. My blood was boiling and even if he had hit me with the Ayresome Park stand I wouldn't have felt it. This was his chance. Surely, he wouldn't back down. I felt nothing but contempt for him when he walked away.

Now he was firing his cheap shots yet again, this time via the press for all of Middlesborough to read. I reached for the phone and dialled his number. 'What's your game, McAndrew?' I seethed. 'You've never been much of a player yourself and now you're blaming others.'

The surprise in his voice seemed genuine and it made me pause. I was compelled to listen. He said none of his references was about me. In fact, they were about more senior players, some of whom were his mates. It seemed I'd grabbed the wrong end of the stick. Suddenly, I felt very calm. What did it matter? I was leaving Boro. All my battles here had now been fought. There was no point looking back. There was nothing to prove. Liverpool wanted me, that was enough in itself. Years later, when John Neal was manager of Chelsea and Tony McAndrew was in his squad, the London club tried to buy me from Liverpool.

'No thanks,' I joked to my former Boro boss, 'not while you've got that bloke playing for you.'

I had returned to Middlesbrough with a handshake commitment to sign for Liverpool. Meanwhile, I wanted to see out my contract and help Boro finish as high on the ladder as possible. Yet, when the team for the upcoming game against West Brom was posted, my name wasn't on the list. As far as Middlesbrough were concerned, I was no longer one of them.

A fortnight after shaking Bob Paisley's hand on the 650 000 pound transfer Liverpool had agreed to pay Boro for my services, I finally turned my back on my old club for good. It had been five years since I had paid my own way to trial with them. I had hoped that our parting would have been amicable. After all, they'd got me

Transfer talk with Bob Paisley

for nothing and now had the highest transfer fee of the season as a return on the faith shown by George Wardle, Bobby Murdoch and John Neal. From a business viewpoint, Middlesbrough had no reason to be unhappy. Not so the fans. They were witnessing the departure of yet another Ayresome 'prodigy' in whom they had invested their faith.

I'd seen the best and the worst of it at Boro but I'll never forget the contributions of those who helped me most — men like Messrs Wardle, Murdoch and Neal plus players like Terry Cooper and Graeme Souness. Jack Charlton had long been on the receiving end from me for once having said that he didn't think I'd make it as a footballer while my rear end pointed to the ground. In fact, I owe him a huge debt of thanks because it was his words which gave me the motivational kick along the road to success.

As for John Neal, he is one of the true gentlemen of the game. It was flattering to be pursued by Liverpool, but how do you turn your back on a man like that? The first thing I did when I finally made it to Merseyside was forward him the thousand quid he had advanced to send me home to see my grandmother before her death.

On the day the transfer had been negotiated my folks and Jenny's family had tried repeatedly to call us to learn of developments. The line had been jammed by calls from reporters in England and Australia, all trying to score a scoop on the transfer deal. And it wasn't just reporters wanting in on the action. There had been a rash of solicitors, agents and accountants all offering their services to manage my career. The one blessing that week was that Liverpool's League Cup Final appearance meant that Middlesbrough, who were down to play the Merseysiders in a league game, had a day off. Jenny and I took the opportunity to escape and celebrate.

The deal remained on a handshake basis until early April, when Bob Paisley phoned to say that they were keen to formalise the agreement. After the cold reception I'd received back at Middlesbrough, there was no reason to procrastinate. Liverpool's home game against Stoke had been brought forward to the Friday night to avoid clashing with the Grand National steeplechase at nearby Aintree on the Saturday afternoon. It was decided that I would be present at Anfield on the Friday to sign and watch the home game. After the signing I was interviewed live on Desmond Lynam's sports show on BBC-TV. Somebody was obviously watching back in Middlesbrough. Jenny and I returned to Teesside to find our house had been burgled again.

Whether experiencing burglaries or generating transfer headlines, my career was rarely anything but eventful. Kicks in the teeth aside, I had enjoyed a charmed existence. Perhaps for the first time, in the heady atmosphere of all that transfer hype, I made the mistake or thinking I was someone special. When I was a tiny kid I used to badger my old man about taking me out on the lake fishing. Dad saw those trips as his piece of solitude away from work and family hassles. He wasn't keen to share it with a precocious kid, but one day he relented. I'd never, caught a fish in my life let alone been out with my father in the boat. I was beside myself with excitement. He baited my hook and tossed it overboard. Nothing happened. Then, there was a blur of silver and a thud in the bottom of the boat. A fat mullet had jumped almost a metre out of the water and landed thrashing amid our tackle and bait. The old man nearly died of a heart attack. Wow, I thought, this fishing is all right. And I automatically assumed I must have been a very special fisherman to have conjured that mullet up out of the depths without the aid of hook and line.

Of course, I was wrong. And I was equally wrong at twenty years of age when I imagined that landing a bunch of transfer headlines would really change my life. Like that little kid who marched up to his mum with his first fish, I assumed that I really must have been something out of the ordinary. Until I could arrange my own housing, Liverpool put me up at the Holiday Inn Hotel. As the biggest transfer signing of the season and the new noise in town, the world came to my door. Representatives of boot and clothing companies chased my endorsement, the nation's leading soccer writers sought interviews and there were plenty of Scouser girls who wanted to be the first to date the new signing. For a young Aussie used to a more spartan existence at Middlesbrough, it was a head-turning experience.

A London sports management firm signed me and was soon extracting its percentage. With the ink barely dry on a contract to wear a certain brand of boots, I was off to fulfil a teenage fantasy. During the dark days at Middlesbrough I had told my mates that one day I'd own a white Porsche with 'ROO 1' numberplates. I mistakenly thought the cheque from the boot contract would cover the cost, but by the time the agents had grabbed their cut of the deal, the cheque was many thousands lighter. I went ahead and bought the Porsche anyway. But that wasn't enough for me. By engaging an inquiry agent I was able to track down the holder of registration plates ROO 1. They were fixed to an old banger gathering dust in a London garage. To secure the plates I had to buy the car as well. The owner wanted 2000 quid, but what's money when you've just been signed as Liverpool's latest star?

Later, when I had really paid my dues at Liverpool, I perceived how critical it was for new players to adopt a low profile when entering the Anfield portals. Some of that money I was spending had come indirectly out of the pockets of Liverpool fans. It would have been better if I'd waited until I could prove I was worthy of the investment.

Being a brash young man, I wasn't astute enough to understand that people were trying to help and guide me. Kenny Dalglish made a point of picking me up outside the hotel on my second day in the city and taking me house hunting. Here was the immortal Dalglish, arguably the finest player ever to pull on a red shirt, going out of his way to make me feel welcome. He wanted me to become part of the Liverpool family. Do you think I was grateful? Not at first. I can remember entertaining the cynical notion that there must have been an ulterior motive. I had much to learn about Liverpool.

The situation would have been better if I'd been fully fit. In fact, I had a serious knee injury. After a few games in reserves I reported the problem to Bob Paisley and he sent me for tests. Like the pelvic damage, the cartilage was wearing away and it would only be a matter of time before it went altogether. It was another legacy of the carpark wear and tear. The outcome was that I wouldn't play again for the rest of the season.

The Boss had always prided himself on being able to pick an injury a mile away. And he must have been furious with himself and especially me when it was revealed that Liverpool had paid a fortune for a player carrying a serious knee problem. No doubt, Bob Paisley had been made abundantly aware that his expensive and injured signing was carving out a bigger reputation on the party and nightclub circuit than he was on the training field. At Anfield they miss very little. In his grandfatherly fashion, the Boss called me into his office for a long overdue chat. He said that now the management had had a chance to see me at close quarters, they were of the opinion that the deal hadn't worked out as sweetly as they would have wished. Manchester United were about to sign Brian Robson from West Brom and the Midlands club was eager to part with some of the proceeds to secure a suitable midfield replacement. Liverpool, said Bob Paisley, would agree to let me go. I was rocked to the soles of my feet. Could they be serious? Were they really showing me the door before I'd had as much as a whiff of the first team action?

I remembered how Souness had warned me not to expect any favours of him, but I was desperate. I went to the bar of my hotel and waited for him to show. When he came breezing in for a drink late that afternoon, I summoned up the nerve to approach him. As embarrassed as I was about my predicament, I was nonetheless in dire need of his advice. He sipped his beer thoughtfully as I related what Bob Paisley had said. Yes, my ex-Boro club-mate offered, he could see the problem from both sides. In fact, my high-life existence had been a pale carbon of his Liverpool entrance. Souey knew all about the good times I'd been enjoying because he was the one who, three years earlier, had founded the party gang which I had inherited. As the latest signing, I was simply carrying on the tradition. The major difference was that, as a footballer, I wasn't in the same class as Souness.

'I wouldn't be surprised if it's a shock tactic,' Graeme said. 'They either want you to knuckle down and get on with the job, or piss off.'

It was all I needed to know. The injury meant there was nothing I could do about my playing form, but I could do something about the party circuit. I knocked it on the head.

The situation was clear to me now. Not being required for duty during those final six weeks, I had been at a loose end with too much cash in my pocket and too much time on my hands. Jenny had gone home to Australia early to prepare for our July wedding, and I had been missing her steadying influence. In that introductory period at Liverpool I stayed out too late, had too many drinks and believed too many people when they told me what a good bloke they thought I was. What I should have been doing was putting my head down and preparing for the day when Liverpool would want some return on their 650 000 quid.

It was Graeme's advice and a trip to Paris that helped me see the light. Liverpool were heading for the French capital and a European Cup Final rendezvous with Real Madrid. As a non-playing member of the squad, I went along for the ride. Our fans were in high spirits and a few hundred of them had selected a Parisian hotel to wet their throats in preparation for a night of vocal support. It was still a couple of hours before kick-off and the air was thick with Scouse accents and singing. Then in walked Shankly.

The place fell silent in an instant. They gathered around him in a circle. The great man, by this stage in retirement, said a few short words on what he expected of Liverpool and their fans that night. I'd never seen anything like it. For me, it was a lesson about a vital ingredient I had overlooked in the heady weeks following my transfer. Respect. I'd seen Dalglish and Paisley at close quarters and observed the esteem in which they were held. But it was nothing like this.

There was another lesson to be learned that night. Liverpool duly won the trophy and I held one of the precious tickets to the celebration about to explode in the Crazy Horse nightclub. Out of a throng of fans singing yet another chorus of 'Gay Paree, Gay Paree . . .' emerged a bloke who proceeded to tell me what a great player I was and how I would be the best thing that ever happened at Anfield. Almost in the same breath he asked me to hand over my ticket to the Liverpool party. Having only one pass, I apologised and said that if I gave it to him I couldn't get in myself. 'You lousy Aussie bastard,' he spat, 'why don't you go back where ya come from!' For somebody who had in the previous few weeks been easily swayed by flattery, it was a salient lesson.

On that Paris trip I roomed with a new squad member from Zimbabwe who had signed on the same day as me. His name was Bruce Grobbelaar. We would be roommates and buddies for the next eight years during which time, largely thanks to Bruce, there would be few dull moments.

In many ways it was a relief to see the season end. Preparations were well under way for the wedding in Australia. Jenny and I were married in style in the family church just a stone's throw from our old Speers Point home. It was great to be back in Australia surrounded by our families and lifetime friends.

We had planned a brief honeymoon on the Barrier Reef before I was required to report for pre-season. Instead, we travelled to Sydney where I was to appear in a media charity game. Jenny was well impressed. We never did get time for that honeymoon, but headed back to England for the start of the new season. I was ready for the challenge. Newly turned twenty-one and a husband to boot, I could handle whatever the Anfield outfit threw at me. Or so I thought.

THE LIVERPOOL **LEGEND**

CHAPTER 6

Allow me to pass on a tip to anyone contemplating a change of employment: take the time to research your new firm. You can bet they've done their homework on you.

What did I know about Liverpool Football Club? Simply, they were the best. So what! This Johnston boy could play too — the newspapers said so. I believed that I was well qualified to make it at Liverpool. Once again I was wide of the mark. Before the new signing would win any real respect he would have to serve what almost amounted to a second apprenticeship learning the Liverpool way.

When I arrived at Anfield the club still followed the tradition of loading the players aboard the team bus each morning for the drive to the training ground at Melwood. With the thermometer hovering around the freezing mark, I was sensibly rugged up in warm-up gear including tracksuit bottoms for what would be my first training session with my new club. 'Don't get caught wearing those,' whispered one of my new club-mates, nodding at my track pants. I looked at the other squad members and noted that to a man they were all in shorts, as were coaches Ronnie Moran and Roy Evans. Then out waddled Paisley and he too was wearing a pair of baggy shorts. It was so cold the veins in his ancient legs stood out bright blue against his white skin. I shook my head in disbelief. Is this how one of the wealthiest clubs in the land treats its staff? In time the new boy would learn that it was all part of the Shankly creed, accepted as holy writ by subsequent Liverpool managers.

'You train as you play,' Shanks used to say. His theory was that come 3 p.m. Saturday, we would have to play football, irrespective of the weather. And we'd play in shorts, not track pants. If you doubt whether it had any real effect on results, take a look at Liverpool's trophy cabinet.

Across Stanley Park, Everton would avoid the worst of winter by training indoors. They had a full-size synthetic pitch in their centrally heated complex, and they wore tracksuits to boot. Not so Liverpool. We'd plough on through snow and ice. And nobody would dare complain. It was so cold during one training session that Ian Rush, notorious for his lack of legwork, paid the penalty for his inactivity when his jaw locked with the cold. Nor did we train on artificial surfaces. With one or two exceptions, the entire season was fought out on turf. Train as you play.

My early training sessions certainly left an impression on Bob Paisley. Liverpool were about to lose the services of striker David Johnson, a prolific goalscorer whose boundless enthusiasm sent him running all over the field during a game. Paisley is said to have watched me train and muttered: 'We're just about to lose one headless chicken — now we've gone and bought another!'

Liverpool had no need for headless chickens. Self-disciplined performers were their stock in trade. There is, however, one essential ingredient that will get a player inside the Anfield door. Courage. I may have been deficient in skill and prone to headless chook acts, but I didn't lack bottle.

No telling of the Liverpool legend is complete without reference to Everton. As any Merseysider well knows, in the beginning there was only one Liverpool club and it was called Everton. Liverpool was created from a split within the ranks at Everton. The rivalry today is the more intense because of that beginning. Civil wars are always more fiercely contested than wars between nations.

The televised English games I'd watched as a kid had shown these mighty clubs in all their glamour. It never occurred to me that these football institutions with their modern grounds, legions of support and highly paid players originated from modest beginnings. Merseysiders are weaned on the history of the two great clubs. For all of us outsiders though, it bears relating.

Everton Football Club grew out of St Domingo's, a Methodist church that fulfilled the civic duty of keeping the local tearaways off the street. They kicked off in 1878 and went so well that they took on an area identity by adopting the name of the local suburb, Everton. The club played its matches on a public pitch at Stanley Park before moving to a rented ground at Priory Road. In 1884 they rented a plot in Anfield Road. Everton grew in power and assets until, in 1888, they were accepted as one of the founding members of the new Football League.

If things looked good at public level, it wasn't so behind the scenes where a power struggle involving strong man and local politician John Houlding was about to split the club apart. In 1892 Houlding's opponents decided to leave Anfield and find a new headquarters. They chose a plot called Goodison Park on the north side of Stanley Park. Ever since that date it has been the headquarters and home ground of Everton Football Club. Houlding was left with a classic business problem: a showroom but no stock. With a ground in his keep but no product to sell, the football entrepreneur pulled a masterstroke — he created his own club. Liverpool Association Football Club was formed in May 1892.

Such were the origins of one of sport's great rivalries. Ask any football fan — you haven't been to Merseyside until you've witnessed a Liverpool versus Everton derby. Playing in one, well, that's something else again.

One of the great Merseyside myths is that part of the Everton-Liverpool rivalry is based on sectarian differences. In the history of football there have been a few religious rivalries, most notably that which has existed between the two great Glasgow clubs, Rangers and Celtic. The story holds that Everton were Catholic and Liverpool Protestant. Club historians give it no credence especially in light of the fact that Everton originated from a Methodist church side and, over the years, played numerous friendlies against that great bastion of the Protestant faith, Rangers of Glasgow. One theory is that the Everton-Catholic link grew from a recruiting period during the 1950s when Everton scouts enlisted players from Eire. In my time at Liverpool nobody paid the religious issue a scrap of consideration. Players in both camps came from either side of the denominational tracks and nobody counted heads nor cared to. At administrative level, there was nothing but cooperation and respect. I never played in a Merseyside derby which wasn't outrageously competitive but, almost without exception, they were conducted in a spirit of good sportsmanship.

Liverpool played its first game on 1 September 1892. Houlding did the honours of kicking off and only a handful of people turned up to watch them beat Rotherham Town 7- 1 in a friendly. Meanwhile, more than 10 000 were crammed into Goodison to see Everton beat Bolton Wanderers. Despite that less than auspicious start, Liverpool's first season was memorable. Fielding a side comprised entirely of Scottish players poached from across the border, they won seventeen out of twenty-two games to run away with the Lancashire League trophy. In 1893 the club, rather cheekily, applied for inclusion in the second division of the Football League. They were accepted. On 2 September that year, Liverpool played their first Football League game, defeating Middlesbrough Ironopolis 2–0 away from home. They returned to Anfield the following week to defeat Lincoln City 4–0 before a noisy crowd of 5000.

By the end of that first season in the Football League Liverpool had played twenty-eight games without loss. In a knockout elimination to determine promotion status, Liverpool won their final match against Newton Heath (later to change their name to Manchester United) to graduate to the first division. They were on their way. Well, almost. The following season saw them plummet straight back to the second division, but they bounced back to the top drawer where, in 1900-01 they hoisted high the championship trophy for the first time.

By then they had discarded their original strip of blue and white quarters for red shirts. The blood red strip has since become one of the great symbols of football excellence, as recognisable as the all white of Real Madrid or the gold shirts of Brazil.

By the time Bill Shankly arrived in 1960, LFC had won five first division titles. In the ensuing twenty-eight seasons they would collect an amazing twelve League Championships and win the European Cup four times, the FA Cup three and the Football League Cup four.

One of the best guides to Liverpool's dominance of the modern era is the number of times they have contested the FA Charity Shield, the traditional new season curtainraiser featuring the reigning League champions versus the FA Cup winners. Since 1964 the Reds have made the trip to Wembley for no less than fifteen Charity Shield matches. As club chairman John Smith was prone to say, 'Liverpool FC is in the business of winning trophies.'

That statement disguises the fact that the English championship is the longest and most competitive football premiership in the world. A typical English season is the footballing equivalent of the Long March. The further you go, the harder it gets. It is a routine of two matches a week for almost forty weeks in conditions which run the gamut from the lushness of autumn to the frozen bogs of deepest winter. It is dreadful terrain. Nobody traverses it better than LFC.

Liverpool's great landmarks reflect the city's role as a busy and successful port of the Empire. Then, square riggers out of my home port of Newcastle in New South Wales would slip into the mouth of the Mersey and unload their cargo at the Pier Head under the shadow of the liver birds atop the impressive Liver Building. Long before LFC came into being, it is said that those birds were a common sight in the Mersey Basin. Now, the liver bird is best known as the centrepiece of the football club's crest.

In those days, the Merseyside docks were alive with industry as dockers unloaded the offerings from the colonies. Directly adjacent to the docks area is the network of streets lined with buildings originally designed as warehouses. Out of the cellar of one such warehouse came the sixties phenomenon known as Beatlemania.

In Liverpool's trading heyday, the dockers drank in the riverside pubs and fought hard to win a five-and-a-half-day week so that they could watch either of the city's two great football clubs. Sometimes visiting merchants would make the trip out to Anfield or Goodison to see what all the fuss was about. Suitably entertained, they would repair to their suites in the gracious Adelphi Hotel in the heart of town. The growing professionalism of football would soon see players, most from humble backgrounds, rubbing shoulders with the Adelphi's wealthy clientele. Regardless of how well they slept, few visiting teams came out of Liverpool with the points. Take Stoke City, for example. In 1902 they stayed at the Adelphi and dined so heartily on expensive fare that most of the team came down with food poisoning. Stoke fielded nine barely fit men and at times were reduced to seven. Liverpool, fortified by more modest tucker, won 7-0.

Old timers will tell you that singing was first heard on the Anfield terraces way back in 1906 as Liverpool strolled to their second first division title. Over the years chanting and singing, especially that emanating from the Kop, has become an Anfield artform. It's spontaneous, humorous and invariably passionate. At times, especially during a poignant moment in a critical game, it can be mesmerising. The Kop in its glory is an awesome thing, rising and roaring like a volcano, obliterating rival supporters and teams alike. I've seen visiting sides, especially those from the Continent, immobilised by the sheer power and passion of the Kop's support for the home side. Just when you need them most they begin again, right on cue: 'Liv-er-pool, Liv-er-pool . . .' Then comes the anthem of a young Scouse soldier dying on the battlefield, softly at first, '*Let me tell you a story of a poor boy who was sent far away from his home . . .*' then growing stronger as the rest of the Kop catches on, '*To fight for his King and his country and also the old folks back home . . .*' The hairs on the nape of your neck begin to stand on end. '*As he lay on the battlefield dying / With the blood rushing out of his head / As he lay on the battlefield dying / These are the last words he said,*' And then everybody joins in, '*Oh, I am a Liverpudlian and I come from the Spion Kop / I love to sing / I love to shout / I get thrown out quite a lot / We support a team that's dressed in red/ And it's a team that you all know / it's a team that we call LIVERPOOL / And to glory we will go . . .*'

As the sound drops away the first phrase of the Rodgers and Hammerstein song that will forever be identified with LFC wells forth; '*Walk on, walk on. . .*' and instantly 30 000 throats are singing with an intensity that defies description. Uplifted by that tide of passion, Liverpool are unstoppable. The Kop's faith knows no limit. The Kop is every bit as much a part of the glory of LFC as any of the great players or managers. With the Kop behind us, we had at least a goal start every time.

Numerous gifted players and characters contributed to the club's colourful history. Take goalkeepers for example. It is little wonder that the club's telex call sign is 'Goalkeeper' in light of the charismatic characters who have stood between the Liverpool sticks over the years. The first of the great keepers was Sam Hardy and he was later followed by a slightly eccentric Irish genius known as Elisha Scott who joined Liverpool in 1914 and held the keeping position for almost twenty years. Irrespective of the weather, Elisha wore three sweaters and two pairs of socks. In his prime the Merseyside derby used to almost invariably come down to a battle between Elisha and the legendary Everton centre-forward Dixie Dean. That tradition of great goalies has been maintained through to the modern era with the likes of Ray Clemence. As for eccentricity, more than a little of Elisha must have rubbed off on Bruce Grobbelaar, the clown prince of goalkeepers.

Managers over the years made some inspired choices of club captains. There must have been a bit of divine intervention involved the day that Jimmy Jackson scored the job. The Reverend James Jackson was a man of the cloth and he led the side admirably during the 1920s. A great crowd favourite, he was dubbed 'Parson' Jackson by the Kop. Jimmy had no time for boozing and gambling and used to tell his club-mates exactly what he thought of those two vices. But on the field he suspended the 'turn the other cheek' dictum to earn a reputation as a tough but fair defender who had the ability to play in almost any position.

Out of the dark days of the Second World War emerged a teenage Scottish left winger who went on to become one of the club's finest. His name was Billy Liddell. He made 492 appearances for Liverpool and anyone who knows anything about the club rates him right up there with Keegan, Dalglish or any of the immortals.

During the same era Liverpool signed a wing half called Bob Paisley. Like Bill Shankly, his career too was interrupted by the war during which he saw action in North Africa. Resourceful and consistent in the Anfield mould, he would eventually leave an indelible stamp on the club's fortunes. This might not have appeared evident in 1950 when, after scoring a vital goal against Everton in the FA Cup semi-final, he was dropped for the final to make way for the return of another player from injury. When Bob Paisley entered his managerial mode years later, this anecdote illustrated that he knew how painful it was for a player to be dropped on the eve of a Wembley final. I know, because he did it to me!

All the trophies and banner headlines tend to disguise the fact that LFC is a very down-to-earth operation. This is exemplified by the legend of the bootroom. In Shankly's day, after the daily training session was done, the manager and his coaching staff would retire to the quiet of the bootroom deep within the Anfield bastion. There, over a few bottles of beer, they would plan a footballing crusade to conquer England and eventually Europe. Why, you might ask, did such strategy meetings not take place around a polished boardroom table, or at least in the comfort of the Boss's office? Liverpool, after all, was a multi-million-pound operation and could certainly afford the best. The answer is that the genius behind the success was basically a working class man who knew how to shoot for the stars while keeping his feet firmly on the ground. There is nothing glamorous about a bootroom, the dark dingy recess where the tools of our trade are stored. It smells of polish, sweat and leather, the real ingredients of our craft. Also there were no distractions to divert the strategists from their obsession. The bootroom is to a football club what the boiler room is to a luxury cruise liner — a dark, inner sanctum, off-limits to the public, from whence comes the real power that drives the colossus.

Bob Paisley was a bootroom fixture as were Joe Fagan, Reuben Bennett, Ronnie Moran, Roy Evans and Tom Saunders. Whether they were ex--Liverpool players or not, all were steeped in the Shankly philosophy and all came from humble origins. Moran, for example, joined the club in 1952 on the recommendation of a postman who delivered mail to the home of a club director. It is many years since Shankly instituted the bootroom tradition but it was still in evidence when I joined the club.

When it came to making the hard decisions, Shankly could be as tough as the situation warranted. After his arrival in 1960 he turned what had become a rather complacent organisation on its head. By the end of that first season twenty-four players had left. One who stayed was Ian Callaghan. He would remain for eighteen years, seeing the club from the second division right through to the first European Cup victory in 1977. Between 1960 and 1977 he played a record 636 League games for Liverpool, collected five League Championship medals and was a member of the victorious 1966 World Cup side.

Most of this colourful backdrop to LFC was taken aboard much later, when I realised its relevance. An understanding of the club's history and traditions serves to remind the individual player of the standards expected of him. Fortunately, I was reasonably familiar with the more immediate history, particularly the fabulous 1970s when Liverpool's playing fortunes had been dominated by the irresistible Kevin Keegan. The Kop was heartbroken in 1977 when Keegan moved to Hamburg. The fans didn't grieve for long. Liverpool spent most of the cash from the Keegan transfer on a twenty-six-year-old Scottish international called Kenny Dalglish. He was an immediate success. In time he would be referred to reverently as King Kenny. It wasn't so much a description but more of a title. Within a decade of the signing, chairman John Smith would describe Dalglish as LFC's greatest acquisition.

In 1981 I was coming to grips with the fact that, far from being Anfield's greatest acquisition, I would be involved in a week-by-week battle for selection for the next seven years. The football media tend to oversimplify the issues. One reporter described me as a '20-year-old midfield dynamo'. Another writer said: 'Nothing is more certain that in the twelve months ahead the tearaway with the style of a young Kevin Keegan will be performing to a far wider audience. Ron Greenwood can barely wait for his British naturalisation plans to be completed to bring him into his England plans.' But Liverpool had many great players on its books and I was hardly one of them.

On the field I never shirked the hard work. Compared to the greatness of Dalglish or Souness and company, sheer grit was all I had to offer at times. And, as it turned out, sheer grit had its place amid the fine pedigrees at LFC. The Liverpool logic was so beautiful in its simplicity. A Liverpool Football Club chairman of the 1920s once said, 'I believe that it is in blending, not in playing, that a club succeeds.' There are many components to the Liverpool legend. Unity is one of them. The notion is that players should respect each other to the extent that they would never see a team-mate embarrassed or let down. It is part of the Liverpool character. During my eight years at the club, the Reds were at their peak when this bond of mateship and mutual respect was strongest. There were times when we were so close that we would go out together for a drink and nobody could break into our circle. Translate this to on-field situations and it meant that you would run an extra mile rather than let your mates down. If a red shirt was under pressure his mates would be busting their guts to make themselves available to receive the pass that got him off the hook. Rival managers couldn't figure it out. Why was it so hard to dispossess Liverpool? The answer was we all worked overtime to help the man on the ball.

Football is a game of eleven versus eleven. Liverpool tipped the odds by enlisting players who would do their own work, and a little bit more. Add eleven 'little bit mores' up and it gives an extra player — we had twelve versus eleven. In some games, when the bond between us was stronger than ever, it could have been twenty-two versus eleven. If a Liverpool manager made the mistake of picking a player who thought he could stroll about without doing the running, 40 000 fans would soon voice their disapproval. LFC means too much to me to name individuals but suffice to say I had my running battles with a few. During one match I asked a certain team-mate to lift his game. His response was to give me the finger. Well, that did me. I did something I'd never done before and have never done since: I did my own work and no more. Within a few minutes our game started to fall away. It was a salient lesson of how the chain is only as strong as its weakest link. It also showed that, for all their wisdom, the men running this mighty organisation sometimes made errors of judgment.

My new club-mates at Liverpool were the same as footballers I'd met anywhere else, save for one crucial difference: they displayed none of the petty jealousies I'd witnessed elsewhere. These guys were winners and they were more than comfortable with that image. Catch them in the players' room after a match, relaxing over a drink, and you'd easily mistake them for a bunch of well-dressed young lawyers, accountants or computer salesmen, confident in the knowledge that they worked for the best firm in the business. Graeme Souness typified the arrogance and style of that particular side. He was class and courage combined in one package.

There would be rough spells ahead but, like Souness, I wanted to stay around long enough to contribute to Liverpool's history. It was a mystery to me how certain players seemed to undergo a transfer at least once a season. In fact, there were a few players who'd had more clubs than Greg Norman. A transfer almost invariably means a change of town and all the attendant problems of dislocation. You kiss your circle of friends goodbye, slap a 'For Sale' sign on the house and go hunting for new digs. It all takes time and can be a huge distraction from knuckling down to the new job.

It says much about the Liverpool style that Dalglish, as one of the senior hands, recognised there was much more to the game than what took place during ninety minutes each Saturday afternoon. Kenny took an interest in the welfare of his fellow players, which partly explains why the club gave him the manager's job. But the managership was still five years away when he appeared at my hotel to take me house hunting.

The choice of where to live requires some thought. Home is more than a roof over the head. It's a refuge. There are few professions in the world that involve your every move being scrutinised with almost microscopic intensity. Soccer is one of them. At training, the coaching staff are constantly weighing up each player's contribution to decide who will be in or out of the team. On match day there are 40 000 fans plus a television audience of millions monitoring every move! It's life in the goldfish bowl. When the job is done, all you want to do is enjoy a quiet drink and retreat to the comfort of home and family where you can put it all back into proportion. One of the first things I did on moving into our new house was to build a dark room. It provided a haven where I could be absorbed in my photography and forget all about the pressure of work for a few hours. Along with music, photography would continue to provide a creative diversion to my daily work.

Most Liverpool and Everton pros lived out of town, away from the public gaze. We chose to live in Sandfield Park, West Derby, deep in the heart of urban Liverpool. Sandfield Park was a relatively new estate built on what was once the grounds of an old school. It was an enclave, a sanctuary in suburbia. Souey had said there was a house available next door to his at Sandfield Park. Liverpool striker David Fairclough lived nearby, too. I decided to take a look. Driving along in the rain, road directory on my lap, I peered out through the wipers trying to spot the house. In fact, I was lost. Pulling up outside what I took to be the right property, I saw a furtive figure, back pressed hard against the side wall of the house, jacket pulled up high hiding his face. How about this, I thought. I've stumbled on a burglary! It was no burglar. It was Colin Bridge, one of this world's great blokes. Typically, he had locked himself out and was trying to get out of the rain. As it turned out, the house next to Bridgey was also for sale, so I bought that. We would be neighbours for the next six years and lifelong friends thereafter. A born comic, he is the funniest fella I've had the pleasure to know. Now a family man fast bearing down on middle age, Bridgey was no dunce when it came to football. He had been an Everton apprentice who never made it to the bright lights. I asked him why and, in typical self-deprecating style, he related the following yarn:

> I was playing in reserves. It was pretty obvious the Boss didn't recognise genuine talent, otherwise I would have been in the firsts. Great news. The Liverpool Echo reported that Everton were

about to change managers. This was my chance. At training I was at my brilliant best and it was no surprise for me when I reported for work the following week to be handed an envelope. Inside was a note from the Boss. It read, 'Please report to my office.' This was it! I went around to the reserves and said, 'See you later; boys. I'm on my way up.' I strolled into the manager's office with a big grin on my face. 'I'm here to sort the wheat out from the chaff' said our new manager, the late, great Harry Catterick, 'and you're chaff. You're sacked! On your bike!'

A couple of second division clubs were interested, but after my treatment at Everton I was leaded for a club where I knew my talent would be appreciated. Skelmersdale. Ever heard of them? No? Nor had I!

Bridgey is a chronic practical joker and during the next six years he would pull some fabulous stunts, many at my expense. Every now and then, though, I'd get one back. It was the practice for sportsmen to drive cars provided by club sponsors. Sometimes the pay-off might be that the vehicle would have the club's name or logo printed on the driver's door. Then all the punters could point and say: 'Isn't that Ian Botharn in that flash motor?' Bridgey's car was an old banger. When he was out I arranged to have 'Colin Bridge — Skelmersdale FC 1967' printed in huge letters along the side of his heap. He loved it!

Sponsors' cars might be one of the perks of the jobs, but not at the price of being easily identified. After having too many supporters from other clubs stub their cigarettes out on the roof of my Porsche, I could see the benefits of auto anonymity.

We were happy in that Sandfield Park house. It was the first home for our two little girls and it formed the backdrop for so much of our early married life. Our neighbours were great. People like to go to work or the pub and tell their mates that a footballer has moved in across the road. But, by and large, my neighbours respected our privacy. The family across the road were staunch Evertonians and they never missed a chance to take the rise out of the so-called Liverpool star who had moved into their street. If we lost to Everton in a derby match I would look across the road to see a supporter's scarf and other blue paraphernalia displayed in the front window. This went on for years, and I was always looking for an opportunity to trump him. My chance came at the end of the 1985–86 season, the year we won the Double. In the week leading up to the Cup Final, my neighbour's front window resembled the display case at the Everton Supporters' Club shop. There was only one answer to this. One morning alter the Wembley Final I was ready for him as he backed his car out of the driveway. Looking up, he couldn't have missed it — I had the curtains pulled back for all to see. There with the red ribbons still attached to its handles, sat the FA Cup in all its glory.

Back in the winter of 1981–82 my personal trophy prospects had looked pretty bleak. Brian Clough was right. It would be some time before Craig Johnston consolidated a first-team berth at Anfield. As Derek Wallis of the *Mirror* noted on 9 December, 1981: 'Johnston's appearances since his 650 000 pound transfer near the end of the season have been so strictly rationed as he serves the required Anfield apprenticeship that all his first-team games this season have been as sub.'

The cause of that observation had been my effort after running on as substitute with eighteen minutes to go of a fourth round League Cup replay against Arsenal. The match remained scoreless until four minutes into extra time when Souness spotted my run into the area and delivered the ball perfectly into my path. The route to goal was acute and the 'keeper looked to have every angle covered, everything except the narrowest of gaps between his body and the near post. I blasted my shot low and hard. 1-0! Terry McDermott scored from a penalty and Dalglish netted an absolute stunner off a Johnston cross. 3-0.

'Craig a Cracker' and 'Fabulous Johnston Breaks Deadlock' trumpeted the press. A warm inner feeling

stemmed from the conviction that my first goal in a Liverpool shirt would put an end to my days as an Anfield fringe-dweller. My self-congratulation was premature.

Bob Paisley told the media that week that the more he saw of me the more he was convinced I might be better playing up front than in midfield. Privately, I couldn't see the wisdom of this because one of the essential ingredients of a midfielder is mobility and when it came to motoring around the park, I was confident nobody could get near me. Yet Paisley had a great record for pulling players into new roles. He had done it with a few at Anfield including Ray Kennedy who had been an out-and-out striker in Arsenal's Double-winning side of 1970-71. Paisley turned him into a midfielder and he went on to become one of the greatest medal winners in Anfield history. There was no way I was going to argue with the Boss's logic. I had subbed in midfield, as striker and even had a go in central defence. By that stage I was prepared to play anywhere for Liverpool — except goalie.

As it turned out, Rushie copped a knock during the Arsenal game and was sidelined for a week. My full Liverpool debut would be as a striker rather than in midfield and the match would be no ordinary league game. Instead, we were bound for Tokyo and the World Club championship showdown between Liverpool, champions of Europe, and Flamengo of Brazil, champions of South America. It would be a real baptism of fire. We arrived jet-lagged and they jumped us with two first half goals from Nunes. We lost 3-0 and were handed a footballing lesson by the outrageously skilled Brazilians. Man-of-the-match was Arthur Antunes Coimbra — the fabulous Zico.

One of the cornerstones of the Liverpool strategy is what our basketball colleagues call bench strength. Quality subs keep the first choice players on their mettle. For that reason that old one-eyed Anfielder Bill Shankly wasn't exactly joking when he used to say: 'There are two great football teams on Merseyside - Liverpool and Liverpool reserves!' One of my proudest possessions is the Central League medal I won for playing in the reserves during that first season at Liverpool. I regard it as a certificate for having served my

The fabulous Zico

Overleaf: Scoring against Nottingham Forest at Anfield

Anfield 'apprenticeship'. Shortly after my move from Middlesbrough I played in a reserves side which included Steve Heighway, Ian Rush, Ronnie Whelan, Avi Cohen, Bruce Grobbelaar, Howard Gayle and Steve Nichol. My memory could be playing tricks on me, but I think I can recall that David Fairclough was the substitute. Some side! Successive Anfield bosses have long been aware that the important part of the season is after Christmas when tiredness, complacency and injury expose the weaknesses in everybody except the best prepared clubs. This is where Liverpool show their stuff, not to mention the quality of their reserve team players. After all, we had our share of injuries including a serious one that sidelined skipper Souness for a month. As a fringe player, I required fourteen first-team appearances to qualify for a championship medal should the Reds finish on top of the heap. Like the great campaign general that he is Bob Paisley threw me into the fray at the business end of the season. Not only did I not let Liverpool or myself down, I helped us jump clear of the pack to place one hand on that precious League Championship trophy. By season's end I had still not played in a losing Liverpool combination, with the one exception of the match in Japan. Our run-in to the trophy included an unbeaten spell of seventeen straight games, fourteen of which we won. For my part, I was happy to contribute. In the midst of this run my tally showed six goals in nine games.

Among my great memories of that spell was a two-goal, man-of-the-match performance against Forest that had the press speculating what might have been had I hooked my star to Cloughie's cause. Ask any Koppite what his major dream in life is, and he might say, 'To score the winner away at Old Trafford.' I did that too as we beat Manchester United 1-0 in a contest that virtually clinched the title. And my first Merseyside derby was made personally memorable by yet another goal. I still have the press clipping of the photo with the caption reading: 'Golden touch from man-of-the-match Craig Johnston as he gratefully accepts Ian Rush's pass to float the ball out of reach of Everton keeper Neville Southall into the top of the net for Liverpool's third goal.'

Interviewed by a television reporter about that goal I was asked if I had meant to chip the keeper. 'Of course,' I replied, tongue in cheek, 'just like Bobby Charlton in the '68 European Cup Final against Benfica!' The truth was I had taken a wild slash at the ball and it had screwed off my left foot and lobbed over the keeper's head.

I might have seen the season out as a first-team regular but for Souey's return from injury. The fact was that he couldn't force his way into a winning side and had told Bob Paisley that if he didn't get a run he would seek another club. We were 2-0 down to Tottenham at half-time when Paisley said to me, 'Get in the bath, son.' Substitute Souness came on for me. Liverpool wound up drawing 2-all.

Accustomed to success since the Shankly days, the Kop can be demanding and impatient with anyone they see as falling short of Liverpool's awesome standards. But whatever the result, the supporters have a tremendous regard for courage and commitment. Right from the start, I gave everything and the fans knew it. For that reason I had a particular affinity with the Koppites. This relationship was established early and, almost immediately, became a bone of contention.

During a match against Sunderland, I was replaced halfway through the second half. The Kop went crazy. Ted MacAuley of the *Daily Mirror* reported it thus;

> *The only puzzling and astonishing move was manager Bob Paisley's decision to pull off Craig Johnston 20 minutes from the end for he was Liverpool's liveliest performer. He knew it too — and was bitterly*

> *disappointed to be substituted when Kenny Dalglish looked a far more suitable case for the treatment.*

> *Fists were waved at manager Paisley, sitting impassively in the stand, and the Liverpool boss was given a rare blast of booing.*

> *Then the mop-haired kid was cheered all the way to the tunnel. His going . . . only served to remove some enticing sparkle and certainly did nothing to enliven Liverpool's work.*

Bob Paisley came out and described the demonstrating Koppites as yobbos not intelligent enough to understand the reasoning behind the move. This was all I needed — to be the centre of a spat involving two of the club's greatest assets: Bob Paisley and the Kop. Happily, I was able to defuse the situation via a newspaper story explaining why I thought I'd been subbed. The logic was that it was a tight game, I'd still to play a full match for Liverpool and my inexperience in helping us defend a 1-0 scoreline was a risk that the manager didn't wish to take. I concluded by saying that it was possible that because I wasn't doing it the Anfield way, I was pulled off against Sunderland. It was all fair and diplomatic but it was the last time I would defend a manager who denied me a first-team place.

The footnote to that particular championship season was supplied, perhaps fittingly, at Middlesbrough where we played our last league game. The reappearance of Messrs Souness and Johnston as League Championship medal winners must have scratched a few old sores, particularly in light of the fact that bottom-of-the-table Boro were about to take the plunge back to the second division. Liverpool have a tremendous regard for the quality of footballers bred in the North-East, viewing the region as England's greatest talent bank. Of that particular side, Souness, Terry McDermott, Alan Kennedy and I had all been recruited from North-East clubs. Sensibly, the soccer scribes did not condemn Liverpool for raiding the vaults, but merely asked when were such clubs as Newcastle United, Sunderland and Middlesbrough going to acquire directors capable of doing justice to the tremendous talent on their very doorstep. By the start of the new season yet another Boro graduate would be at Anfield. David Hodgson had served his apprenticeship with me at Ayresome Park and we had both stepped up to the first team during the same season. Blessed with natural speed, he would join the strong pool of goal-scoring talent at Anfield. Unluckily for him, the presence of Ian Rush and company would mean few first team chances.

For my return to Ayresome I was granted the honour of leading Liverpool onto the field. The fans who had once cheered me delivered a hostile reception with chants of 'Money-grabber' greeting my appearance. It annoyed me that Boro had branded me a money-grabber. After all, I had paid my own way to England, enabling Boro to secure a midfielder for nil outlay. Within a few short seasons, they had managed to sell me for three-quarters of a million quid. It seemed to me that the club was not the slightest bit interested in retaining young players and building a side. But they didn't have the guts to spell that attitude out to the fans. Instead, they laid the blame on those players who hit the transfer trail. What went on in the boardroom and what the club told the supporters via the press were two different stories. Boro made a killing out of the Craig Johnston deal. They were the money grabbers, not me.

With the championship already ours the result was inconsequential. But not for the home side. Boro, after drawing at Anfield early in the season, were desperate to knock over the new champs. We held on for a draw. The season was over and I'd collected my first League Championship medal. Satisfied that the job was done, we went out for the night and got righteously drunk.

LETTERS FROM **LIVERPOOL** CHAPTER 7

The people who run LFC are obsessive about their product. That's why they're the best. They believe totally in what they're doing, almost to the point of fanaticism.

This unswerving allegiance is best illustrated by an apocryphal tale about the great Shankly. Anfield mythology holds that Shanks was making his way to his seat in the dugout before a Liverpool versus Everton match at Anfield. As with each derby, there was barely an inch of standing room left in the ground. To gain a vantage point, one supporter had scrambled up some scaffolding where he balanced precariously high above the crowd. A minute before kick-off the desperate fan lost his footing and plummeted earthward only to be jerked to a halt a few feet from the ground by a television cable tangled around his neck. Among the first to spot the man's predicament was Shanks. 'For God's sake, cut that fellow down,' bellowed the Liverpool boss. 'Can't ye see he's turning blue!'

The problem with any obsession is that it tends to exclude just about everything else. The average professional footballer doesn't have to know a lot about anything besides football. And that's a pity. Yet it is even more tragic that clubs do not encourage players to make better use of their abundant free time. Tertiary education is rare and definitely not high on anybody's list of priorities. A rough thumb sketch of the average pro soccer player depicts a working class boy who never wanted to be anything other than a footballer. To achieve his goal, he has had to give away any other athletic pursuits, education and alternative employment prospects. Yet there were many pursuits at which they excelled. I've never met a pro footballer who wasn't a card sharp, pool hall wizard, master of the dart board or expert judge of horseflesh.

At the end of every training session Ronnie Moran would shout: 'Straight home and get your feet up in front of the telly!' As a result Liverpool footballers became armchair experts on almost every sport imaginable. As for televised football, Dalglish was an absolute scholar of the game and knew every British player by name and characteristics. Kenny was capable of boring us rigid on away trips by running videos of obscure Scottish fixtures. Nobody was game to complain but it paid to take a good book just in case. Kenny's data bank extended to the Continent after I supplied a newspaper with a picture story featuring him with a satellite dish. A grateful manufacturer furnished Kenny with his own dish which meant he could then monitor matches from Spain, Italy, Germany, France or wherever football was televised in Europe. Gone were the days when the cloth-capped manager went abroad an spying missions.

I sometimes wished I'd come out of the same mould as the other lads. Perhaps the difference was that most of the hobbies enjoyed by my team-mates came under the heading of indoor entertainment. Being Australian, my childhood fun had been found outdoors. It was a cultural difference and it singled me out from the rest and regularly excluded me from the clique. They often interpreted my solitude as a snub of their culture. In reality, I wanted to be one of the boys, but there was always another guitar lesson, a book I wanted to read or a piece of photographic gear to master. It wasn't that I had a great plan for self-improvement. There was simply too much happening in the world to limit myself exclusively to football.

One of my great distractions was music. It was a joy to come home from a training session, drop an album on the deck, crank up the sound system and lose myself in the magic of the photographer's darkroom I'd built in our Liverpool home. Before I bought a house or a single stick of furniture, there was always the sound system. Its quality and sophistication became a yardstick for the wages I was earning.

During an adolescent introduction to modern music I'd slowly worked my way through the rock greats. In my apprenticeship years at Middlesbrough, my mate Peter Tredinnick had introduced me to the genius of Bob

Dylan. 'If you like Dylan,' somebody said, 'try this.' It was Bruce Springsteen's landmark 'Born To Run' album. As a teenager Springsteen had said he wanted to write like Dylan and sing like Roy Orbison. He probably made b cAmerican dream'. This bloke, who had grown up amid the industrial sameness of New Jersey, understood that there was a road out of the mundane. I could relate to that. 'Born To Run' and subsequent Springsteen albums were played to death on my stereo. When Bruce and his E Street Band crossed the Atlantic for his 1980–81 UK tour, I had just arrived at Liverpool. On the day I bought the Porsche, I drove to London to catch Springsteen at Wembley Arena. The British critics, locked into the New Romance craze, weren't overly impressed, but he blew me away. Springsteen came back in 1985 and I flew to Ireland to catch him at the mystical setting of Slane Castle in the country, an hour's drive from Dublin. This time, they were ready for Bruce. More than 90 000 packed the grassed amphitheatre for the show set against the backdrop of a brilliant sunny day and the awe-inspiring green of rural Ireland. It was one of the most magical days of my life and the ultimate diversion from the pressures of football.

When the tour moved onto England, I pulled a few strings to work my way into the photographers' pit for the Tyneside concert at St James's Park, home ground of Newcastle United. Conveniently, I knew the promoter, Harvey Goldsmith, and he introduced me to Jon Landau, the former *Rolling Stone* journalist who had gone to a small rock venue on the Jersey shore and came away to write: 'I've seen the future of rock 'n' roll and its name is Bruce Springsteen!' Landau packed away his typewriter to take over the full-time management of Bruce and his band. It was a happy collision. The literary Landau introduced the street-wise Jersey rocker to some of the finer things denied him by a modest education. I could see parallels between professional football and rock 'n' roll here.

Landau and I were chatting before the concert started and he invited me backstage to meet Springsteen. I gave it a second's thought and then declined the offer, Legends are better left alone. However, I asked if he could get me into the photographers' pit. He was reluctant. Only four passes were issued worldwide to cover the tour and the privilege was closely guarded.

'You've got the first song,' said Jon Landau, 'then get the hell outta there!'

I was so overcome by the occasion that I hardly got a single picture in focus.

Music was an abiding passion and I added everything to my collection. With the acoustic guitar Jenny had bought I strummed laboriously at the exercises until I could pick out a few chords. My progress improved when I found a professional teacher. By then I'd given away an earlier flirtation with the trumpet and was concentrating on guitar, both acoustic and electric. Later would come a set of keyboards, a drum machine and a four-track recording system. Here were the makings of a do-it-yourself recording studio. But more of that later. Meanwhile, I was adding to my music collection and taking the opportunity to chat wherever possible with anyone in the business.

One day we were playing at Vicarage Road, home ground of Watford, and were out inspecting the pitch before kick-off when 'One Perfect Day' by the Australian band Little Heroes came over the public address system. Wow, who put this on, I wondered. It was cold and drizzling and when it got to the part 'And tell me, is it still raining there in England?' I thought, how bloody appropriate.

So, who do you think would be in charge of the music at Watford's home games? Into the midst of the post-match drinks session strolled the club chairman, Elton John. Just back from an Australian tour, he looked tanned and relaxed. He didn't want to talk music or football, but made a beeline for me because he wanted to chat about Australia and how much he was in love with the place. When I said I was envious of the fact that his profession was played in summertime while mine was exclusively a winter pursuit, he laughed: 'What are you doing this for when you could be down in Aussie rolling around in the surf?'

My job for team morale was to take care of the music, whether it was for prematch inspiration or post-

The photographer at work, with models Jenny and Chelsea Johnston

match relaxation. I was the club's honorary dee jay and thrived on the responsibility. Unlike certain Aussie bands, Cold Chisel were relatively unknown in the UK. At LFC, however, they had a pocket of support generated by my habit of playing Chisel hits over the team bus sound system. One or two songs became so much in demand that the players could sing along with every word, especially 'Forever Now', a huge hit with the card school.

In 1988 an Australian Aboriginal XI cricket side toured England under the leadership of rugby union great Mark Ella. I was picked in a Sport Aid team to play them in a charity fixture at Southampton. Our side included Jimmy Barnes (the ex-Chisel lead singer), Bill Wyman, David Essex, Aussie Test player Steve Waugh, Bruce Grobbelaar — who had been a handy cricketer and baseballer as a kid — and former England soccer great Mick Channon, all under the distinguished leadership of Clive Lloyd. When my grandchildren ask me if I was any good at cricket, I will be able to say in all honesty: 'Cricket? You're only talking to a man who shared the crease with Clive Lloyd!' It was a match made memorable not by the standard of cricket, but the number of beers consumed later.

I found photography and music more mentally stimulating than football. When it came to learning the intricacies of the single lens reflex camera, I wanted to know it all. I subscribed to photographic magazines, studied the manuals and, in time, emerged from the darkroom with a collection of black and whites worth keeping. Later, I would even master the magic of developing colour in my own home. Standing there in my small darkroom for hours on end whiffing developing chemicals could not have been good for me. But it was infinitely more stimulating than sitting on my arse watching televised horse-racing.

The privileged life enjoyed by a footballer put me in the perfect position to snare some exclusive shots. In April 1982 the Liverpool squad was invited out to nearby Aintree for the running of the Grand National Steeple classic. I took my camera along and, when we were treated to an inspection of the course, snapped Alan Kennedy, Bruce Grobbelaar and Terry McDermott taking a leap at one of the jumps. The *Sun* newspaper heard about the photo and bought it to run with their next Liverpool match preview.

When it came to photographic opportunities, the fish kept leaping into my boat. On a return trip to England after the close season break in Australia, I found myself seated next to a very pregnant Jenny Gibb, a fellow Australian bound for Britain. I nearly leapt out of my seat when she started screaming. She had gone into labour 30 000 feet above the Indian Ocean! The birth was imminent and all I could think of was what a photo story this will make! The problem was that my camera was tucked away in the locker above our heads and I had to vacate my seat to give the mum-to-be a bit of room. Thinking quickly, I took over the directing job and talked a fellow passenger into taking the shots. While anxious dad Robert Gibb looked on, flight stewardess and trained nurse Rita Ellis played midwife and delivered a 5 lb baby girl. The flight was diverted to Lanarca, Cyprus to drop mother and child at the local hospital. Within twenty-four hours our exclusive photos of the jumbo jet drama and the stewardess who performed the delivery — cradling the newborn babe — were splashed across the pages of a national paper.

Speaking of babies, Liverpool counts among its most loyal fans a certain lady called Winifred Francis. When not at Anfield supporting the Reds, Mrs Francis is likely to be found performing her role as one of Europe's leading obstetricians. She has delivered many of the offspring of Liverpool players and was in charge of the birth of our second daughter, Cassie.

It is Mrs Francis we had to thank in December 1982 when the Liverpool squad members suddenly found themselves jetting out of mid-winter Britain for a flying visit to Khartoum, capital of Sudan. It seems the eminent medico had worked a miracle to guarantee the lineage of President Nimeiri and the head of state was keen to show his gratitude. While in the UK, he had been invited by Mrs Francis to an Anfield match and he in turn had become a Liverpool fan. If the president couldn't come to the players, then the players would have to come to the president, at his expense. And that's exactly what happened when we touched down in Sudan for an especially arranged mid-season match against a local representative side.

We were feted in a style befitting royalty and the Sudanese people gave us a wonderful reception. Fortunately, I packed my camera and managed to snap a few fabulous memories of our trip. The *Daily Mail* thought my shots were worth reproducing and bought a series of pictures of the Liverpool lads enjoying the sunshine and the hotel pool while our football rivals were shivering back in Britain.

A few more published works and I was prepared to believe that my future beyond football would involve a career in professional photography. With almost a third of our household living space turned over to darkroom and studio, I formed a company to operate as a photographic business. The move appeared premature when I ran head first into a demarcation issue that looked certain to terminate my shutterbugging career before it had a chance to develop. The regular appearance of my by-line in the national press was creating murmurings in the ranks of the pro photographers. They didn't appreciate the idea of a footballer using his entree to provide pictures. After all, I was in a privileged position being inside England's number one club. And I wasn't even in the photographers' union. In the space of a year or so I had almost thirty photos published in the national press, including a couple of front pages. On receipt of an indirect warning from the union, I was obliged to curtail most of my submissions for publication. But I wasn't trading exclusively on my name. At least three photos, including one front pager published in the national press, appeared without my by-line which meant they had made it entirely on their own merits.

The setback didn't blunt my enthusiasm. I kept clicking away, taking family shots, snaps of our dogs, Bluey and Skippy, team photos, and portraits for my club-mates. I even snapped a shot of Kenny's son, Paul, in a Liverpool strip and superimposed him on a backdrop of a packed Anfield. Now here was an idea. Soon I was taking orders from friends and fans who wanted a photo of themselves 'playing' for Liverpool. Again, the lads accepted this as one of my eccentricities and utilised my services. I took shots of Sammy Lee's wine bar for his submission to council for approval, numerous shots for Rushie's and Bruce's autobiographies and more family portraits than I can count. The big shot of the year, however, was always the LFC lads' Christmas Party picture. The show was fancy dress and the photographic evidence became an institution as it graced the back page of the Christmas Eve edition of one of Britain's larger circulation tabloids.

Working in a studio within an environment that can be easily controlled makes for exciting results. My mentor became Harry Ormesher, Merseysider and one of Britain's leading fashion and glamour photographers. By concentrating hard on my studio work I was able to pick up a few jobs shooting fashion and sportswear. It was gratifying but, for sheer excitement, I preferred more spontaneous challenges — like rock concerts. My camera went along for the ride for Drums Over The Mersey, a thirty-six-hour anti-heroin drum marathon featuring Merseyside's and some of Britain's best bands. We had just beaten Spurs on the Saturday and I turned up on stage on the Sunday to lend LFC's support to the anti-drug campaign.

Just before my departure from England in 1988, I slipped backstage at the Nelson Mandela concert at Wembley. By now, my camera and I were well known back stage and somebody slapped a pass into my hand. It was Sting's who had already been on and done his bit. Sliding in between the speaker banks and the curtain, I cut a hole in the material and poked my camera lens through to gain the best camera angle of the lot. With the music pumping, a capacity crowd in full voice and my motor drive whirring away, I was as alive as I'd ever been in any football situation. This was living! Along with a range of fabulous shots, my souvenirs from that concert include Sting's backstage pass and Eric Clapton's guitar pick.

When the touring Aussie Kangaroos rugby league side appeared in Britain I was on the sideline at a few matches snapping away with my camera. I've always enjoyed the pace and sheer confrontation of rugby league and was gratified to see the 1982 Kangaroos waltz through Britain. Grabbing my camera bag, I went over to Leeds for the Third Test of the tour and banged off a roll of keepsakes of that fine Australian side.

From the Johnston portfolio -- fashion shots ...

Somewhere in the recesses of most professional athletes' minds lurks the constant question: what will I do when my playing days are over? An athletic career is a short one. Once the legs start to go you'd better have a secure outlet in mind because you're a long time gone. Some lend their names to sports stores, an awful lot become publicans. The lucky ones remain in the game in one capacity or other. Too many, however, finish on the bones of their arse.

Professional photography was starting to appear a likely career bet for me until June 1982 when I was invited aboard the Australian Broadcasting Commission's television commentary panel for the 1982 World Cup telecast. The prospect of doing live television brought home the truth of that old maxim: the human brain starts working the moment you are born and never stops until you stand up to speak in public. Nerves aside, I came to appreciate what it was like to be on the other side of the football fence. In this game, adequate preparation, research and giving both players and referees the benefit of the doubt were tricks of the trade I soon had to learn. Maybe I didn't set the world alight but there were a few favourable reviews both from within the Australian television industry and from outside. The commentary stint gave me the chance to see how a show came together. I was fascinated by the production team's skill and the technology involved. The magic of instant moving pictures had me hooked. Perhaps I would have to revise my plans about becoming a photographer.

My appearance on ABC-TV and Australia's absence from the World Cup Finals raised an issue I would rather have avoided. Would Liverpool's Australian midfielder make himself available for the Socceroos?

The matter had been raised on a seasonal basis ever since I'd made my Middlesbrough debut at the age of seventeen. First cab off the rank had been Australian Soccer Federation strongman Sir Arthur George. The long-time ASF president was used to getting his own way. He telephoned on a number of occasions imploring me to accept the offer of a green and gold shirt, but I was not interested in being stampeded into something that might jeopardise my career in England.

A year later, the controversial West German coach Rudi Gutendorf had the Australian national job and he flew to London to watch me play. I had an absolute shocker but that didn't prevent him repeating the offer. The matter was complicated by my appearances in the England under-21 side, and because I had both Irish and Scottish antecedents, there were overtures from both of those associations for my services. This national tug-of-war caused a great deal of personal torment for reasons that perhaps only my dad could understand. Ever since I was a kid I'd dreamed about representing my country. Mine was a generation weaned on the Olympic exploits of the great Australian athletes of the 1950–60s, our Davis Cup and rugby league heroes, swimming champions and cricketing giants. Sadly, soccer didn't fit into that frame. Until Rale Rasic guided the 1974 Socceroos into the World Cup Finals in West Germany, Australian soccer's national profile was virtually non-existent. When I went to Britain to chase my soccer dream, I was influenced by my father's advice — play at the highest level possible. Despite my rampant nationalism, I knew that a move into the Socceroo ranks from the English professional scene would be a retrograde step. I wanted to play for Australia, but not at the risk of what I had achieved. The advice coming from the wise old heads in England was that I'd have to be crazy to even think about the Australian offer.

Back then there were very few none-British players in the English professional ranks and FIFA was yet to start censuring clubs who did not release players for international duty. Most pros would be incredulous at the idea of, say, an Australian or South African forsaking a starting place at a professional club to return home for an international against New Zealand or Nigeria, especially when it meant missing games for the club that paid his wages. Remember, at that time there were no designated international breaks in the season schedule allowing players to return to their country of origin for national duty without risking their club careers.

This personal and public debate over my international call raged season in and season out. It became a sideshow and, eventually, a monumental distraction to my career. As if the pressure from Australia wasn't enough, England manager Bobby Robson was desperately keen to see me take out British citizenship so that

... and Footballer of the Year, Ian Rush

he could draft me into the England squad. I can recall flying home from a European Cup-tie in Eastern Europe where I had really hit my straps. Robson, who had made the journey to watch a couple of Liverpool players figuring in his England considerations, expressed his interest in me on the return flight. I was tempted and flattered, but I wasn't ready. Churning around in my mind was the possibility that I could still play for Australia.

While the Socceroos were exiting from the 1982 World Cup qualifiers, I was desperately striving to establish myself at Liverpool. From then on Aussie soccer scribes regularly raised the question of whether or not I was available and/or eligible for Australia. Some felt that I had forfeited my right to play for my home country by making those two under-21 appearances for England. Few journalists actually consulted me on the matter. If they had they would have learned that I still considered myself eligible for Australia because not only did I carry an Australian passport, I was still an Aussie national.

By 1984 Frank Arok had been appointed national coach with the awesome task of ensuring that Australia qualified for the 1986 World Cup Finals. Arok was doubtlessly aware of the debate surrounding my eligibility. Early in the Australian winter of 1984, he travelled to Newcastle, New South Wales, where I was holidaying with my family during the close season. The coach's mission was to determine what role Craig Johnston might play in Australia's Cup campaign. It was not a meeting I welcomed. The prospect of being called on to throw in my lot with a national team 20 000 kilometres from Anfield raised all sorts of worrying possibilities. At that stage I was experiencing a stormy passage with the Liverpool management, and a first-team place and, therefore, my livelihood, were anything but secure. Moreover, Jenny was pregnant and we would soon have other demands to consider. My career, mortgage and immediate financial well-being were in England, and I could not put those at risk.

Arok had played and coached at the highest level in Yugoslavia. He knew the score. Firstly, he made a point of keeping our meeting strictly secret. Instead of rendezvousing on soccer territory, the meeting took place at Newcastle Rugby Club. The coach laid his cards on the table. He had no wish to make unnecessary demands on Liverpool for my time. He didn't want me for all the eight preliminaries, but only for the crucial away game against Israel in Tel Aviv, and both the home and away matches against Scotland. The offer seemed relatively simple and appealing, but I was loath to make a commitment until I had had a chance to discuss the situation with Liverpool.

'As far as I understand,' I told Frank Arok, 'I'm eligible to play for Australia.'

'Good,' he said with enthusiasm, 'because we need your big-match experience.'

We shook hands and went our separate ways, both contemplating what had to be done to bring our plans to fruition. Unfortunately, our good intent was wasted. Within a fortnight of that meeting a story declaring that I was ineligible to play for Australia appeared in a Sydney newspaper. It was sourced to an ASF administrator who had said that the situation had been investigated by FIFA, the governing body of world football, and that Johnston was definitely out of contention. I was incredulous and angry. They hadn't even bothered to consult me to ask whether I considered myself ineligible or not. I was convinced that the ASF had its wires crossed. The fact remained that, despite the England under-21 appearances, I was still an Australian national bearing an Australian passport. And that, by my reading of it, made me eligible.

One columnist who didn't buy the ASF line was Johnny Warren, a former national team captain and one of Australia's greatest soccer sons. As a kid my prize possession had been a Johnny Warren signature ball. Warren didn't mince his words in letting the ASF know it was operating under cock-eyed logic. In an article entitled 'Let's Get Johnston!' Warren said: 'Such a widely held misconception is not good for the Socceroos or for that matter the future of the game here. It is my belief that should Australian soccer get off its backside and take the obvious and necessary initiatives, Craig Johnston could well contribute directly to the Socceroos for the next ten years, and, more importantly, to the development of the game for the rest of his life.'

My only recourse was to call on the ASF and ask to see the document detailing the ruling. It would have to carry the imprimatur of FIFA if that body had indeed adjudicated on the matter or, if not FIFA, then the English Football Association, as this was the body which supposedly had international claims on my services. The ASF assured me that the newspaper report was correct. Moreover, I was informed that the ASF had contacted English Football Association secretary Ted Croker to affirm the ruling. However, I was not shown the document supporting the press report. As far as I could determine, nobody had sighted this vital piece of correspondence. Did it exist? I suspected not.

The visit did nothing to allay my feeling that the ASF's stance was absolutely wrong. The national coach wanted Johnston, yet the national administrators were saying the player wasn't eligible. If the same situation had arisen in almost any other country, rather than ruling the player out of consideration, the football association would have moved heaven and hell to prove he was eligible! I made up my mind that I wouldn't let the matter rest until I sighted documentary evidence that proved who was right and who was wrong. The chance came in December 1984 when Liverpool flew to Japan to play South American champions Independiente in the World Club Championship.

On the flight was the secretary of the English Football Association, Ted Croker. I approached him in the foyer of the Tokyo Prince Hotel, explained my dilemma and asked for a ruling.

'I believe the Australian Soccer Federation has already approached you about this,' I said.

He flatly denied having received any word from the ASF on the matter. But he promised he would investigate and give me an official ruling. His written reply arrived in January 1985. It completely substantiated my suspicions, proving beyond doubt that Australia, not England or any other country, had first call on my services. The relevant portion of the letter read:

Further to our discussion in Japan, I have now investigated the situation regarding your international appearances for our under-21 team.

I have a positive assurance now from FIFA that these matches will not in any way prejudice your eligibility to play for Australia, assuming that, as I believe you stated, you have an Australian passport and are a national of that country.

For me, the matter was resolved in more ways than one. So disheartened was I by the Australian body's attitude, that I made a resolution. There was no way Craig Johnston would be involved with any side under that particular ASF administration's jurisdiction. It meant I would never play for Australia.

For good reason Liverpool became known as 'the United Nations'. Our 1983 side was a blend of Scots, Welsh, Irish, English, Zimbabwean and Australian. Grobbelaar, the Zimbabwean, and Johnston were often referred to as 'the colonials'. This exclusive club would gain another member in 1987 when Jamaican-born John 'Digger' Barnes joined from Watford.

Media fanfares invariably preceded the arrival of yet another big star at the club while our rivals would gnash their teeth at Anfield's buying power. Liverpool almost always bought well, but the club rarely received the credit it deserved for the less public purchases. Liverpool has a policy of identifying promising players in the lower divisions, buying them and then putting the Anfield polish on their game with a long stint in the reserves. This was Shankly's method and it prevails today. Take a look at any Liverpool reserve side and it is a younger version of the first team. The club scouts for player types and steadily grooms the second stringer until he is ready to be slotted straight into the first team. In this way Liverpool has maintained its awesome standards, season after season. For that reason, ex-Anfielders are always a much sought after commodity when the time comes for them

to leave Liverpool. Players differ in skills and ability but the one characteristic common to true Liverpool players is courage. It is the last and most vital ingredient a scout seeks before he tables a favourable report on a player headed for Anfield.

There is always an element of risk in buying players, but Liverpool makes fewer mistakes than most clubs. Hindsight reveals the 1979–80 season to be one of the most monumental recruiting periods in the club's history, not so much for the huge outlay on the transfer of Craig Johnston, but for two more modest buys. The first was an unassuming youth by the name of Ronnie Whelan from the Irish club Home Farm. Even in football strip he looked like a trainee insurance clerk out for a weekend run with the firm's social team. By 1989 the Irish international midfielder would be wearing the captain's armband for Liverpool, if only for a while. Still looking deceptively young and fresh-faced, he would emerge as one of the pivotal players in the club's 1980s dominance. Ronnie, or Dusty as we called him, was the archetypal footballing personality: quick-witted though cynical, with a love for the horses, snooker and cards. His Irish impudence enabled him to get away with murder and he had the clever knack of always staying on the right side of management and players alike.

The other quiet signing that year was Ronnie's room partner, a greyhound-like striker with a crop of black spiky hair and a toothbrush moustache. Liverpool scout Geoff Twentyman had spotted the eighteen-year-old Ian Rush dashing about in his first season with fourth division Chester City and had pleaded with Liverpool to sign him. After just thirty-three appearances with Chester, this unlikely looking Welsh striker found himself in Liverpool's reserves courtesy of a 300 000 pound transfer. Within a few short seasons Ian Rush would develop into one of the greatest strikers of all time.

Rushie was the quietest guy I'd ever met. He was six months at Liverpool before anyone heard him say a word. My nickname for him was Flapjaw. He called me Bald Eagle. I still haven't figured out why. It would have been a mistake to assume Flap's apparent shyness had anything to do with a soft centre. He came from a no-nonsense North Wales family and could be as hard as he was quick. I saw a few people step it up to Rushie and all of them backed down.

Flap made his first-team debut late in the 1980–81 season and didn't exactly set the world alight, failing to score in seven appearances. The following season he scored thirty goals in all competitions. By 1983 he and Dalglish were considered the most formidable partnership in European football. When he departed for Italy in 1987 I had a feeling we'd be seeing him back on Merseyside before too long. He was hardly a renaissance man. Flap's idea of bliss was a pint of beer, a packet of crisps and the company of his mates. He was an uncomplicated bloke and a certifiable football genius. Get him out with the boys and he could be a merciless mickey-taker; but man-to-man he was a true gentleman and a good mate.

The 1982–83 season started on an unsettling note for me with the story that I might be on my way to Newcastle United. The North-East club had just stunned the soccer world by signing Kevin Keegan who had returned from Hamburg via a brief spell at Southampton. As the story went, Newcastle wanted 'to sign Keegan's look-alike — Liverpool's Craig Johnston'. Newcastle boss, Arthur Cox, had been keen to sign me direct from Middlesbrough. Undeterred, he had since approached Liverpool with an offer. Newcastle's neighbours, Sunderland, had made overtures for me the previous season and now United were hoping they could do the trick. I was far from an automatic choice at Anfield and the prospect of partnering Keegan in midfield was attractive, but it was not half as attractive as working my way with the best club in the land. My career goal was to play at the highest level and, as far as I was concerned, Liverpool was the pinnacle. Anything else was second best. However, as I would learn, being a fringe player at Liverpool always left one open to transfer rumours. I put the speculation out of my mind and knuckled down to the task of helping the Reds defend the League Championship trophy collected the previous season.

It was to be a watershed year in the history of LFC. By season's end we would have another two titles

for the trophy cabinet, a fitting finale to the great career of Bob Paisley who would stand down as manager in May 1983. However, in the optimistic days of autumn, trophies and retirements were many months away.

Manchester United jumped to an early lead that lasted the better part of three months and gave rise to the belief that the big-spending club, always promising so much, might be about to deliver a championship. That impression lasted only as long as it took Liverpool to hit our customary mid-season high. Like a long distance truck driver winding his machine out through the gears, Bob Paisley had Liverpool revving sweetly in top range by mid-November. Come April we were sixteen points clear at the top. Even thoroughbreds that far in front can lose concentration. We did, failing to win once in our final ten outings. It didn't matter, we still finished eleven points clear of the field.

Historically, the FA Cup has been the hardest trophy for Liverpool to win. While consistently making the final rounds, the Reds had traditionally been cursed with bad luck when it came to claiming that priceless piece of silverware. By 1983, the most successful outfit in England could count a mere two FA Cup wins among its credits. They had played in six finals all told, losing four. The bad luck continued in 1983 when the fifth round draw saw unfashionable Brighton make their way to Anfield. Under normal circumstances Liverpool dismisses such challenges with the nonchalance of a Clydesdale brushing off a fly with a swish of the tail. But this was no ordinary fly. The Brighton manager was former Liverpool player Jimmy Melia and the on-field inspiration came from a bloke called Jimmy Case who was as hard a case as ever pulled on a boot. Jimmy was a Scouser who had fulfilled every Liverpool lad's dream by serving a long and distinguished career at Anfield before slipping off to Brighton for his remaining years at the top. Manager and player planned to unseat their former employer.

From the kick-off it was a torrid contest. Brighton stretched us all the way. They led 1-0 until I came on and equalised with an overhead scissors kick. It looked like we were going all the way when Liverpool were awarded a penalty. The keeper saved Phil Neal's side-footed attempt. With minutes to go we clung to a 1–all scoreline and the prospect of a replay at their ground. Then Jimmy Case ruled out the possibility of a replay when his speculative long-range shot deflected off a defender and looped over Bruce's head into the net. We were out of the Cup.

Our agony was compounded by a less than auspicious showing in the European Cup when for the second year in succession we were shot down by an Eastern European side, this time by Lodz of Poland who couldn't believe their luck as we blundered our way to defeat. That left us in contention for two trophies — the League Championship and the League Cup. We set out to win them both.

The League, or Milk Cup as it was known under a sponsorship deal, had stood in the Anfield showcase for the previous two years. A hat-trick would make it ours to keep. We put Ipswich to the sword in the first round and then scraped home against lowly Rotherham when I scored the only goal of the game. Norwich, West Ham and Burnley came and went and suddenly we were at the gates of Wembley. It was late March and we enjoyed a seemingly unassailable lead in the championship race. Here was a chance to wipe out the FA and European Cup disappointments and collect two trophies in the one season. Doubtless our opponents would have something to say about that. We had drawn Manchester United for the final and, after having lost their way in the championship, they were hell bent on extracting some reward from the season.

Phil Neal and Alan Kennedy were the only survivors from the 1977 Liverpool side which had outplayed Manchester United for almost the entire game only to go down 2–1 in the Wembley FA Cup Final of that year. Six years later our two veteran fullbacks must have been wondering if United would prove our nemesis again as Norman Whiteside shot them into an early lead. It was Kennedy who put Liverpool back on terms while Ronnie Whelan provided the winner in extra time.

That match won't be remembered so much for its football as for the sight of skipper Graeme Souness shoving Bob Paisley in front of him to become the first manager ever to lead a winning Wembley side up those steps to receive a trophy, it was the Boss's last official act as manager. He would not be steering the ship in the new season, but what a legacy he left behind! Who could have imagined that the man who filled Shankly's shoes would eclipse his predecessor's stupendous record? The nine Paisley years reaped thirteen trophies including six League Championships, three Milk Cups, a UEFA Cup and three European Cups. The FA Cup — so elusive for Anfield managers — had slipped through Bob Paisley's grasp. For a man who had won everything else, the disappointment went deep. Three years later, however, his contribution would be very much in evidence when the team he had helped build finally lifted that trophy.

NOT GOOD **ENOUGH** CHAPTER 8

O
n 22 February, 1985 the *Daily Mirror* ran a back-page story bearing the banner headline 'I Don't Like You, Mr Fagan'. The sub-heading declared 'Listed Johnston lashes boss'. The story was the culmination of an eighteen-month battle to convince the man who replaced Bob Paisley that I didn't deserve the shoddy treatment he'd been dishing out to me. Ultimately, it came down to personalities. I gathered Joe Fagan didn't like me. And, as I told the media, I wasn't particularly rapt in him.

When Bob Paisley chose the spring of 1983 to slip serenely into retirement, my future at Anfield looked nothing but rosy. The previous season had finished on a sweet note as we had successfully defended both the League Championship and League Cup. After two years with the Reds I was confident I'd found a first-team niche. There had been one or two bumpy spells along the way, but mainly I had seen eye to eye with Bob Paisley. When he retired he had shaken nay hand and said, 'Thanks very much for giving it your best.'

Joe Fagan had been part of the Anfield bootroom scene for twenty-six years when, at the age of sixty-two, he stepped into the manager's chair. His two-year stint at the helm of Europe's greatest side would coincide with a traumatic period in the club's history. For other reasons, it would prove the most painful and frustrating two seasons of my entire career. On trophy count alone, the 1983-84 season must go down as one of Liverpool's finest. We collected the mighty treble of the League Championship, League Cup and European Cup in a season fraught with difficulties and injury. In the process we overtook Bayern Munich and Ajax of Amsterdam to be second only to Real Madrid in European Cup victories, Ian Rush revealed his awesome potential by outstripping the thirty goals he had scored the previous season with an astonishing forty-five, and, more than ever, Liverpool became equated with invincibility. Yet, all was not well at Fortress Anfield.

Liverpool had worked feverishly during the close season to restock its shelves to cover the impending departures of senior players of the calibre of Souness, Kennedy, Neal and, eventually, Dalglish. Nothing is more flattering than being pursued by an Anfield manager waving a contract. Yet, to the surprise of the Kop, Liverpool returned virtually empty-handed from its foray into the transfer market. Michael Robinson, the burly Brighton striker, and Gary Gillespie, a tall and talented defender from Coventry City, were the only new signings. The really big fish were hooked by rival clubs.

Nobody knows why the nation's most sought after players shunned the Liverpool overtures. The popular theory was that the Reds were suffering from their own success. It was well known that the average new signing might spend up to two years in Liverpool reserves with no guarantees of a first-team appearance. Our rivals offered the near certainty that a talented recruit would walk straight into the firsts. A player who joins Liverpool as a full England international might spend his first season in reserves. Then, before he can say 'What about me?' he finds he has disappeared from England selection calculations. That's exactly what happened to Paul Walsh two seasons later when he joined from Luton Town. Later still, a stint in the reserves would cost me an England shirt. The conclusion was that the players Liverpool had in its sights were simply intimidated by the competition for berths at Anfield.

On reporting for pre-season in July, those of us who had battled to keep the League Championship trophy and League Cup in the Anfield cabinet were privately pleased that there were no new faces likely to disturb our unity let alone our pay packets. But, as with almost every other season at Liverpool, there would be no automatic first-team start for Craig Johnston. No matter how well I had played at the end of the previous pre-season and no matter that I was always the player to beat in the training sprints or stamina work, I was never in the starting line-up when a new season kicked off. On the bench for the Charity Shield opener against Manchester

Shooting for goal against Manchester United, Charity Shield, Wembley 1983

United at Wembley, I watched us heading for defeat before being given a run late in the match. We lost but I did well enough to find myself back in contention.

With Ronnie Whelan recovering from a pelvic operation, I slotted into the left midfield role to bring to five the number of different positions I'd played at Liverpool. Being a natural right-footer, I'd rather have been on the right side of the park or in central midfield, but those considerations were trivial alongside the fact that I was wearing a first-team shirt. I was fit and in form. There were a few problems looming, however, which were capable of ripping that shirt off my back.

One of the players to slip through the Liverpool net during the close season hunt was Glasgow Celtic's genius Charlie Nicholas. North of the border they said he was better than Dalglish. The colourful Scot had thrown in his lot with Arsenal and was already a crowd favourite with the Highbury faithful. Liverpool's miss and Arsenal's gain added an extra edge to the contest when we travelled to London to meet the Gunners in the autumn of 1983. Champagne Charlie Nick hit the bar after fifteen minutes but that was as close as Arsenal came to repelling the Red tide. I opened the scoring with a goal from close range and Dalglish showed who was Celtic's finest by scoring a cracker. As a team, Liverpool were absolutely brilliant. The match was televised and I was grabbed for an interview after we had changed. It was a bad choice as I could hardly speak, so choked was I with a bout of flu. Jimmy Hill said: 'The lad has obviously got off his sick bed to play for fear of losing his place.' He was right.

I'd been trying to hide my condition from the Boss. At stake was not merely my spot in a buzzing team but a seat aboard the aircraft for the European Cup away tie against BK Odense of Denmark. I'd kept the illness a secret before the Arsenal game but it soon became obvious how unwell I was when I failed to attend training. Reluctant at that stage to upset his winning combination, the Boss heeded my plea and included me in the travelling party of sixteen. We returned from Odense Stadium with a 1–0 victory which we were to convert to a six-goal margin by flogging the part-timers 5–0 in the second leg at Anfield.

By early winter the League Championship was bearing the hallmarks of a Lancashire party as Liverpool and Manchester United skipped clear of the bunch. As champions, we were naturally the one side everybody wanted to beat and there were no easy games. My role on the left was to play as a conventional wing half, support the attack and provide cover for left back Kennedy whenever he went forward. One of my strengths was that of a hustler which meant that I'd get through plenty of physical contact. The more challenges you put in, the greater the chance of bringing down an opponent and upsetting the referee.

We were well into a 3-I demolition of West Ham at Upton Park when I went in to dispossess Billy Bonds. I mistimed the challenge on a greasy playing surface, caught his heel and tripped the Hammers skipper. There was nothing malicious about the tackle. Having been booked earlier in the game, I'd been deliberately cautious. Nobody could believe it when the ref dipped into his pocket and produced the red card. I was off! Bonds protested long and loud on my behalf, West Ham manager John Lyall said later that it wasn't the sort of game that deserved a sending off, and one newspaper report described it as a 'stupidly harsh dismissal'. The protests didn't help. I faced a one-match ban that looked like stretching into three once my penalty points for the season were tallied. Nobody could have put my predicament better than the journalist who wrote: 'A lengthy ban would be disastrous for Johnston who has won the hearts of the Liverpool supporters this season with his gutsy performances.'

Worried sick about losing my place in the team while serving the suspension, I had been assured on the trip home by Joe Fagan that my position was secure. While my team-mates jokingly dubbed me 'The Butcher of West Derby', Joe Fagan went into bat for me by telling the media that I was normally the sort of player who steers clear of referee trouble.

'Craig is the victim of his own enthusiasm,' explained the Boss. 'He is naturally aggressive and competitive, but never dirty.'

In their usual thorough way the Anfield backroom staff went to work on the problem and found that I had a total of fourteen penalty points. Under the new suspension rules that still left me seven points short of the total required before the end of November to warrant an automatic three-match ban. Three or ten matches, it didn't matter. Miss one game at Liverpool and you may never make it back.

One match was all it took. The Boss moved Steve Nicol into left midfield as Liverpool blitzed Luton Town 6–0 that Saturday while I watched numbly from the stand. The next game was the away leg of our European Cup clash against Spanish champions Athletic Bilbao and, with Ronnie Whelan back from injury, competition for first-team places was going to be white hot. There were three of us — Whelan, Johnston and Nicol — in the frame for left midfield. Nonetheless, recalling the Boss's words, I was confident of regaining my place. As the media kept noting, Johnston had been in commanding form for the opening fifteen games up to the suspension. What's more, I knew that I'd been one of our most effective players in the first Euro leg despite Bilbao having held us to a scoreless draw. On the eve of Liverpool's departure for Spain, the *Daily Star* carried a back page headline declaring 'The Best in Britain'. It was supported by a sub-head: 'We fear Johnston, admits Bilbao boss.' The exclusive story quoted Bilbao manager Javier Clemente who said: 'Johnston is the big danger. Dalglish and Rush are great players but Johnston is in a class of his own. He's strong and aggressive. He's everywhere. He's the best midfield player in Britain.'

It was flattery beyond belief and I could well have done without it. When Joe Fagan named his side to do battle with the Basques, I was not included. The lads did brilliantly to not only overcome the opposition but the hostile home crowd. Being excluded from this important chapter of the European campaign made me feel like an outsider as the players celebrated on the return flight.

The weeks dragged by and with each day came the deepening conviction that I was back among the fringe-dwellers. Liverpool were clear at the top by November and I knew that my role in the first fifteen games of the season had helped get them there. Surely that counted for something. Reduced to the too familiar position of bench warmer, I had plenty of time to think. It was unbelievable! That tackle on Billy Bonds could not have been miscued by anything more than an inch or two, yet it had cost me dearly. When I won that first-team shirt, I privately vowed that anybody else who wanted it would have to shoot me to get it off my back. Not for one moment did I think I'd lose it without a fight, yet, here I was back on the bench powerless to do anything about it.

Opportunities were passing me by. The first round derby clash against Everton came and went minus the presence of Craig Johnston, it was followed by one of the glamour fixtures of the season: Tottenham Hotspur versus Liverpool in London. When the team sheet for the match was posted, I wasn't even included as substitute. Instead I would have to travel with the team in the unlikely event that somebody took ill the night before the match. If there was one thing I couldn't stand it was watching my club in action while I sat motionless. It was sheer torture. There were players in the squad who loved the idea of sitting on their arses and collecting the first-team win bonuses without raising a sweat or getting their boots dirty. But not me. As a professional athlete the whole week's training is geared to that ninety minutes on Saturday afternoon. You're full of adrenalin and you need that weekly kill. If you don't get it you go crazy. You can't sleep at night. While the others would be enjoying a deserved post-match drink and the celebration of the team effort, I'd be out running the streets of my neighbourhood just to let off steam. I felt that I hadn't contributed therefore I had no right to join my mates for a drink. In certain circles I was perceived as a loner. Nothing was further from the truth. More than any other player, I wanted to come in from the cold.

I fronted the Boss and told him to leave me out of the Spurs trip. It meant losing first-team wages but I'd rather play in reserves than sit in the stand. When I came out of the manager's office, Kenny Dalglish, who used to sit next to me in the dressing room, saw the look of disappointment on my face. When I told him I'd opted to stay behind and do some extra training he said, 'You're making a big mistake.' He was saying it as a friend and a senior player because he genuinely cared for my welfare. I respected the advice, but, as I told Kenny, we were made of different stuff. I couldn't deal with the idea that I wasn't even a sub. The team headed for London. With no reserves match scheduled, I jumped in the car and drove north to Middlesborough and one of my old brick training walls. It wasn't apparent then, but I'd just fired off the first round in a battle that would develop into one of the most acrimonious manager-player confrontations in Anfield history.

Nobody had to remind me that competition for first-team spots was part of the Liverpool formula. And I knew that nobody had a God-given right to a red shirt week in and week out. Many a knowledgeable fan had consoled me with stories of more talented players than me who'd had to bide their time. The one thing that I didn't understand, however, was why form was never good enough to secure me a place in the side. This trend began to emerge in the first half of the 1983-84 season and would almost drive me crazy with frustration.

We met Birmingham at home on 5 December and, in one of our worst performances, scrambled to a 1–0 win which stretched our lead to four points. The only reason I was in the side was because Kenny was out with torn stomach muscles. I'd bounced in against Fulham in a Cup-tie and had played well, flicking on the ball for Souness to score the winner. Against Birmingham, I was retained in my favourite position just behind the two strikers and performed creditably in a Liverpool side glaringly out of touch. It is one of the Reds' trademarks that when the magic deserts them, they can often summon enough character to see them through. In its match summary the *Liverpool Sports Echo* observed: 'Only three or four Liverpool players played up to their full potential but one who did was Craig Johnston deputising for the injured Dalglish. He was behind most of his side's attacking moves and it was his flicked header that opened the way for the winning goal,'

When the team was named for the ensuing away game against Coventry City, I was back on the bench. Didn't form count for anything? Why, when at least seven regulars had been below average against Birmingham, did the Boss decide to drop me?

On hearing the news on the Friday morning I stormed into the players' lounge, still wearing my muddy training gear, grabbed a pen and a blank sheet of paper and scribbled out a transfer request. I handed the note to Joe Fagan and told him in no uncertain terms that I didn't think he'd been fair to me. My contract was due to expire at the end of the season and my future at Anfield did not look settled enough to induce me to sign the new three-year contract the club had slipped under my nose. On the matter of my non-selection, the Liverpool boss told reporters: 'Craig has given me a letter asking for a transfer and doesn't feel that I've been fair to him. He has a case. He's played in most of this season's games, done well and I can understand how he feels. He's entitled to his opinion and is quite right to express it. [Dropping him] was not easy and I might find out that I've done the wrong thing,'

Liverpool fans who didn't make the trip to Coventry couldn't believe the result: Coventry 4, Liverpool 0.

My transfer request posed real problems for the Boss. Unable to restock the ranks during the close season he needed all the quality reserves he could get. Ten days before my request, a disillusioned David Hodgson, one of the recruits from the Middlesbrough class of 1980–81, had also asked for a transfer. Joe Fagan's response was to flatly deny us a move. I can understand his attitude. The great Liverpool winning dynasty was getting on towards twenty years and everybody was wondering who would be the unlucky guy on the throne when the castle began to crumble. Joe Fagan didn't want to be the one. For the time being, nobody would be leaving Anfield.

The Christmas-New Year period is considered the halfway mark of the football season's long cold march. Rather than being a resting point, it is probably the toughest week of the entire season. While the rest of England is lapping up the Yuletide pleasures before a warm fire, pro footballers are ploughing through the mud and sleet playing up to three games in the hectic holiday week. Do well that week and you can grab the jump on your opposition. Flop and you can suddenly find yourself among the trundlers. After the Coventry flogging and before you could say 'Season's Greetings' I was pitched back into the side. We immediately whopped Notts County 5–0 at home and scrambled to an untidy win over Brian Clough's youthful Forest side at their City Ground on New Year's Day. We were back at Anfield two days later for the top-of-the-table clash against Manchester United. This contest between two of Britain's greatest football institutions would be a pulsating contest chock full of commitment and passion. When the starting line-ups were read out by the ground announcer, I was the only one on the park who was not an international. What an array of talent, from the likes of Dalglish through to United's Dutch international Arnold Muhren. There would be much more than the competition points riding on this one.

The two sides tore into each other from the outset and the intensity of the battle soon took its toll. United's giant defender Gordon McQueen was the first casualty when he turned himself inside out to block my shot midway through the first half. He had fallen awkwardly and was obviously in trouble as the substitute came off the bench. Only minutes after goalkeeper Gary Bailey had made a brilliant one-handed save from Dalglish, Kenny prodded a corner kick into the path of Souness who hammered his angled drive from outside the box. It had goal written all over it until Arthur Albiston lunged to block it on the line. Anticipating the rebound, I swooped on the chance and knocked it past Bailey into the net.

Our celebrations were short-lived. A minute before half-time, Dalglish, whose guile had made him the

target of some bovine defending, went up for a headed ball. Out from the back four to meet the challenge came the uncompromising Kevin Moran. The beefy defender got his header in all right, but as he went up his elbow smacked into the side of Kenny's face. With a sound like a hammer striking a water melon, his cheekbone was shattered.

I was nearest to him as he slumped to his haunches. By the time I reached him his left eye was already closed, the side of his face was misshapen and starting to swell. He would be out for a critical part of the season. Could Liverpool still win it without Dalglish? How good were Joe Fagan's fringe dwellers?

Norman Whiteside scored United's equaliser right on the stroke of full time to send them back to Manchester with their dignity intact. The draw still left Liverpool clear at the top. As we visited Kenny in hospital that week we were alarmed by the extent of the damage. His face had blown up like a balloon. In his six years at Anfield he had barely missed a game. Now he would be out for quite a few. His absence would be a test of Liverpool's mettle as the pack chased us all the way to the wire.

The omens looked bad when lowly Wolverhampton Wanderers made the journey to Anfield in mid-January and scored the winning goal with their first attacking move of the match. Pit us against Real Madrid, Bayern Munich, Tottenham or Manchester United and we'd set the ground ablaze. But stack us up against the cellar dwellers and we inexplicably came unstuck. It was a problem and we knew that there would be no trophies for the Reds unless we found a solution.

It came just three days later when we travelled to deepest Yorkshire for the first leg of our Milk Cup quarter-final tie with Sheffield Wednesday. It was a bitterly cold night, courtesy of a gale-force Arctic wind. The pre-match pitch inspection suggested that any activity on the playing surface would soon turn it into a sea of freezing mud. Just the sort of conditions tailor-made to bring a champion team undone. Despite the near zero temperatures almost 50 000 fans packed the Hillsborough Ground. They'd turned up perhaps expecting a display of cool classical football: what they got was a red-hot Cup-tie. Stevie Nicol stung Wednesday into action with a beautifully chipped goal and from that moment the battle of Hillsborough was on. Running into the teeth of the gale, Wednesday hurled themselves at our penalty area and within ten minutes were back on equal terms. What ensued was a half hour of merciless football as both sides contested every ball, defended fanatically and rampaged forward at every opportunity. In the second half, with the wind and crowd at their backs, Wednesday hit the lead on the hour when Gary Bannister's shot deflected in off Mark Lawrenson's legs. Bruce Grobbelaar, who had played brilliantly in goal, was left stranded.

If attacking zeal and sheer commitment counted for anything, Wednesday would have swamped a lesser side on that bitter January night. But this was Liverpool. When the home side committed the cardinal sin of relaxing momentarily after hitting the lead, we sprang the offside trap. I unleashed a ball through the middle that set Rushie on his way. The keeper dragged him down in the box and Phil Neal calmly stepped up to ram home the equaliser from the spot. We headed home to Merseyside in high spirits. By drawing we had wiped out Wednesday's home advantage thereby making it doubly difficult for them in the second leg at Anfield. More importantly, we had convinced everybody, especially ourselves, that we could do more than just mind the store during Kenny's absence. Fortress Liverpool was intact.

But could we also do without Souness? We were to find out during February when our skipper and one of the game's born leaders was sidelined by injury. With the two great Scots went much of the creativity and fluency that gave Liverpool the edge. Creativity severely rationed, we fell back on Liverpool's greatest asset: character.

Everybody talks about the classic Liverpool performances when the Reds, at their arrogant best, trample the opposition into the turf. But for my money the matches that really stand out are those games that aren't so pretty. I'm talking about the times when the team doesn't play well, when nothing goes right and the only available strategy is to battle and to keep on battling. This is the ugly, cruel side of the season when injuries take their toll and the matches that count most always seem to be scheduled for the coldest recesses of winter and are played on frozen mudheaps far from the glamorous glare of the television lights. These are the games that really win championships.

The slog was on when we met Sunderland at Roker Park in early February. It coincided with a goal drought for Rushie, our defence was going through a horror patch, Michael Robinson was still adjusting to the Liverpool style and the rest of us were understandably wrong-footed by the absence of Souness and Dalglish. Sunderland were justifiably optimistic. In the end we gave them nothing. I had a goal disallowed and was flattered when the great Jackie Milburn gave me his man-of-the-match nomination. More importantly, the lads battled it out right to the end and came home with a draw that kept us on course for the title, five points clear at the top.

By this stage, everybody in footballdom knew that, despite good form, my grip on a Liverpool spot was still tenuous. John Donoghue of the *Daily Express* observed in his Sunderland match report: 'It must gall some first division managers that here is a player who spends most of his time fighting to stay in the side when he could comfortably walk into almost any other . . . as much as it needles Johnston himself.' My attitude was that there were two players in the team who wouldn't have been there if Souness and Dalglish had been fit. I was determined that when they returned, I'd still be wearing the number 10 shirt.

Sunderland boss Alan Durban remarked; 'The more I see of him the more he reminds me of Kevin Keegan,' That embarrassing observation carried added weight in light of our third round FA Cup-tie with Keegan's Newcastle United. The Keegan comparisons had continued on and off virtually from the season I'd stepped into the first team at Middlesbrough. We were similar in height and stature, had curly hair and buzzed around the park like blowflies in a bottle. But Keegan was a twotime European Player of the Year and at Liverpool had been elevated to the status of living legend. As I kept saying, labelling anyone the next Kevin Keegan was like slapping a 'Bradman' tag on a young batsman from the bush — a career curse you could well do without.

Far from being a Keegan clone, I barely knew the man. He had left Liverpool for Hamburg before I stepped into the frame and much of his football since returning to England had been played in the second tier. Yet our paths were destined to cross when we drew Newcastle in the Cup. United were top of the second division, it was to be Keegan's Anfield homecoming and the match would be the first non-final to be shown live on television.

Under the twin headings of 'Kopy Kat Craig' and 'Liverpool triumph as Johnston does a Keegan', the *Daily Mirror*'s match report began; 'Craig Johnston buried Kevin Keegan's ambition to lead Newcastle to a famous FA Cup victory by giving a stunning impersonation of the Anfield master last night.' If you asked me to nominate career highlights, this match would certainly make my short list. I scored one goal and had a hand in two others as we triumphed 4-0. This is how Derek Wallis of the *Mirror* saw it:

> *Liverpool's second goal after 29 minutes was the result of powerful running by Johnston which was so reminiscent of Keegan. He brushed aside Glenn Roeder before crossing the ball for Rush to score unchallenged. Newcastle's supporters still roared their team's every touch before Johnston scored his classic goal after 63 minutes. When Lee sent a choice pass along the right, Johnston left Kenny Wharton stranded with a burst towards the post and somehow squeezed the ball between the woodwork and the goalkeeper.*

'Where do you get your hair permed?' Kevin Keegan, FA Cup third round, 1983

Heady stuff, but in the fourth round of the FA Cup, our bogey side Brighton, for the second year in succession, brought us crashing back to earth as they trounced us 2–0. Our trophy hunt was reduced to three.

No matter how good my form or how many first-team games I played, I lived in constant fear of rejection. Harsh experience told me that even if I played out of my skin, I could just as easily be dropped for the next game. Every team meeting was a trial. The Boss would name the side starting with the goalkeeper and by the time he had completed the back four my palms would be sweating. It was nerve-racking, not just for me but those closest. I felt sorry for my roommate Bruce Grobbelaar who must have been driven crazy by my paranoia, especially after I'd kept him awake with my troubles before the crucial away European Cup-tie against Bilbao.

If it was hard on Bruce, it was harder on Jenny. The average Liverpool fan couldn't explain why Skippy, as I'd been dubbed by the Kop, was in and out of the team. It certainly had nothing to do with form. There had to be another, more sinister reason. We heard them all from 'He was caught in bed with a director's daughter', to 'He had a punch up with Fagan'. None was true but that didn't stop the rumours. Not surprisingly, in a community like Merseyside where football is everything, this placed crippling pressures on our personal lives.

Being the constant target of transfer speculation was also not conducive to a settled home life, particularly when we were expecting our first child. When the pressure reached a peak late in 1983, neither of us was sleeping well and our nerves were very much on edge. Jenny was experiencing complications with the pregnancy and we were both feeling very much like two lost kids a long way from home. It was a bleak Christmas made the more so when Jenny, four months pregnant, lost the baby. We'd experienced a few rough passages during the short time we'd been together, but that was about the worst. Jenny lost the baby on the Thursday morning, on Friday I was dropped for the Coventry game, handed in the transfer request and later that day learned that my best buddy, Bruce Grobbelaar, had requested and was granted a change of roommate.

Jenny was inconsolable and needed her parents. I was resigned to the belief that I was about to leave as a failure. While my wife headed for the family refuge back at Lake Macquarie, I moved in with my neighbours Colin and Eileen Bridge and their three kids.

Fortunately, Jenny's return and the arrival of the New Year brought a positive change to our personal lives. Jenny fell pregnant again. There would be more turbulent waters ahead, but this time we were determined they wouldn't impose upon our family life.

Towards the end of that season Dalglish achieved Anfield immortality by signing on for four more years thus ensuring that he would see out his playing days with Liverpool. The club approached me with a four-year contract but I was wary, and with justification.

The peaks and pits of that particular season were no better illustrated than by one week late in March. On 21 March we strode into the Stadium of Light in downtown Lisbon to do battle with Benfica, champions of Portugal. There were 80 000 packed into the ground and the reception, set against a barrage of flares, was enough to terrify lesser men. The atmosphere was volcanic. Yet, in the tradition of great Liverpool sides of the past, we rose to the occasion by shooting down the Benfica Eagles to the tune of 4–1. It might well have been Liverpool's greatest Euro performance. The Benfica fans sat in stunned disbelief. My own contribution came in the form of a very satisfying all-round game capped off by our second goal - a screamer from outside the box.

Three days later found us at Wembley where we were to meet Everton in the League Cup Final. Merseyside's football faithful ignored the rain to support their heroes. The atmosphere was wonderful and a tremendous tribute to the fans and sportsmanship of both clubs. Unhappily for me, what could have been an idyllic afternoon turned decidedly sour. According to the following day's press reports, I had been one of Liverpool's better players. It cut no ice with the Boss. With the match poised to enter extra time, he gave me the flick and sent on Michael Robinson. I did something unheard of: I pleaded with the manager. He was unmoved. It had happened yet again, and at Wembley of all places. I was gutted.

As the teams returned for the kick-off, the substitution was announced over the public address. For the second time in my years with Liverpool, a manager was booed. In my anger and frustration I said to Fagan: 'Now's ya chance to get Warky in,' referring to the midweek purchase of midfield scoring machine John Wark from Ipswich. Enraged, Joe Fagan turned to me and said: 'Do you think this game's all about you, son? Go on, piss off now!' gesturing towards the dressing room.

One of the lads on the subs bench put a blanket around my shoulders to shelter me from the rain. I've never felt so dispirited in all my life. At the end of extra time, with the sodden blanket about my shoulders, I trudged disconsolately towards the tunnel oblivious to the fact that both sides were involved in a post-match presentation to the Queen Mother. And that's how I became the centre of a 'Queen Mum snubbed' furore. What an embarrassment! The press and public gave me heaps. In a game devoid of great highlights the focus fell glaringly on the 'ungrateful colonial' who had turned his back on royalty. Fortunately, a few reporters understood my disappointment and gave me the chance to explain what had gone wrong. Bruised by the experience, however, I pledged that there would be no repeats. There weren't.

We met Everton in the replay at Maine Road, one of my favourite grounds. The outcome was settled in the twenty-second minute when Graeme Souness turned away from Kevin Ratcliffe to lash an unstoppable drive from outside the box into the Everton net. We triumphed 1-0 to lift the trophy yet again. This time I started and finished the match.

Whenever I had fronted the Boss about my non-selection problems he would fall back on the standard quote of managers and coaches the world over: 'I will never change a winning team.' I made the mistake of taking Joe Fagan at his word. When it came to me, he made exceptions to his own rules. I sat in the team meeting two days after the League Cup triumph feeling confident I had secured my place for another week at least. The Boss spoke; 'The only change is Wark in Johnston out.' The *Sunday Express* reported:

> The chop fell on Craig Johnston who delayed signing a three-year contract and last week made clear his displeasure at being substituted at Wembley. Last night Fagan stressed, 'I am pleased for John Wark and disappointed for Craig, and that is a statement from the heart . . . Craig has taken it with quiet dignity. Before when I left him out he came storming in. This time I said to him, 'Would you like to be sub?' and he just said 'Yes, please. ' I was almost too embarrassed to tell him he wasn't playing because players have to have feelings and emotions. I sincerely hope he stays with us because he is a very good player.

Tell me I'm not going crazy, I said to myself. How much rejection can one body stand? By this stage I was wondering whether my paranoia had got the better of me. This yo-yo existence was making me unhinged. What was wrong with my play? Was there something I was overlooking that must have been obvious to Joe Fagan?

Just when I was feeling totally isolated, the Kop came to my rescue. The *Liverpool Sports Echo* devoted an entire column to letters on the subject and the support for me was overwhelming. D. Hughes of Bundle Road, Liverpool wrote: 'I was disgusted but not surprised by Joe Fagan's decision to drop Craig Johnston to make way for John Wark to make his debut at Watford. Whenever a key player recovers from injury it is usually Johnston who makes way for him, and when a substitution is made it is Johnston who comes off, no matter how well he is playing.' S. Brown of Queen's Drive, Liverpool, asked: 'What has Craig Johnston done to get in Joe Fagan's bad books? It seems that Johnston is always made the scapegoat when things aren't going well.' Unhappy Liverpool fan, Billy Jones of Cantril Farm, Liverpool, concluded with the observation: 'Johnston

So proud of that red shirt

EURO GLORY!

It's six of the best
for British Soccer

BRITAIN'S super Soccer teams swept the board last night with all six reaching European semi-finals.

Liverpool swept aside Portugal's Benfica 4—1 in the European Cup with two goals by Ronnie Whelan and one each from Ian Rush and Craig Johnston.

Delighted manager Joe Fagan said "We've had some good results in Europe —but this must rate top of the list."

He added "I feel very proud I thought we were magnificent although I imagine the Portuguese

STAR REPORTER

fans will be disappointed with Benfica

In the Cup Winners Cup Manchester United stormed to a sensational 3—0 victory over their crions to go through 3—2 on aggregate. Skipper Bryan Robson got two and Frank Stapleton added the third

United played before an ecstatic packed crowd

Daily Star, 22 March 1988

CRAIG'S CRISIS

The wet
blanket

HE DOESN'T look too happy, does he?

Indeed, Liverpool's midfield star Craig Johnston was the ONLY person to look less than delighted at Wembley.

As the players gathered at the end of normal time, Anfield boss Joe Fagan and Johnston had a brief exchange of words.

Johnston was clearly unhappy at being replaced by Michael Robinson for the extra-time stint against Everton.

At the end of extra time, Johnston trooped off the pitch as the rest of both teams went up the steps to shake hands with the Queen Mother.

And here he is pictured, a lone and disconsolate figure at the Wembley carnival.

Later, Johnston said: "I didn't know anything about going up the steps. I didn't know we had to go up into the Royal Box if the game ended in a draw."

Daily Post, 29 March 1988

Milk for seconds!

Happy Craig proud to be part of a wonderful occasion

☐ CRAIG JOHNSTON: "As an outsider not only from Merseyside but from Britain I'm just proud to be part of such a wonderful occasion, especially after the misunderstanding of Sunday.

"The fans were absolutely marvellous and I'm a much happier man than I was after the match on Sunday."

INSIDE: 8-page Replay Special

☐ PHIL NEAL said: "The fans from both clubs have been marvellous. I take my hat off to them all.

"I just hope the Everton lads' heads don't drop now because I would like to see them get to the FA Cup Final and win it for Merseyside.

"Tonight's game wasn't a classic in football but it must have been very exciting. It was a game of true grit."

KOP THAT! Craig Johnston strikes silver

The Sun, 31 March 1988

CHOP FOR HERO CRAIG

MILK CUP hero Craig Johnston was axed by Liverpool yesterday.

Less than 48 hours after collecting a Cup winners medal, he was told he is out of today's match at Watford.

Manager Joe Fagan, who gives £450,000 John Wark his debut, admitted — "It was my first really tough decision since I got the job — to talk to Craig Johnston last night as he went into Anfield but he went up to the meeting not again

Refused

He asked for a transfer in December and his written request and his stained in Fagan's office Fagan has refused to sign a new three-year contract.

JOHN WARK ... debut at Watford

By MIKE ELLIS

Cup Final last Sunday. Fagan said "Craig has not been playing badly but John Wark may give us more solidity in midfield and his scoring flair is unquestioned.

"I could have taken the easy way out by naming an

26 March 1988

Craig Johnston after Wembley   Picture: PETER JAY

THE 'DIGNITY' OF JOHNSTON

by JAMES MOSSOP
Watford 0, Liverpool 2

THEY used to have a naughty name for that tussle - headed young Scot, Johnny Wark, in the Liverpool backroom.

The pest, they called him, because of the damage he habitually inflicted on them in the blue of Ipswich.

Manager Joe Fagan's remedy was to sign him for £450,000 and pitch him into a Vicarage Road debut— and then watch him score the crucial first goal.

QUOTE BY FAGAN ON JOHNSTON

So three days after they had collected the Milk Cup, Liverpool went shooting back to the top of the First Division.

After the two rousing matches against Everton, Fagan had to decide who should make way for Wark.

The chop fell on Craig Johnston, who delayed signing a three-year contract and last weekend made clear his displeasure at being substituted at Wembley.

Last night Fagan stressed "I am pleased for John Wark

and disappointed for Craig—and that is a statement from the heart.

"Today Wark was a yard short of fitness. You always get that with a player at a new club I expected it—but I also expected him to score.

"Craig has taken it with quiet dignity. Before when I left him out he came storming in. This time I said to him 'Would you like to be sub'? and he just said 'Yes, please'.

"I was almost too embarrassed to tell him he wasn't playing because players have to have fee tags and emotions. I sincerely hope he stays with us, because he is a very good player.

"Today was a peculiar game. There was no excitement. We like to keep the crowd

WATFORD: Steel, Hardsley, Sinnott, Callaghan, Johnston, Reilly, Barnes, Hodson, Taylor, Jackett, Atkinson. Sub: Richardson.

The message at our team meeting was it took about a minute it was as a long meeting was that we must be aggressive. We were determined not to be beaten."

(81), were both created by that master of deception Kenny Dalglish, whose spontaneous magic defied his lack of full fitness.

Wark's goal altered the course of the game. It was the first time he had scored since November 26 and that was against Liverpool at Portman Road.

But here he was in Liverpool's famous red, back in the old routine — pushing forward, eluding his marker by stealth, plonking the ball past the goalkeeper.

He was in at the beginning of the move, stealing into the penalty area while Dalglish was collecting the ball from Sammy Lee.

LIVERPOOL: Grobbelaar, Neal, Kennedy, Lawrenson, Whelan, Hansen, Dalglish, Lee, Rush, Wark, Souness. Sub: Johnston.

Referee: T. J. Holbrook, Wolverhampton.

With a flourish that was fateful to Watford, Dalglish shielded the ball and turned away to thread it into Wark's stride. It was beating Eric Steve in an instant.

Liverpool were in control. Dalglish provided Rush with the pass that brought him his solo goal of the season and from the moment he swept past the defender everyone knew he would be on target.

It must have been all desperately mystifying for two men from Third Division Plymouth Argyle, manager John Hore and coach Martin Harvey. They may have felt that Watford, their FA Cup semi-final opponents on April 14

'G'day Ma'am'. Most people didn't realise that I met the Queen Mother before the game

has been playing great this season. He has not put a foot wrong.' Support came from further afield. A travelling fan from Worcester wrote:

> *'I was so amazed and upset at Mr Fagan's decision to drop Craig Johnston from the team that I felt I must put pen to paper. Sports commentators, football fans in general and Liverpool supporters have all recently spoken of Craig's effectiveness in the Liverpool team. I find his will to give a hundred per cent in every game, his footballing skill and his great natural enthusiasm for the game enjoyable and refreshing. When I arrived at the match on Saturday and read Mr Fagan's page in the program, I found him saying that you 'Can't ask any more of a player than that. He gives of his best throughout the whole ninety minutes.' On that score Johnston should always feature in Mr Fagan's team. Why is he always the scapegoat when Liverpool have a bad run? Come on Mr Fagan give Craig a fair crack of the whip, please.'*

I sincerely appreciated what the fans had to say, but I had my own thoughts on the matter. For starters, other managers who did appreciate my input officially and covertly approached me to leave Liverpool. To a man they asked: 'How can you put up with that sort of treatment?' But instead of luring me away from Anfield, their approaches merely strengthened my resolve to stay and beat this guy. However, set against that was something Terry McDermott had said not long after I made my Liverpool debut. The England international by that stage was in Liverpool reserves and about to return to his native North-East. Terry was a bit of a rebel and I considered him a mate so I took it very seriously when, on the bus back to Anfield after training, he said: 'If they've got it in for you, you might as well pack it in now. No matter what you do, you will never be truly accepted by them [the management]. You're different.'

The incident that weighed on my mind was that dreadful scene in my first full season at Liverpool when the Kop had booed Bob Paisley for replacing me. Despite being dragged off the field, I had taken the Boss's side on the issue. After all, he was the football strategist. But he was not the only influence. There were others on the bench who also had an input. Those bodies on the bench are a team in themselves. Whatever the Kop or Craig Johnston thought didn't really matter; the result of that demonstration had been to align the player with the fans against the management. It was an impression that I never managed to shed during my time at Anfield. For much of the time I would remain an outsider.

What did I know? Despite the controversy, I played in more than forty games that season including the Milk and European Cup Finals. At the end of it all Joe Fagan stepped up to be crowned Manager of the Year. For the first time in the club's history Liverpool won three major prizes: the Championship, League Cup and European Cup. With the team he had inherited from Bob Paisley, the new manager had virtually wiped the board clean. From whichever way you looked at it, Fortress Anfield was more impregnable than ever. Or was it?

LIFE AND **DEATH** CHAPTER 9

Chelsea Cara Johnston was born in the Mater Misericordiae Hospital, Newcastle, New South Wales on 11 October 1984. The fact that I was there for the birth instead of back in England playing soccer created more than a ripple of consternation on Merseyside.

With the European Cup Final extending Liverpool's 1983–84 season on into June, the team had undertaken a shortened end-of-season trip to Swaziland where we played their national side and Tottenham Hotspur in a mini tournament. On our return to Merseyside, a Liverpool select was invited by an Israeli agent to take part in what we were led to believe would be a fairly social and lowkey five-a-side friendly in Tel Aviv. Not until the event was primed to kick off, and we witnessed the pre-publicity and the size of the crowd, did we realise what was afoot. Israel was in the grip of election fever and, in the tradition of bread and circuses, the political machinery wanted to put on a show. We were the main event. The penny finally dropped when the national anthem was played, everyone stood up and in walked the prime minister.

Liverpool might have been kings of Europe but this indoor business was totally alien to us. The Israeli side played us off the court. Our compensation was a fully paid two-week holiday at the Red Sea resort of Eilat on Israel's southern border. Relaxing in the sun out of range of the usual attendant media corps, we were totally unaware that we'd become the subjects of an official bun fight back in England. Apparently, the correct channels had not been pursued to obtain clearance for the Liverpool crew to play in Israel. We were to learn that not only had Ian Rush, Phil Thompson, Alan Hansen, Graeme Souness, Craig Johnston, Steve Nicol, plus Newcastle United's Terry McDermott and David McCreery not been cleared to play, none of us had even been insured. That's million of pounds worth of football livestock running around one of the world's trouble spots without cover! The stink took a long time to settle when news reached Anfield and the Football Association's headquarters back in England.

I lost myself in Israel. When the others returned to Britain, I stayed on and immersed myself in the culture and lifestyle of the Holy Land. Jerusalem, Bethlehem, Nazareth, the Sea of Galilee — all those old Sunday school names were suddenly no longer ancient fables. I was fascinated. The real-life tale of this land made the endeavours of a highly paid athlete and a religion called football seem insignificant. The opportunity to study the Hebrew culture at first hand reminded me of the enormous gaps in my education as a result of having quit school at fifteen years of age. Before I knew it, a month had flown by. It was almost time to resume pre-season and I had not yet rejoined my pregnant wife in Australia.

It took me just a few days with Jenny to realise that my plan to collect her and fly back to Merseyside for the birth simply wasn't on. Scarred by the failure of the first pregnancy, Jenny felt secure with her family, particularly her mother and married sisters, close at hand. She was under the care of the family doctor and all appeared to be proceeding well. Jenny made it clear that she wanted to give birth in Australia. She suggested I return to England without her.

The proposal created a crisis for me. All along I had mentally budgeted that I would be there for the birth of our first child. The prospect of returning to England without Jenny simply had not entered my head. Having already witnessed one midflight birth, I was unwilling to subject Jenny to a twenty-four-hour flight back to England. My decision was to remain in Australia until the baby was born.

Despite the troubles of the previous season, never in my time at Anfield had a first team place looked more secure. I couldn't believe I was contemplating knocking back the one thing I'd wanted: the chance to start the season as a regular first-teamer! Liverpool had again found little joy in the transfer market and there were no major signings to strengthen the competition for berths. In fact, the biggest close season transfer drama had involved the departure of one of Liverpool's and the world's finest footballers.

After leading the Reds to victory in the European Cup Final, Graeme Souness had flown to Genoa to talk terms with the management of Italian first division club Sampdoria. As captain of Liverpool and Scotland, Souness had a strong bargaining hand. He knew how to take care of himself in the negotiating room and was resolved that he wouldn't accept one lira less than he thought he was worth. As he told me later, he had emerged from the negotiations white-faced. Souey had a figure in mind, expecting the Italians to beat him down. Instead they upped it beyond even his bank manager's wildest expectations. For once the famed composure was rocked. He nodded numbly and signed on the dotted line.

So, Souness was gone leaving a gap as wide as Sydney Heads in the heart of the Liverpool midfield. On top of that Ian Rush was recovering from surgery and David Hodgson had hit the transfer trail to Sunderland. The situation meant that Craig Johnston was no longer an option, he was a necessity. Staring me in the face was the biggest chance I'd ever have of staking my claim to the prize that mattered most: a permanent first-team role.

I picked up the phone and dialled the club. Joe Fagan came on the line and with my heart in my mouth I told him I wouldn't be returning to Liverpool until the baby had been born. There was numbed silence on the line and then an outburst of pure disbelief. Faced with an unprecedented situation, the Boss said he would have to speak to the board. He'd get back to me.

The offer was to fly a specialist out to Jenny when and if she needed it. Meanwhile, they wanted me back on Merseyside, pronto. If not, they would stop my wages and think seriously about pulling down the shutters on my Anfield career. I knew what was at stake but the bitterness of our previous confrontations influenced my thinking. The Boss had let me know before that I was sublimely superfluous to needs, so why all the fuss now?

Word of the stay-put Aussie was soon out on Merseyside and in all the papers. It caused a sensation. Craig Johnston was dubbed 'The Bad Boy of British Football'.

Examining my motives years after the event, I now know that as much as I wanted to stay with Jenny, the birth wasn't my only consideration. Under any circumstances I would have wanted to be there for the baby's arrival, but had it been anyone other than Joe Fagan on the other end of the line, I might have been able to see beyond the bitterness that clouded my thinking. Instead, I dug in my heels and risked my career.

When the initial shock of my announcement blew over, the club and others mistakenly assumed that I was using the break as a chance to negotiate a transfer. I was contacted by three top drawer English managers and several Continental clubs. Ken Bates, chairman of Chelsea, was on a business trip to Australia and made a point of inviting me to dinner in Sydney. I accepted the invitation but not his offer to throw in my lot with the West London outfit. I can't say I wasn't tempted, particularly in light of the fact that John Neal was managing Chelsea. But sensing that my former Boro boss might not be there too much longer, I abandoned the notion. In a totally different way, however, the name 'Chelsea' was foremost in my thoughts. The inflight movie on the way home had been On Golden Pond starring Jane Fonda who played a character called Chelsea. I thought, what a lovely name! On the way to the hospital, we took a wrong turn and drove into a street called Chelsea Close. It was an omen. When our firstborn duly arrived she was dubbed 'Chelsea Cara'. It took less than a day for some wag to ask me: 'What are you gonna call your second — Arsenal?'

By the time of the birth, the reality of the situation had finally hit home at Anfield. Yes, I was sincere in my stated intention to remain in Australia until the birth and, no, I would not be signing for any other clubs. I would be returning to Liverpool. The club management realised they still had an asset, if an erratic one, on their hands. He was 20 000 kilometres away and woefully short on match fitness, but he had given his word to return.

Unlike suggestions from sections of the English press, I was not sitting on a beach working on a tan.

I knew that there was no way I could jump back into the battle after four months away from the action without putting in some serious fitness work. Taking to the sandhills I built up my stamina and endurance. With no Saturday match as an incentive to train, I needed a focus and found one in Sydney's annual City to Surf fun run. Happily anonymous among the 25 000 other starters I ploughed over the course finishing in 1580th position after taking a minute or so to hop a fence and check on the welfare of the crew of a news chopper that had made a crash landing on an adjacent cricket field. At nights I worked out in a gym, played squash and put in vital sprint training at a nearby park. Being mid-winter, there was no great temptation to resume my surfing career.

Chelsea was born near midday on 11 October amid much press fanfare. The birth was not without complications. Jenny required a last-minute caesarean section and within seconds of the doctor producing our beautiful daughter I fainted. At Tottenham on the Saturday afternoon, the travelling Liverpool fans chanted, 'We love you Chelsea, oh yes we do . . .'

The day after the birth found me aboard an England-bound Qantas flight. Liverpool were floundering in twentieth position in the league and welcomed anything that amounted to reinforcements. The Boss promptly threw me into the action as substitute in the home leg of our European Cup-tie against Benfica. As the press reported: 'To the chant of "Skippy is back, Skippy is back . . ." Johnston set up both second half goals in Liverpool's 3–1 victory.'

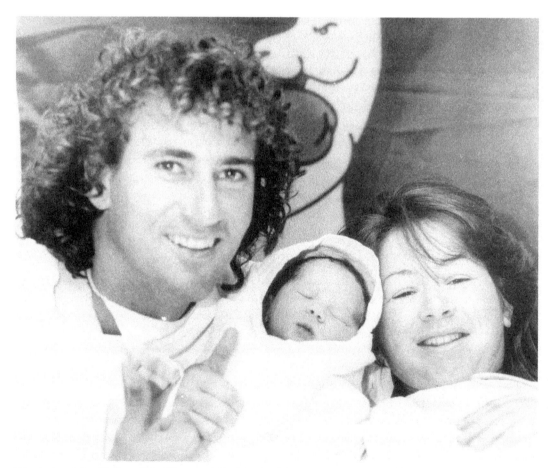

Worth the wait – Chelsea Cara Johnston with the proud parents

In the league it was looking a woefully grim season for Liverpool. Our unfamiliar position in the lower climes was made all the more embarrassing by Everton's runaway lead at the top. Three days before the Benfica game, Anfield had been the venue for the Merseyside derby and the Kop looked on demoralised as Everton repeated their Charity Shield effort by beating Liverpool.

For Liverpool's next thirteen games Craig Johnston was named in the starting line-up wearing the number 10 shirt. I had signed a year's contract, Jenny and Chelsea had arrived and Liverpool had climbed to sixth place. We were still a shadow of the treble-winning side but we were on our way back. With a new contract and a place in a winning side, I was confident about my position. As far as I was concerned, the hatchet had been buried.

On a live television game featuring Liverpool and Queens Park Rangers, commentator and former England great Bobby Charlton nominated me as his man-of-the match, reserving particular praise for my defensive contribution. Ironically, my perceived defensive deficiencies were about to cost me my first-team place and throw my Anfield future right back in the melting pot. We lost 2–1 to lowly Leicester at Anfield on Boxing Day. My first job at Middlesbrough and Liverpool had been to stop the opposition from playing and, despite the result against Leicester, I had done exactly that. In his own autobiography, where he catalogues the Fagan years, Bruce Grobbelaar recalled the fateful team meeting following that defeat:

> 'He [Joe Fagan] was seen by the world as a marvellous, benign uncle figure who was always ready and willing to praise an opponent and underplay his own success. He was not like that all of the time, however. When he was angry he was not a very nice man at all as my roommate Craig Johnston once discovered. Craig annoyed Joe with things he said and did and I am convinced that that is why Craig played so little for the team under Joe and why he did not realise his undoubted potential during those two seasons. It must be said that Craig deserved a lot of the treatment but he was, and still is, a talented footballer who simply needed a little help and guidance. Joe seemed unable to give it to him even though he would show his respect for Craig's football abilities by selecting him at crucial times for important matches. They had so many rows I could only imagine it was one of those unavoidable clashes of personality which sometimes occur. It reached a climax during one particularly bad run when Joe told the media that there would have to be changes at the back because of our leaky defence. Instead, when he read out the team for the next match, he left Craig and Jan Molby out of a midfield that had played well and named another midfielder, Kevin MacDonald, at the back. At this I shouted out 'Who?' in an incredulous voice and quickly turned away to do up my shoe laces. But when Craig discovered he had been dropped again he sighed and swore under his breath. Nothing was said to me but Craig was asked to stay back and, no doubt, they had another head-on collision.'
>
> (More Than Somewhat by Bruce Grobbelaar, Collins Willow, London, 1986)

Joe Fagan justified his stance by telling the press he wanted ball winners rather than ball players. If anything, hustling opponents into losing possession was one of my strengths. On the evening following the team meeting I phoned Phil Neal. The Liverpool and England right back was in the twilight of his career and I had made it my duty to see that no jumped-up winger with speed to burn would ever take him to the cleaners. My self-imposed assignment was to not only take care of my opposing midfielder but to use my younger legs to help Nealy keep the winger quiet. I had seen Villa's flyer Mark Walters zip past Phil one day and neither of us wanted to see it happen again. The Liverpool veteran appreciated my covering role and had many occasions to thank me. I felt Phil would more than willingly come to my defence in light of the Boss's comments. I was wrong. My skipper and teammate didn't want to know.

Craig Johnston's name didn't appear in the starting line-up for more than three months. Despite

Liverpool's climb back to respectability and my part in the recovery, and despite my having signed a new contract, it was apparent the old nightmare had returned bigger and uglier than ever. Since the previous season I had started in no more than thirteen games for Liverpool. When I did get a game I was so nervous and frantic to do well that I wasn't the same player. My lack of composure must have put my team-mates under pressure, a factor that would not have gone unnoticed by the coaching staff. Knowing that they were aware of that situation only made me more nervous. My paranoia was such that I thought only Pele-like performances would ensure my place in the side. Consequently, a certain amount of greed, which wasn't appreciated by my team-mates, became evident in my game. After the stay in Australia and the latest round of my much-publicised bust-up with the Boss, I'd been branded a rebel and a bad boy. Liverpool had no apparent need for me and nor did other teams. My value on the transfer market slipped to 250 000 pounds.

All this was a great source of amusement to those who had cemented a place on the team. After the Milk Cup saga at Wembley the lads suggested I should ask our strip sponsor to supply me with a special Adidas blanket, complete with the familiar three stripes. Even Joe Fagan would have a laugh about it. When he named the substitute at our regular team meetings, instead of saying who would wear the number 12 shirt, he would say: 'And the blanket goes to . . .' It became part of Anfield folklore. At a glittering footballing function at which the guest of honour was England boss, Bobby Robson, Rushie was presented with the Golden Boot award as the season's leading marksman, which went over very well. When comedian Stan Boardman presented Craig Johnston with the Golden Bench award, it brought the house down. Even I had learned to laugh at the situation.

The entire soap opera was bound to come to a climax. After three months on the outer I slapped a transfer request on the table and did something I have since regretted. I went public with my feud. 'I DON'T LIKE YOU MR FAGAN' screamed the *Daily Mirror* headline atop a story detailing my disenchantment with the Boss. *The Sun* reported: 'Craig Johnston's turbulent career at Liverpool ended yesterday when he launched a scathing attack on manager Joe Fagan after having a transfer request granted. Johnston, who lost his place in the Kop team at Christmas, stormed:

"Over the years the manager has made it obvious he does not like me — and I like him even less."'

Before the stories appeared I phoned Joe Fagan and told him what was about to break so that he could exercise his right of reply,.He told *The Sun*: 'I have no personal axe to grind. The poor devil is not in the team. He is a good player and he has done his best for Liverpool. It is all right for him to say things about me as long as he doesn't degrade the club. I have been expecting him to ask for a move and I think it would be better for all concerned if he went somewhere else.'

The lads thought it a great joke. Knowing my penchant for changing the words to popular songs, Bruce prepared a special rendition of 'Please Release Me', with Ian Rush and Ronnie Whelan on back-up vocals.

The 'bad boy' tag stuck. As tabloid genius Ted MacAuley so lyrically put it: 'GOOD RIDDANCE — clear off Craig and keep on going. And if that British message is not clear enough for an Aussie too dumb to know good manners when he sees them, I'll translate: On yer bike, mate — and keep pedalling! Johnston, I feel, will be missed at Anfield like Scargill at Mrs Thatcher's next Downing St party.' I was resigned to the fact that at the end of the season, when my contract expired, I would be saying goodbye to Anfield for good. The management threw me in for a couple of games as Liverpool struggled on to finish a distant second in the league, thirteen points behind Everton. For the first time in years, Liverpool were struggling to win a single trophy as the Reds slipped out of Cup contention after losing a semi-final replay to Manchester United. Ronnie Whelan and Paul Walsh had saved Liverpool's blushes in a thriller at Goodison Park. After the replay at Maine Road football critics agreed that the bench blundered by pulling off Dalglish in favour of a defender. United went on to win 2–1 and then denied Everton the Double by beating them at Wembley.

Earlier in the season Spurs had dispelled all hope of another League Cup by putting the skids under

'Oh, what a feeling!'

a below-strength Liverpool. Again, we had gone into the World Club Championship in Tokyo against South American hot shots Independiente under-prepared and jet-lagged and lost 1–0 to their superior skill and aggression. Anfield's final hope of refurbishing its dwindling trophy stocks rested with the European Cup.

Liverpool beat Panathinaikos 5–0 on aggregate over the two legs to book a berth in Belgium for what would be the club's fifth European Cup Final. Our fellow qualifiers were the mighty Juventus of Turin, featuring Platini, Boniek and Cabrini. Having won all previous finals in which they had appeared, Liverpool were nonetheless determined to prevail as kings of Europe.

The recent history of the European Cup had been one of the great fairytale chapters in the annals of LFC. When the idea of a series between the champion clubs of each European country was introduced in 1955, the English snubbed the proposal, choosing not to enter until the following year. The majestic Real Madrid, with Ferenc Puskas and Di Stefano, dominated the Cup from the outset, winning the trophy five times in succession from 1955 to 1960. They were succeeded by Benfica of Lisbon who paraded the magical skills of Eusebio, the man dubbed the European Pele. Inter of Milan won back-to-back titles before Celtic (1967) and Manchester United (1968) set up a British double.

By now the Cup, already the exclusive domain of champions, had developed a reputation as the forum of European football's great artists. Puskas, Di Stefano, Eusebio, Charlton and Best were succeeded by the likes of Neeskens, Cruyff (Ajax), Muller, Beckenbauer (Bayern Munich), Keegan, Clemence (Liverpool), Shilton and Francis (Nottingham Forest). As one commentator would remark, the European Champions Clubs' Cup, to use its full original title, had truly become 'the province of the privileged'.

We're not talking about a bunch of grubby blokes from a couple of pit-towns kicking the shit out of each other here - the European Cup is for the true princes of football. This is the beautiful game played at its most rarefied level. Its standards and traditions transcend all borders and cultural differences. For example, when Don Revie built his famous Leeds United side of the late 1960s, he dispensed with the club's traditional blue and gold in favour of all white like Real Madrid, in recognition of the unmatched excellence of Europe's first football rulers.

In addition to the sheer honour of playing and winning in Europe, there are the financial considerations. For successful clubs, the Cup is a horn of plenty. The prospect of as many as four or five home games per season featuring the likes of Real Madrid, Benfica, Bayern, AC Milan or Moscow Dynamo means bumper crowds and huge receipts. European giants have reinforced their invincibility by virtue of the cash receipts gleaned from their Continental conquests. For the premier clubs of Europe, a series which started out as an honour to enter, soon became an integral part of the winning business.

Shankly and Manchester United's Matt Busby were among the first British managers to recognise the Cup's importance. The United boss was seriously injured when half of the team known as Busby's Babes died in the Munich air disaster on the way back from a 1958 away leg. Out of the ashes of that tragedy Sir Matt rebuilt United. Ten years later, Bobby Charlton and the remnants of that side, combined with the likes of George Best, defeated Benfica 4–1 in an emotional final at Wembley.

Perhaps the one great frustration of Shanks' managerial career was that he didn't win the European Cup. God knows, he tried hard enough. His effort over almost fourteen years, however, was all money in the bootroom bank. In 1977 Bob Paisley took the Reds to Rome where Kevin Keegan dominated proceedings as Liverpool beat Borussia Moenchengladbach 3–1. At Wembley the following season, Keegan's heir-apparent, Kenny Dalglish, grabbed the winner when Liverpool triumphed 1–0 over Bruges of Belgium.

After a two-year reign by Nottingham Forest, Liverpool and Real Madrid met in Paris in 1981. As a newly signed, non-playing member of the squad, the occasion offered me a rare insight into the drama and refined atmosphere of the Continental final. On a perfect Parisian night the Parc des Princes was bedecked in the

Nice legs, shame about the face!

The horror of Brussels, May 1985

Littlewoods Cup Final, against Arsenal, Wembley 1987

On assignment in the pits at Adelaide

LIVERPOOL SCRAPBOOK

Grand National 1982

Bruce.
King of
Spectacular
dives
Sudan 1983

EXIT ➔

Supersub Davie
Fairclough
on the way out!

Would the
real John Barnes
please stand forward

Insiders view of the Treble

Captain Kennedy. Would you trust
this man with your btle Life?

Sammy Lee - EXCESS baggage

Bruce losing his pre match nerves! - ¼ final European Cup. Benfica 81

RED HOT RAP

Who cant walk on water? Dead Sea Israel 1984

League Championship

young Paul Dalglish looks perfectly at home

Digger and Son

white of Real and the blood red of Liverpool. The Kop had decamped across the Channel to sing their side into European Cup immortality. A third win would rank Liverpool alongside three-time winners Ajax and Bayern. In my years as a professional footballer I'd never witnessed anything to match the occasion. What the game lacked in fluent football, it more than made up for in sheer tension. The atmosphere was contagious. I turned around to see who the vociferous Liverpudlian was sitting immediately behind me and was stunned to recognise the lord mayor of Liverpool, resplendent in his chains of office, shaking his fist at the referee and swearing like a trooper.

The outcome was decided by the unlikeliest of heroes. In the eighty-second minute, Alan 'Barney Rubble' Kennedy chested down a throw-in and, from the acutest of angles, drilled a stunning shot into the Real net. Un-Real! The fans were ecstatic and Barney, fittingly, took the Cup and the boys into town to show the French a thing or two about drinking champagne. Some of my sweetest memories of football have been the European campaigns. It was on the trips to the Continent that we would forge the strongest ties with the hard-core Liverpool fans.

I enjoyed a drink more than most and, after any victorious away Euro tie, there was always a happy Scouser or three with whom to sample the local brew. Returning to our Lisbon hotel in the wee small hours, I switched on my room light to behold a scene that resembled the battlefield at Spion Kop. There were bodies everywhere! Sammy Lee's famous travelling mates had made it to Portugal and had taken Bruce at his word that they would be right for the night. Ten of them, well-primed on Lisbon lager, were strewn around the room. A couple had grabbed blankets and pillows. The rest needed nothing but Liverpool scarves for bedding. I was dead tired and not short of a beer or two myself, but I scored barely a wink's sleep thanks to the cacophony of snoring and farting from our sozzled Scouse squatters. On the plane ride home, I spotted a bleary-eyed Sammy trying to catch a cat-nap. I had to laugh. Obviously, a similar fate had befallen one of Liverpool's favourite sons.

But my most memorable times involved the Liverpool players themselves. I'll never forget the home-tie against Dinamo Bucharest in 1984–85 when their hatchet man Movila was given far too much rope by the referee. He was up to all the tricks off the ball — spitting, punching, kicking — and nearly had Bruce stretchered off when he stomped on our goalkeeper's leg. But Movila was a mere clod-hopper compared to the finesse of Souness. The Liverpool skipper put an end to the nonsense in one telling incident. There were no witnesses but the Romanian exited with his jaw broken in two places.

There was a lot more to playing in Europe than what took place on the field. We used to take our own chef and food abroad. There was so much at stake that, in some countries, cheating was a way of life. Abroad we weren't allowed to eat salads or anything that had come in contact with water. If the home side supplied a half-time refreshment, Bob Paisley would go crazy if he saw one of us go near it. With some justification, he was paranoid about his thoroughbreds being nobbled.

Rome was the venue for the 1985 Final and we were giving away a tremendous advantage to AS Roma who would be meeting us in their own backyard. While they tuned up on their home turf, Liverpool acclimatised themselves to the anticipated heat and humidity of Rome with a week in Israel. I'd like to say we were the very essence of professionals with our minds fixed firmly on the prize, but I'd be lying. We hit the booze from the outset in Tel Aviv, repairing from one drinking session to the next. What the hell! It had been a tough season, we'd already won two trophies and nobody rated us a bolter's chance of rolling Roma on their own patch.

In fact, our relaxed state was the best pre-match preparation of them all. Souness, as assuredly as he directed on-field proceedings, took charge of the social program as well. The result of that week of fun in Israel was a reaffirmation of the camaraderie and respect that bonded our team tighter than any other.

Our every action was monitored by Italian reporters who doubtless told everybody at home just how relaxed and loose the Liverpool lads looked. Quite by chance, we were to convey that very mood to our opponents in the vital moments before the match. I'd given Chris Rea's album 'Wired To The Moon' a hiding to

'I don't know what it is
(but I love it).'
European Cup Final, Rome 1984

such an extent that all the players knew the songs off by heart, especially 'I Don't Know What It Is (But I Love It)'. It seemed an oblique reference to the intangible ingredient that set our team apart from the rest. When one of us would sing a verse, the rest would come in on the chorus, clapping and chanting, evoking those images of unity and victory. After the pitch inspection we made the long trek down the tunnel back to our dressing room deep within the bowels of Rome's Olympic Stadium. The tension among the squad was palpable as we walked in silence down that dark corridor. Inexplicably, Davey Hodgson broke into a solo rendition of the opening verse of the Chris Rea song. One or two joined in and by the time we drew abreast of the Romans' dressing room, the whole Liverpool squad was chanting and singing 'I don't know what it is but I love it . . . I don't know what it is but I want it to stay …'

The AS Roma players looked on bemused. This must be the super-relaxed Liverpool side they'd heard about! We were already one up on them before a ball had been kicked. The nerves never returned. Ronnie Moran saw to that. The Liverpool coach was rubbing one of his charges down just minutes before we were to run out when he launched into one of his marvellously obscure 'This-reminds-me-when' stories. It was about yet another village game on a windy common in Lancashire and was so well told that for a minute or two we all felt we were there, the immediate challenge forgotten. At the end of the story we laughed at the incongruity of it all. Ronnie's juxtaposition of football at its humblest and highest levels, although probably unintended, did the trick. At that point the team was tighter than ever and at perfect pitch for the biggest one of them all: the European Cup Final.

We ran out to a reception of smoke bombs, flares, klaxons and waving flags as 20 000 Koppites for once found themselves outshouted.

Phil Neal scored for us in the fifteenth minute off my cross and Pruzzo equalised on the stroke of half-time. The scores remained deadlocked even after extra time. The contest would be decided on penalties. Who had the superior nerve? Phil Neal was our penalty specialist but instead it was Steve Nicol who came forward first to place the ball on the spot. His blasted shot flew high over the bar. The Italians did better by finding the net but Nealy made certain with Liverpool's second. Roma's golden boy Bruno Conti stepped up and, with his famed left foot, hit the same advertising hoarding as Stevie Nicol. 1–all.

Souness, Righetti and Rushie were all bang on target as the tension built. Then Italy's World Cup

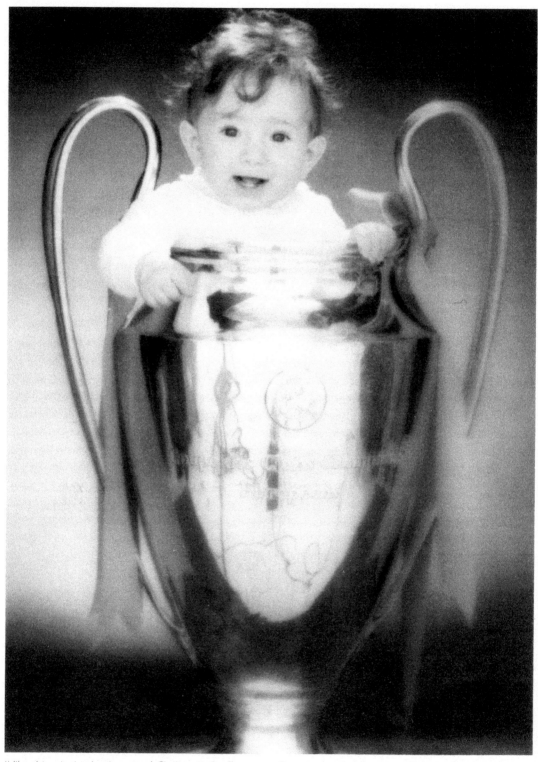

'I like this winning business too.' Chelsea in the European Cup

veteran, the super cool Graziani, took the ball and strode confidently towards the spot. He was stopped dead in his tracks by the sight of my mad roommate, the clown prince of goalkeepers, feigning fright. Bruce was standing there on the goal-line with his knees trembling in mock terror and his body slumping like a rag doll in a near faint. To this day I don't think it was gamesmanship on Bruce's part. It was merely his way of deflating the over-charged tension. Maybe Graziani was still blinking in disbelief when he struck the ball. Whatever the reason, his kick sailed harmlessly over the crossbar.

If Alan Kennedy could convert his chance, the Cup was ours. The affable Geordie, who had missed every penalty he had taken in practice that week, collected the ball, placed it on the spot, took a couple of backward steps and made football history. Liverpool had overtaken Ajax and Bayern and, with four, victories, remained second only to six-time winners, Real Madrid.

Our celebrations were delayed for at least two hours while two of our lads were subjected to the obligatory drug tests. I'm certain the swab revealed they were both still high on team spirit. We finally celebrated at a private villa atop one of Rome's seven hills. With the lights of the Eternal City below us, and the European Cup on the table, the number of drink rounds was almost eclipsed by the number of times we chorused the anthem for the season: 'I Don't Know What It Is (But I Love It)'.

It was George the Fish who sensed it first.

'There's gonna be a lotta trouble here today,' said the Merseyside fishmonger and friend of the lads. As a privileged member of Sammy Lee's gang, we had sneaked George into Brussels' Heysel Stadium for the pre-match pitch inspection before the kick-off to the 1986 Final against Italian champions Juventus. The match build-up had taken place amid a delightful carnival atmosphere set against a balmy June afternoon. Two hours before the game, George had strolled out as one of the lads for the pitch inspection and the chance to wave at his Mersey mates gathering on the terraces.

I can remember it so vividly. An hour or so before the scheduled kick-off, I was sitting next to George near the mouth of the wire-meshed tunnel facing out onto the pitch. That's when he voiced his fears.

'There's gonna be a lotta trouble here today.'

'What do you mean?' I queried.

'Look at that fence over there,' he said, pointing to the flimsy structure segregating the ill-fated Sector Z from where the bulk of the Liverpool fans were gathering. 'A lot of the tickets have gone into the wrong hands,' he said. I knew what he meant. During our pitch inspection I had noticed that one of the cardinal rules of crowd control had been broken. Opposing fans, instead of being segregated, were mixing on common ground. At best, all that separated two large bodies of supporters was the frail fence referred to by George.

As a long-time observer of football tribes, George the Fish's opinions were respected by the lads. But, for the time being, we had other things on our mind. We were in the countdown mode to another European Cup Final.

We were below deck in the dressing room in a state of semi-undress when I first heard the uproar. I darted up the stairs and looked out through the mesh at the sight of Juventus supporters fleeing in the path of a group of Liverpool fans. Panic shot through the crowd like an electric current, triggering a mass stampede towards the retaining brick wall at the opposite end to the Liverpool section. I called out to Bruce and, with Sammy Lee in tow, he joined me at the top of the stairs. As George had predicted, the fence had given way. It was a chaotic scene and the panicked crowd appeared to be bearing down on us. I belted back down the stairs to tell Ronnie Moran to close the top window to our dressing room annexe to ensure the security of the players. Returning to the top of the stairs, I could see that the tide of fleeing fans was banking up against the brick wall not 60 metres from where we stood. The wall was heaving and buckling under the pressure until, with an awful noise, it came crashing down. From out of the melee rushed a young man in the black and white colours of Juventus. He had blood on his face and, seeing the red of a Liverpool player beyond the mesh, flung himself at the wire screaming, 'Animals, animals!' At that moment police in riot gear arrived at the mouth of the tunnel and shoved us back down the stairs.

No matter what stories you have heard or read elsewhere, I can honestly say that no Liverpool player witnessed any of the thirty-nine deaths that took place at the foot of that wall — the confusion was too great, our view was limited and most of the squad had remained downstairs. Snatchy reports filtered down the stairwell that people were dying. The estimated body count mounted — eight, fifteen, twenty. We didn't know what to believe. People in different coloured uniforms appeared from time to time and all gave varying reports in various languages. The players' major worry was for the welfare of their wives and families who were sitting above in the stand. Then word came down that the trouble was well removed from the stand area. Thankfully for me, Jenny was safe at home in Australia.

Outside, total pandemonium had broken loose. The riot police were unable to cope with the crisis and there was speculation that the game might be called off. By this time Joe Fagan, escorted by martial arts

Brussels 1985 – if we hadn't played, there would have been more bloodshed

expert and personal LFC bodyguard Tony Chinn, had moved to the Liverpool end. In tears, the Boss made an impassioned plea to the fans. They abused him. Sporadic fighting still flared on the terraces but the major damage had already been done. Thirty-nine people lay dead in the vicinity of the collapsed wall.

There was no question whatsoever that the game had to be played. Thousands of people had travelled from two countries to witness a football event. Instead, they had been treated to a scene straight from Hell. If we didn't give them what they had come for who knows what would have happened. Like professional soldiers sent into battle we played the game.

If we had known the full magnitude of the horror, I think it would have been near impossible for us to even go through the motions of playing, but we had not seen what those watching on television or the rescue crews on the spot had witnessed. The sophistication of long-range lenses and saturation television coverage had relayed the entire drama to a watching worldwide audience. We were right on the spot but we knew little of what had really happened.

The bare statistics of the match were that Juventus won 1–0 via a Platini penalty. In light of what happened that afternoon it seems churlish to say that the penalty should never have been given. The score that will always be remembered from that evening is thirty-nine dead.

I was kept awake throughout the night by the phone ringing in my Brussels hotel room. On the other end were reporters from Australia and Britain. The afternoon's events were the last thing I wanted to discuss, but there was no dodging it, however, when our aircraft set down at Speke. We were met by a huge media corps. The whole of Liverpool was in mourning. A deathly silence had enveloped the entire city. There was only one word to describe the mood: shame. How could Liverpool, the club that for so long had flown the flag of good sportsmanship, have been reduced to such barbarism? Liverpool, the club that more than any other had worked overtime to vet the credentials of its travelling supporters and check the ground security of away venues, stood condemned. Until Heysel, none of the stigma of football hooliganism that had made England supporters the scourge of Europe had touched Liverpool. But this was beyond football hooliganism, this was manslaughter, and the whole city felt ashamed.

There were lesser victims of Brussels. Not surprisingly, all English clubs, after a deplorable record of crowd behaviour, were kicked out of European competition indefinitely. As for Liverpool, they may never get another chance to prove that it was only a handful of mindless criminals, rather than genuine supporters, who had violated the club's honour.

Joe Fagan had announced his intention to retire before the game. The rumour was that Kenny Dalglish would be taking over as player-manager. Despite the acrimony of our relationship I felt deeply for Joe Fagan as, in tears, he stepped off that return flight from Brussels. His whole world had fallen apart.

THE TIES THAT **BIND** CHAPTER 10

The phone rang in my parents' Lake Macquarie home. It was an international call for me.

'Springsteen!' said a cheery voice on the other end.

It was Kenny Dalglish. Liverpool's new manager wanted me back. With the changing of the guard at Anfield and, particularly, the Brussels aftermath, my transfer crisis had all but been forgotten. Now, with the new season about to begin, Liverpool's youngest ever manager faced the job of restoring the club's shattered image. Dalglish was marshalling his troops. My woes under his predecessor didn't rate a mention. As far as Kenny was concerned, I was off the transfer list and back in consideration.

What had been a rumour when we travelled to Brussels for that ill-fated final had been confirmed on our return to Liverpool. Kenny Dalglish would be the new boss. With the season effectively over, I was on my way to Slane Castle, Dublin, to see Bruce Springsteen when I learned I was required at Anfield to talk to the new manager. Few had been more aware of my woes than Dalglish. His dressing room hanger was next to mine and

'Now listen here, Springsteen.' A word of advice from new boss, Kenny Dalglish

he had watched the entire drama unfold over the past four years. He had sympathised at times and chastised me when I deserved it.

At this stage, as far as I was concerned it was game, set and match. The Liverpool party was over and I was off to find another club. Dalglish had other ideas. Solving the Johnston problem was his first managerial task. We sat down and I told him that my plan was to head back to Australia for the close season and to think about my future. Kenny was frank. He thought there had been times when I had been treated unfairly and times when I'd been at fault.

'Remember QPR away,' he said. 'It wasn't so much what you did on the ball but what you did off the ball that I liked.' I knew what he was talking about. 'I can't promise you anything other than a fair go,' he said.

This was music to my ears. I resolved to give it a try.

The critics had queued up to pour scorn on Liverpool's decision to appoint a player to manage the top club in the land. After all, it was a departure from the bootroom tradition that had witnessed the baton pass from Shankly to Paisley and then to Fagan. By Anfield's conservative standards, the appointment of the boyish faced Dalglish was seen, at best, as a desperate punt. There was even talk of a Souness-Dalglish coalition. As it turned out, the quiet figure who slotted comfortably into the background as Kenny's adviser was none other than the semi-retired Bob Paisley.

Despite training well in pre-season and hitting top form in the trial games, I was disappointed to find myself on the bench for the opening three matches of the 1985–86 season. Thrown into the action as substitute in two of those games, I did enough to convince Kenny that my pre-season form wasn't a flash in the pan. As far as the Kop was concerned, the Boss could have shown no greater sign of faith than by entrusting me to wear his own famous number seven shirt for the next five games. This was the shirt made famous by Keegan and then Dalglish and it obviously carried some of the magic as I grabbed goals against Ipswich, West Ham, Watford and Oxford. It was the start of a run of thirty-two successive games for Craig Johnston in the Liverpool first team.

I'd found another ace in a change of diet gleaned from reading about Ivan Lendl. His dietitian was Dr Robert Haas. When I learned the medico had written a book, I went and bought it. Lendl had said he'd never won a major competition before he went on this strictly controlled diet. The super-fit Czech tennis star prescribed a special high-fibre intake. It was 80 per cent carbohydrate, 15 per cent protein and 5 per cent fat. There was no red meat, salt, sugar or most dairy foods. It allowed as much fruit, fresh vegetables and water as you could consume, and, fortunately, the odd beer. All the things that I had imagined were fattening and bad were prescribed in the diet: potatoes, brown rice, brown bread, pasta. The effects were stunning and, for one whose job called for super-fitness, easily monitored. For a kid who'd been raised on steak and eggs as the food of champions, this was a revelation.

My pre-match meal, which Jenny would prepare, always adhered to Dr Haas' nutritional equation. The sight of me tucking into nuts, wholemeal pasta and dried fruit was the cause of great hilarity at first. As time wore on and my performances spoke for themselves, my diet became a topic of discussion at team meetings. Before long Kenny, Ronnie Moran and Roy Evans were on the diet, Sammy Lee had filed a standing order for his pre-match meal and Jenny had quite a few players' wives phoning her for recipes.

When the commentator on a live telecast of a match against Spurs, said 'If you're wondering where Craig Johnston gets his energy from, I believe he's on a special diet and even brings his own pre-match meal whenever he plays away from home.' I was in big demand. For the next month or so I was absolutely inundated with enquiries from ambitious youngsters, social sportsmen, Sunday joggers and even fellow pros. For the benefit of all those who might be interested, here's my exclusive pre-match meal:

INGREDIENTS
1½ cups brown rice
2 tablespoons vegetable oil
3 egg whites
1 medium onion, diced
1 cup frozen or fresh peas
soya bacon chips
soy sauce
cooked prawns or chicken pieces
METHOD:

Boil rice for approximately 20 minutes then drain and spread onto tray and place in refrigerator overnight. Heat 1 tablespoon of oil in wok or frypan and stir fry onions and peas approximately 3 minutes and place on dish. Heat additional oil in wok and cook egg whites pancake style. When cooked remove and dice. Place rice in wok and stir fry for a couple of minutes. Add onions, peas and egg whites and stir for 2 minutes. Add 2 teaspoons of soy sauce and bacon chips. Add meat last and stir for further 5 minutes to heat. Serve with a side salad. Serves 4-6.
DESSERT:
Fresh fruit salad.

For once, a Craig Johnston eccentricity was working for the team's benefit. If I failed to get back in time to support the defence, somebody would shout from the bench, 'You should have eaten more brown rice!'

Fit, relaxed and confident in the belief that I had again found a manager who believed in me plus a diet that worked, I was playing some of the best football of my career. Unfortunately for my memoirs, it fell in the midst of a dispute between the television networks and the Football League and none of our early season games was televised.

Injury brought the run to a halt. I'd taken a knock at Watford and the osteo scar on my left thigh developed a nasty egg. Roy Evans came to my hotel room in the middle of the night to check on the damage. It was only a scare. Fortunately, I missed just one game until we met Queens Park Rangers in the second leg of the League Cup semi-final in February.

They had won 1–0 at Loftus Road and we had the job ahead of us in the return leg. Steve McMahon put us back on terms until, amazingly, we conceded an own goal. We forged back into the attack. Sprinting after a long clearance that bounced high on the bumpy pitch, I managed to get my toe to the ball a split second before colliding with their goalkeeper. His momentum flicked me in the air causing me to crash awkwardly in the goalmouth. I was momentarily knocked out and didn't know we'd scored until Roy Evans came to my assistance and said: 'Good goal, now get on with it.' I could barely move. Something had gone in my lower back and I was in terrible pain. We were level again, but not for long. With six minutes remaining luck deserted us yet again. Gary Gillespie watched in horror as the ball screwed off his foot and into our net for yet another own goal. We had scored all four goals in the tie but it was QPR who marched on to Wembley.

I was dropped for the next two games and was genuinely worried that I had fallen from favour courtesy of a sore back incurred against QPR. A vertebra had jammed against the sciatic nerve causing me great pain and discomfort. Thankfully, manipulative therapy eased the problem and I was soon back in the side.

One of the pivotal points in that most memorable of seasons came in February. Early in the season Manchester United had jumped to a ten-point lead. It really gave us the pip. The title race was barely a third run

The bread and butter – winning the League at Stamford Bridge, May 1986...

...the icing on the cake – beating Roma in their own backyard, European Cup, 1984

My final game - FA Cup Final against Wimbledon, 1988

What better reason to give up football?

Dear Bruce and Barnsie
A tough day at the office – yet another board meeting!

and already Man United were being acclaimed as champions. By Christmas, however, their train had run out of steam. Come the New Year and the battle at the top had settled down to a slug-fest between the two Merseyside giants, Liverpool and Everton. We were on song with Rushie and Paul Walsh scoring goals at will. But, as dramatically as we had hit form, the magic suddenly deserted us. We crashed to Manchester City and Ipswich and could do no better than draw with Man United. The widely held belief was that the championship battle would swing on the February derby between Liverpool and Everton at Anfield. It was to be my 250th career game and one we were desperate to win. Maybe our desperation got the better of us.

After Liverpool had dominated early proceedings, Everton defender Kevin Ratcliffe attempted a speculative shot at goal. To his and our disbelief the ball squeezed under Bruce's body for one of the softest goals of the season. Gary Lineker added another to complete our humiliation. Everton immediately jumped five points clear with games in hand. If that wasn't enough, press reports the next day labelled Dalglish's men as 'Liverpool's worst side in twenty years'.

On the night of the loss we attended a function to celebrate Sammy Lee's testimonial year. The worst thing you can do in Liverpool is appear in public on the evening you have lost a derby match. But we were there for a cause and were determined to tough it out. We had a big drink that night and the mood among the lads was one of steely resolve. Again, the ties of team spirit began to forge as tightly as ever. Stung by the ensuing media criticism of our derby display we drew close together. We knew what had to be done.

The campaign proper started at Tottenham where we beat Spurs 1-0 with a late goal from Rush. The three points were priceless following Everton's midweek mauling of Manchester City which enabled the Blues to open up an eight-point lead. We exacted league revenge on QPR by hammering them 4–1 at home. The Dell is not the place to go if you are in desperate need of points, yet we emerged from the Southampton encounter with the maximum. We then watched in anticipation as Everton did no better than draw with Chelsea in the televised match the following day.

All we could do was win, but we did more than that at Oxford by hammering them 6–0. That certainly improved our goal difference record. Meanwhile, Everton fell victims to the plastic perils of Luton's synthetic pitch. Still, our cross-town rivals had a game in hand. Sheffield Wednesday broke our stride when they caught us on a mudheap at Hillsborough to hold us to a scoreless draw. We arrived back on Merseyside, turned on 'Match of the Day' and watched Newcastle hit the post, the bar, and just about everything except the Everton net.

The Easter Monday featured a tale of two soccer-mad cities: Liverpool v Manchester City and Manchester United v Everton. Steve McMahon scored a pair as we won 2–0 while United held the Blues to a draw at Old Trafford. There may have been no time for busy footballers to enjoy their Easter eggs but we were more than happy with the two-point nest egg we had collected from the holiday schedule. The table showed the leaders with seventy points apiece; but our superior goal difference meant that, for the first time, Liverpool were on top. High drama. Everton still had a game in hand but we couldn't afford to think about it. All we could do was keep on winning. Under no circumstances could we afford to lose.

As the season careered towards its conclusion Merseyside was starting to simmer. The planets were aligning for what could well be the most dramatic conclusion to an English season since the game's inception. At the top of the table, Everton and Liverpool were locked in a neck-and-neck battle for the Championship. Following the draw for the FA Cup semi-finals, it became evident that the undreamed of scenario was taking shape. The two clubs might yet meet at Wembley Stadium for the first all-Merseyside FA Cup Final. If that shoot-out were to eventuate, there would be more than another trophy at stake. By then one of the Cup Finalists might be playing to win the Double.

Despite the semblance of good-natured rivalry that existed between most Merseyside fans, at street level the tension was all too real. Among the players there was no love lost either. As far as the Liverpool lads were concerned, we wouldn't be taking any prisoners.

YULE NEVER WALK ALONE

Baby Face Barney

Unclean thoughts from Leper Dalglish and Devil Hansen!

Million Pound Smile

Boy Thompson

Hello Possums

While you're down there...

Party Animals

Punk fullback

Hey Gringo. Give me your medals

The sheik of Shimmys

Ku Klux Fan

Kid* Creole Coconuts

Tube of the year Contest 1st Walsh 2nd Want 3rd Rush Judged by last years winner on the left Brucie!

← Guess who →

Pre match* meal

Eye Eye Cap'n*

The Boss impersonating

In the semi-finals Everton overcame Sheffield Wednesday at Villa Park. All eyes swung to the result of the other match at White Hart Lane in North London . . . Liverpool 2, Southampton 0. We were there, we were there! A slow, deliberate nod from Ronnie Moran as we tumbled ecstatically into the dressing room confirmed the answer to the question we didn't have to ask. Everton had made it too. The unprecedented was primed to happen. By the time both team and supporters returned to Merseyside on the Saturday night, the town was in carnival mode. We headed out to celebrate and keep the nightclubs open till dawn.

Pushing thoughts of Wembley aside, the rival clubs returned to the job of winning the league. On the following Saturday Liverpool trounced Coventry 5–0 while Everton had a magnificent result, beating Arsenal at Highbury. Both clubs faced nerve-racking away games midweek — Watford v Everton on Tuesday 15 April and Luton v Liverpool twenty-four hours later. Our rivals shot three points clear by beating Watford. Luton had brought Everton undone on the plastic and were freely tipped to make it a Merseyside double by beating us. With the season fast running out of games, Everton had the jump on us again. Or did they? Liverpool's Australian midfielder has scored better goals, but few more important, said the press after we beat Luton 1–0. Psychologically, it was a blow Everton could have done without.

The prevailing mood in our camp wasn't so much one of celebration but of, 'Well, that's another one out of the way.' We were totally focused, cocooned in a shell of commitment. It had been a long, tense season and the over-riding desire was, 'Let's get it over with.' The prospect of playing relegation-doomed West Bromwich away in what was sure to be a kicking match wasn't a pleasant one. The last thing we needed was an injury. We came away with a clean bill of health and three points from a 2–1 win. Everton stayed gallantly on course with a victory over Ipswich at Goodison.

At our next home game Liverpool started hesitantly against a Birmingham side battling to avoid the relegation plunge. The end result was satisfying, however, as stand-in centre-back Gary Gillespie scored a hat-trick in our 5–0 win. Everton rode into Nottingham Forest that Saturday afternoon and emerged two points light after being bailed up by Cloughie's men.

After forty games Liverpool had eighty-two points while Everton, still with a game in hand, were just two points behind. We were down to the final rounds of the title bout and the tension in red and blue corners was almost overpowering. The pressure to win was one thing, but the competition for first-team places was something else again. Our full squad travelled everywhere. Each man was important to the cause but we all wanted a share of the glory. The lads went full steam to win every game but nobody could afford to cop a knock that might cost him his place. Take Mark Lawrenson, for example. The champion defender had stepped aside the week before to rest an ankle injury and Gary Gillespie had promptly moved in to score a hat-trick against Birmingham. The upshot was that Lawro, one of the world's finest defenders, was reduced to a spectator's role on the bench, a fortnight before the Cup Final. As it transpired, however, he would still play at Wembley. But the lesson was lost on none of us, especially me. The thought of not playing scared me half to death.

We were drawn to play Leicester City midweek at Filbert Street in what would be the second last league game of the season, a mere week and a half away from Wembley. On the day we were to travel down to Leicester, I rolled over in bed to switch off the alarm clock and was seized by a paralysing spasm at the base of my spine. It was the back problem again. For months I'd been having manipulation after training and before games to keep my back moving freely.

While I was stretched out on the floor unable to move, Jenny reported the bad news to Ronnie Moran. Not only would I miss the important training session that morning, there was no chance of my being aboard the bus for Leicester that afternoon. In fact, Ronnie told me to forget about the game. They would get me to the specialist when they returned. Stuff that! I thought. Somehow or other I would get off the floor, struggle down to Leicester and retain my place in the side. Jenny asked Ronnie if I could visit my own physiotherapist. He

'Oi, what's your game, son!'

reluctantly agreed, sending youth coach Chris Lawler around to collect me. I couldn't walk let alone drive! Half an hour on the manipulating table did the trick. I was stiff and sore, but at least I was mobile. Knowing the Boss would have already pencilled in my replacement, I told him that I would drive down to Leicester that night. Kenny agreed and said he would delay his team selection. At the crucial training session at Leicester on the morning of the match, I was desperately relieved to come through with no recurrence of the back problem. Thank God, I was still in the side.

It was to prove a night of high drama as Everton had also drawn away to play little Oxford United at the Manor Ground. The delay caused by a capacity crowd trying to gain access to Filbert Street set our kick-off back fifteen minutes, and this meant that our fans could monitor the progress at Oxford courtesy of thousands of portable radios and would know the result there a full quarter of an hour before our game was due to finish.

At 8.03 Rushie put Liverpool ahead and at 8.14 Ronnie Whelan stretched the lead. Still no score at Oxford. At 9.08, as the ball rolled uneventfully across the Liverpool midfield, an almighty roar erupted from our fans. It was followed by ecstatic singing and chanting. The news spread throughout the team in an instant: *Everton were behind at Oxford!* To the bemusement of the Leicester lads, several of our players punched the air. The fans were chanting 'Champions, champions!' and 'We love you Oxford, oh yes we do . . .' Embraced by exuberant fans as we came off the field, we learned that Les Phillips had bobbed up virtually on the stroke of full time to score the winner at the Manor Ground. Oxford 1, Everton 0. A win at Chelsea on the Saturday would bring the championship back to Anfield. A draw would be enough to put paid to Everton but there was still the outside chance that West Ham, on a late surge, could pip us both at the post by winning their two remaining games.

Meanwhile, back at Leicester, there was no time for sore backs or celebratory beers. While the others returned home by bus, I had to make the trip in my car. On the outskirts of Leicester I was stopped by the police.

'Where are you off to in such a hurry at this time of night?' they asked.

'Sorry officer,' I said, 'my wife's having a baby.'

Cassie Lee Johnston was born in Oxford Street Women's Hospital the next morning. Even though the omens were right, I resisted the urge to name our new daughter 'Oxford'. Two days later, we were playing Cassie's sister's namesake — Chelsea — with the League Championship on the line.

Nothing brightens a Londoner's day more than watching his side roll Liverpool. The Chelsea faithful were out in force, their numbers swollen by the thousands who had bought match tickets in anticipation of seeing the championship decided, one way or another.

Nerves and an atrocious playing surface spoilt any chance of classic football being played. Instead, what ensued was a tense, brittle, often bad-tempered encounter. The one-on-one physical clashes were fearsome. I was wasting time late in the game when Doug Rougvie, their big defender, collected me with an elbow that all but broke my nose, set the claret flowing and knocked my front teeth out of plumb. However, the outcome and the championship were resolved by a classic goal scored by a classic footballer. In the twenty-sixth minute Jimmy Beglin's pass picked out Dalglish on the edge of the box. Chesting the ball down, Kenny volleyed a curling shot into the back of the net. How fitting it should be that the man chosen to manage Liverpool in its greatest hour of need should provide the clincher.

While the celebrations raged on in the Liverpool dressing room, most of those quaffing the champers were oblivious to the fact that almost all the lads had slipped quietly away. Some of us sat in silent introspection aboard the team bus, others had gone to spend a few minutes with family and friends. We left the bubbly gang to do our partying for us. As far as we were concerned, the season was not over. Our partying would have to wait. Liverpool were to play Norwich on the Tuesday night in a semi-final of the Screen Sport Super Cup series, a money-spinner arranged for the English clubs excluded from Europe. For certain squad members it would be the final screen test before Wembley. We paraded the League Championship trophy before the game in which I played up front. Midway through the first half I felt a painful twinge in my back and looked expectantly at the bench. 'Get, on with it,' was the barked response. I didn't need telling twice. As the substitutes warmed up I lifted my game accordingly and scored a cracking header. It meant that I had found the net in every competition that season . . . except the FA Cup.

On Cup Final eve Bruce Potter of the Mojo advertising agency in Australia phoned me at our hotel outside

London. Two seasons before I'd featured in a television commercial for Toohey's beer. The theme was that this Aussie boy wouldn't sign the forms that made him a Pom. Yet, such was my form that season, Kenny Dalglish had asked me to take out British citizenship, which I subsequently did, so that I could represent Scotland at international level. I didn't play for Scotland but it had ruined the commercial and cost Toohey's a fortune. The only way to redeem the deal, said the Mojo man was for me to score at Wembley.

'Not a problem,' I laughed, 'Draw up the contract.'

To win the Double Liverpool had slogged through the last nineteen games of the season without defeat. The second half of winter had been an unrelenting passage of pressure for the players and management of a club used to the demands of being on top. It would take us a long time to unwind. In an article in the Newcastle Herald, Neil Jameson wrote:

> 'At approximately 11 p.m. on the night of the Cup victory, Sammy Lee strolled into the piano bar of the Mountbatten Hotel in London's Covent Garden where his team-mates were quietly drinking. Unattended on top of the grand piano sat the red-and-white ribboned FA Cup, still half full of champagne.

> 'Look at this lot,' observed Lee good naturedly, 'You wouldn't believe we'd just won the Double. Call this a party? Come on lads, drink up!'
> The weight of expectation had become a habit. Instead of celebration, the mood was more akin to the quiet relief sometimes shared by survivors of an ordeal. Much later that night, after alcohol had leached the stress from the system, the young men of Liverpool would celebrate until dawn.'

In retrospect, it was a grave mistake not to rest during the close season. I'd just come out of what felt like a war zone and had committed myself to Bob Geldof's Sport Aid campaign followed by an intensive month of live television for the ABC's World Cup coverage. It was a fatal mistake not to party with the boys in Spain, return home, rest and spend time with my family and folks in Australia.

By the time we returned for pre-season in July, without realising it, I was in no frame of mind to tackle another arduous winter of football. Also, there had been one particular moment in Australia that I would later live to regret. My younger sister Faye had recently suffered a sad loss when her husband Kevin, twenty-one, had died while undertaking relief work in Pakistan. He was a wonderful man and he left behind a grieving widow and an infant daughter. In the midst of my frenetic close season visit, Faye had wanted to talk to me about her loss. With the FA Cup in hand, I had whizzed in and out of the family home, barely finding time to sit down with my folks.

'Can we talk about it later, Faye?' I had said. They were to prove fateful words indeed.

Four months into the new football season found me in form and in the first team. My back, however, was troubling me again and, although I was delivering the goods on the park, I felt mentally jaded. Then I injured my big toe and, when X-rays revealed that the bone was broken, instead of being upset at the prospect of not playing, I found I was quietly relieved. At last I could take a genuine break. The club slipped me straight into hospital where I was subjected to an epidural to ease the back problem. With a plaster cast on my toe I checked myself out of hospital so I could join the lads for the not-to-be-missed LFC fancy dress Christmas Eve party,

I was at home climbing into my Dame Edna Everage costume when the phone rang. The extended pips suggested it was a call from Australia. Mum's voice came on the line. In her deliberate, unflappable way she said:

'Craig, it's Faye. She's had an accident. They don't think she'll live . . .'

'Walking on sunshine . . . and don't it feel good!'

Happier times with my sister Faye

'An accident? What sort of accident?' I said, panicking. 'Mum, where is she?'

A couple of weeks earlier we'd received a letter from my sister Faye. She was in Morocco with her two-year-old daughter and was on her way to England to visit us before returning to Australia. I couldn't believe what Mum was telling me, Faye had been taking a shower when the flame on the gas hot water system had blown out. Overcome by fumes she had collapsed and crashed her head as she fell. She had stayed on the shower floor inhaling the deadly fumes for possibly as long as an hour before anyone found her. My little sister was now in a coma in a Tangier hospital, seemingly beyond hope. For my family back in Australia, there was nothing they could do. The details were sketchy and the language problem almost impossible down thousands of kilometres of telephone line. Mum was at the point of despair. What could we do? Was there any way I could arrange for an English-speaking doctor to fly to the scene?

The realisation hit me: *I had to get there*.

We phoned the airlines. It was a Thursday afternoon and there were no flights before Saturday. My mind was racing. Maybe I could charter a plane! But what about the qualified medical help that I would need to care for Faye should I be able to bring her out of Morocco? Then I recalled having heard about a Lear jet service that came equipped with its own paramedics and life support system — the world's fastest ambulance they had called it. Leafing frantically through the phone bank for relevant numbers, we made a series of calls until we were on the right track. Yes, such a service did exist but it was not available in Britain. The nearest aircraft on standby was at Le Bourget.

'Where's that?' I asked.

'Just outside Paris,' came the reply. 'But you will have to confirm and fly tonight because that's the only time the jet will be available.'

It was already late afternoon, and there was no way I could make it to an airport near Paris within the allotted time. Or was there? If I could charter a private flight to France . . .

For anyone wishing to find out how hard you can squeeze a credit card, try booking a medivac jet and a private connecting flight at short notice. As for the paramedics and emergency equipment, well, all I can say is that your financial standing had better be damned good. Before they would confirm my booking they put me through the credit rating version of the Spanish Inquisition.

Running through the checklist of things I needed to take with me, I came to 'passport' and panicked. Where was my passport? The club had it! Grabbing a swift look at the clock I wondered how I could possibly drive to Anfield, collect the passport and still make it out to Speke Airport in time to meet the flight to France.

'Leave it to me.' The offer came from my next-door neighbour, Colin Bridge, who had been present when my mother had phoned. Bridgey jumped into my car and returned in no time at all clutching the passport. The club hadn't wanted to part with it so he had driven into the city to find Peter Robinson at a Liverpool restaurant and had persuaded the Anfield executive to direct his office staff to hand it over.

An hour later I was boarding the chartered plane at Speke. With its twin props clawing at the bitter evening air, the aircraft climbed and headed east towards Le Bourget where we would be met by a team of French-speaking paramedics. Ploughing through a dense cloud pattern over the English Channel we ran into a ferocious electrical storm that set our tiny aircraft bucking and heaving like a sailboat in a hurricane. I couldn't believe my eyes when the pilot produced a torch and shone the beam out the window at the engines to check whether the props were stiff rotating!

It seemed an eternity before we were taxiing towards the services terminal at Le Bourget. Alighting, I was pointed towards the sleek outline of a Lear jet, its engines already whistling at low revs. An anxious looking paramedic, white trousers showing beneath the heavy overcoat that protected him from the bitter cold, stood at the foot of the stairs, casting impatient looks at his watch. I sprinted for the light that defined the jet's passenger door.

'Ello Mr Johnston?' he queried before ushering me up the stairs where I hurriedly shook hands with the other members of his team.

The flight across the Mediterranean to Tangier took about two hours. The pilot had radioed ahead to explain the nature of the mercy dash and persuade Tangier security to keep the airport open for another couple of hours. No sooner had the jet rolled to a halt than we were out the door, and down the stairs in search of transport into the city. The paramedics were gripping metal cases containing their emergency equipment. All I had was a scrap of paper on which I had scrawled the address of the Christian hospice where Faye had been taken. We found a taxi whose driver, like most of his countrymen, was fluent in French. On the instructions of the chief paramedic, the cabbie took us straight to the hospice.

The scene that greeted us was like something out of the movie *Midnight Express*. We found Faye on the second floor of an antiquated building, lying comatose on a bed in a crowded ward. Her eyelids were blistered, her face was puffed up and discoloured red and yellow. Tubes ran from her nose and mouth. Her body had already begun to waste. I looked at her, thinking of how my little sister had asked me to sit and talk with her so soon after her husband's death and I'd been too busy to give her the time. Would we ever have that talk? That's when something inside me gave way.

'Faye, Faye!' I was sobbing and screaming at once. It was no use. She didn't stir.

A gentle but firm hand on my shoulder drew me to one side. Then the paramedics went to work. I watched with a mixture of apprehension and awe as they tapped a vein in her forearm and administered an injection. Then came the oxygen mask. In her present state she was too weak to move, yet if they didn't move her soon she would die right there on that ancient bed in that dilapidated hospice. What they needed was a stronger heartbeat if they were to attempt to move her. The paramedics spoke rapidly to each other in French as they

Despite pessimistic medical predictions, Faye continues to take slow steps towards rehabilitation

worked over her body. What were they saying? What were her chances?

'Will she live?' I was shouting at them now. 'Will she live?' The paramedics were grim-faced. Then one lifted his eyes momentarily until they met mine. Sadly, he shook his head and returned to his task.

Before I had time to feel the impact of his gesture, I sensed a tiny tug at my trouser leg. Looking down, I saw Faye's two-year-old daughter, Jamillah. I picked her up and hugged her. Fighting back my tears, I said: 'Mummy will be all right,'

The paramedics spent almost an hour readying Faye for the journey. She was hooked up to a veritable grapevine of tubes and life-support systems. Linking arms, they lifted her gently onto a stretcher. While the French team completed their preparations, I took my niece down to the tiny ground-floor chapel and prayed.

With me nursing Jamillah and Faye on the stretcher in the back, we rode the taxi back to Tangier airport where we ran into a major problem. The airport was closed, we were told, and the authorities would not clear us for departure. It was obvious what they wanted but I'd already given all my spare cash to the nuns who had cared for Faye. It was still pre-dawn and freezing cold. We lowered the stretcher and stood on the tarmac while our pilot haggled with the authorities in French. None of us had visas and we were aware that the immigration officers could make real trouble for us if we refused to cooperate. A half hour dragged by and I could tell by the apprehensive looks exchanged by the paramedics that the situation was getting critical. Just when I was thinking that we might have to make a run for it and fly without clearance, the pilot and the officer-in-charge were shaking hands. I didn't see any money nor do I know what transpired but I wasn't sticking around to ask.

Faye with her daughter, Jamillah

In that freezing half hour on the tarmac, Faye developed pneumonia. On the flight I held my sister's hand, nursed Jamillah and kept a worried eye on the meter monitoring Faye's heartbeat. As we were landing at Heathrow the beat fluttered and stopped. The paramedics unstrapped their seat belts and went frantically to work to restore the pulse.

No sooner had the jet's door swung open than an ambulance was pulling alongside. With the siren blaring, it raced through the deserted early morning streets to St Mary's Hospital, Paddington. They can say what they like about the British health system, but it was such a relief to be back in a society with a sophisticated medical service. I sat forlornly with Jamillah, who by now was exhausted and too confused to understand, while Faye underwent a CAT scan and other neurological tests. After what seemed like hours, a doctor appeared in the corridor, a sheaf of print-out paper in his hand. The report was devastating. Although she hadn't fractured her skull as first expected, the gas had restricted oxygen to the brain for God knows how long. She had suffered massive brain damage. Just then the doors swung back on their hinges and four robed figures appeared pushing a trolley bed. On it was the inert form of Faye. The doctor spun on his heel to follow.

'But will she live?' I almost shouted at his back.

He half turned to reply: 'The chances are less than fifty-fifty. Prepare yourself for the worst.'

I phoned Mum from the hospital. I was crying as I said: 'You have to come and see her before she dies.'

Mum and Dad arrived in London four days later. Faye was still in a coma as we mounted a bedside vigil. Jenny came down to London to collect Jamillah who was blissfully unaware of the tragedy that had befallen her mother.

The Anfield management had covered for my absence by saying I was injured. I was grateful for that. Nonetheless, come Christmas, I was called back for a game at Anfield against Manchester United. Over the next week I was up and down the motorway like a yo-yo trying to do my job for Liverpool and to do the right thing by my family. After five or six days the immediate threat to Faye's life abated. But the coma persisted. We were willing to try anything to produce a spark of recognition. I even pinched Jamillah, taped her cries and played them back to Faye hoping she would recognise her daughter in distress. Mum and Dad told her stories, recounting incidents from her childhood. Nothing seemed to work.

It was a bitterly cold winter. We had set up camp in a hotel at nearby Marble Arch. Meanwhile, my life revolved between the St Mary's intensive care ward and my duties at Liverpool. Despite my personal worries, I made certain that once I stepped out onto the park, I didn't let my family problems impinge on my football. I was playing good soccer and the fans had no way of knowing the trauma I was going through.

We met Luton in an FA Cup round on their plastic turf. It was freezing cold, snow was falling and those punters watching the live telecast would have appreciated being in out of the elements. Somehow I managed to scoop what looked like a certain goal off our line to force Luton to a replay at Anfield. I phoned my dad after the game. He was in tears.

'You played well, Reg,' he said. 'The good news is that Faye picked up today.'

We were grateful that the press hadn't run the story. It wasn't that they didn't know. In fact, my erratic departures from Liverpool and frequent appearances in St Mary's had soon put them on the trail. As the news was about to break, I phoned every paper and Merseyside radio and television, only to find that Kenny Dalglish had beaten me to it. My elder sister, Charmaine, who had not been told about Faye's accident, was about to give birth in Australia. She and Faye were very close. News of the tragedy would have devastated Charmaine and we were very much concerned for her health and that of her unborn baby. To their eternal credit, the British media sat on the story.

By the end of January Faye was off the critical list. Mum and Dad had to return home to work, so it was decided that Faye would return to Australia too. Also Faye's care was costing an absolute fortune because she wasn't insured outside of Australia. Then we learned that all flights to Australia were fully booked for three months. We were about to book Faye into a Merseyside nursing home when Qantas miraculously made up to nine seats available not just for Faye, who was on a stretcher and a saline drip, but a registered nurse, my parents and little Jamillah.

Back in Australia, Mum and Dad were enraged by medical advice which suggested their daughter would never walk or talk again. On 2 March 1988 Faye walked unaided across the breadth of Martinsville soccer pitch near my parents' Lake Macquarie home. Due to a wonderful Australian therapist, Ian Hunter, the selfless love and dedication of my parents, and a team of volunteer helpers, Faye was taking slow but hopeful steps.

On the football front, Liverpool were optimistic they could recapture some of the magic of the previous season. But Kenny's words were prophetic: 'It doesn't get any better than this, son.'

He was right. Luton tipped us out of the FA Cup in a second replay. We went down at Wembley to Arsenal in the Littlewood's Cup Final. That left the league. Poised right behind the leaders coming into the home straight, the Boss had us perfectly positioned to pounce. Instead we stumbled at the vital moment, losing to Spurs away, Wimbledon at home and, the most memorable of the lot, Norwich away. The latter sticks in my mind because of the extraordinary events after that match. The management shut us away in the dressing room for about an hour after the game to let us conduct our own post mortem. Then Ronnie Moran cut through the hubbub with his opinion on our failings.

'The simple fact is that some players aren't pulling their weight,' he said.

That day I knew I'd had a stinker and I knew that Ronnie was right. For some weeks there had been a few not pulling their weight. We might have had the same collection of players as the previous season, but it wasn't the same team. The unity was gone.

For other reasons, I was additionally upset by our failure that season. I had written and coproduced a record called 'The Pride of Merseyside', optimistic that we'd finish on a high note. The song, eulogising the feats of LFC, was due for release on Littlewood's Cup Final eve. We lost to Arsenal and then fell on our faces in the League Championship. Not surprisingly, nobody bought the record, particularly after Everton deservingly went on to win the championship. I was 32 000 quid out of pocket but at least I'd learned something about the recording business. My idea had been to capture on record and video the glory of the Double through the eyes of a hard-bitten, out-of-work Scouser who couldn't afford a ticket for Wembley. I'd taken a traditional Kop song and revamped it with Sammy Lee's travelling gang playing starring roles in the video. The product might have struck a better chord if the team had been able to recapture the spirit of 1985–86. I'd tried to capture that spirit in the words of the song. Grabbing the first record off the press, I delivered a Royal Command performance for Sammy's mates in a dockland pub. Sung to the tune of 'The Green Beret' it went:

No work, no hope, one chance for fame,
It's our life, not just a game.
For the Reds grown men have cried,
They're the pride of Merseyside.

Chorus
Liver birds upon their chests,
Liverpool — the world's best,

This great team trusted and tried,
They're the pride of Merseyside,

The angels came took Shanks away
And from above we heard him say,
'Give me men whose hearts have bled,
Make them proud to wear the red.'
(Chorus)

And now our glory won't ever stop
We've got King Kenny, We've got the Kop
One thing we have they'll never hide,
We're the pride of Merseyside
(Chorus)

It was a mega-flop.

Despite the setbacks, the closing images of the 1986–87 season were all pleasant. Rushie was Juventus-bound and we saw him off in style with a day out at Chester races. It coincided with Everton's title clincher and the sentimental on-course tip was for a long shot called Come On The Blues. Everybody on the course, with the exception of Flapjaw's farewell gang comprising Aldridge, McMahon and Johnston, must have been on it as it romped home.

For our end-of-season tour, King Kenny led us back to the Promised Land, Israel, perhaps in the hope of re-forging the ties that had bound us. While we were sitting in the square at Tel Aviv, a member of the travelling press party came strolling towards us waving a telex. I was on stand-by for England.

'If Spurs and Coventry have to go to a replay in the Cup Final,' the journalist said, 'you'll be playing for England against Brazil next Wednesday night you Pommie bastard!'

As it happened there was no replay. With the Spurs stars available, England fielded a full-strength side. While I made plans to return to Australia and Faye, I reflected on how the rocky season on and off the field had still finished on a note of optimism. Bobby Robson had enough faith in me as a footballer to include me in his England calculations.

THE FINAL **WHISTLE** CHAPTER 11

T he journey is often more interesting than the arriving. On Thursday, 12 May 1988, just three days before Liverpool's FA Cup Final appointment with Wimbledon at Wembley, a national tabloid dropped the bombshell that Craig Johnston was quitting football.

'I Hate Being A Footballer' the headline screamed.

The report was largely correct, although I'd never actually said I hated being a footballer. I'd given the story to the paper only to learn within a few days that the editors intended breaking it before, instead of after, the Cup Final as had been agreed.

When I heard that the paper was reneging on its promise, my immediate response was to warn Kenny Dalglish of the storm about to break. As the Liverpool manager would later relate in his official diary of that season:

> *'It was a shock, to say the least. In my view he should not have gone near the newspapers until after Wembley to prevent any possibility of this happening. He is entitled to his point of view and obviously his own future is up to him. You have to respect that. But I also have the responsibility to Liverpool FC to consider as my first priority and nothing will be allowed to interfere with the match we have coming up against Wimbledon on Saturday.'*

With the benefit of hindsight, I was disgusted that I'd allowed myself to land in that position. I swear on my life that the deal I struck was that the story would not appear until after we'd played Wimbledon in the Cup Final. With the way the British media operates, I had a choice of making a general statement about my retirement and having to fend off the barrage of questions and innuendo certain to ensue, or do a first-person exclusive for money. I chose the latter and 25 000 pounds. The fact of the matter was that they never really had the story. All I had told the journalist I was dealing with was that I intended to retire and I would give him the full story after Wembley. But they had the headline, and that was enough for them. They told me that they were running with the headline on the Thursday morning and that I could deny the story on the Friday. I was in a corner. There was no choice but to give them the full story. By breaking its word the newspaper had portrayed me as a Judas. I would have gladly paid ten times the amount I received for the story to have run after Wembley. To say that I was devastated at the turn of events would be an understatement. I was crazy with anger that my confidence had been betrayed and that I might be held responsible for diverting the squad's attention during the crucial Cup build-up.

In fact, I did divert the lads' attention, but in a positive way. Nigel Spackman and Gary Gillespie were both under an injury cloud after having collided with each other in a match the previous week. Both suffered head wounds and their possible non-selection was the focus of media attention, that is until my little story broke. Instantly, the pressure was off the other lads and on me. As usual, humour provided the perfect antidote. With photographers keen to grab shots of Dizzy and Spacko's head dressings, the lads cut up lengths of elastoplast and applied them to themselves. They stuck them on foreheads, eyes, ears and even on their boots. No prizes for guessing where they suggest I tape mine: over my big mouth.

The reaction among the lads and coaching staff to my announcement was one of disbelief. Everybody, with the exception of Bruce, was convinced that I was taking the piss and that as soon as the Cup Final was over I'd have another story in another newspaper denying the original yarn. In hindsight, maybe I should have. The

Sun SPORT

Thursday, May 12, 1988 ☆ ☆ ☆ ☆ ☆

LIVERPOOL FOOTBALL CLUB

I QUIT SOCCER

By CRAIG JOHNSTON

crown paints

'People will call me crazy but I will not care'

FERGIE'S £¾m SWOOP FOR SCOTS KEEPER-P39

INTERVIEW by MIKE ELLIS

CRAIG JOHNSTON stunned the football world last night when he announced: "I'm quitting the game and going home to Australia after the FA Cup Final."

The £1million-rated Liverpool star is starting a new life in New South Wales with his wife and two children.

Johnston said last night: "My only regret is I've had to make this announcement now.

"It was my intention not to say anything until the Cup Final had been decided because I didn't want to put any pressure on the club or my mates.

"But there had been rumours flying around in Australia and I felt it right that I should put the record straight.

"I sincerely hope the timing of this decision does not affect Liverpool this weekend. I would hate to think that might happen but it is out of my hands now."

Fallen

Johnston, who broke into the England squad last November, is one of the top earners in the game and stands to collect £120,000 from this season alone.

But he added: "I have fallen out of love with football. I have started to hate some aspects of it and I know this is the right decision for me and my family.

"It is not a spur of the

KENNY DALGLISH . . . Kop boss will be stunned by news

moment thing. I have been thinking about it for over two years and I know this is the time to get out.

"People will think I'm crazy but I don't care. My schoolmaster in Australia said the same thing when I told him as a 14-year-old I wanted to go to England and play football.

"Well, I've done it and I've got a million memories to keep me warm in my old age.

"For ten years I have been responsible to the man in the street who has had the right to criticise when I made a mistake on or off the field.

Stun

"Now it is time for me to be responsible to the man who lives in my house – me."

The bombshell news will stun Kenny Dalglish as he prepares for Saturday's Wembley showdown with Wimbledon.

But Johnston said: "I'll walk out of Anfield with my head held high and with a clear conscience.

"But I do regret I had no other choice but to make this announcement now. The last thing in the world I want to do is rock the boat with the Cup Final coming up
● Turn to Page 39

Printed by News International Newspapers Limited, 1 Virginia St, London E1. © News Group Newspapers Ltd. 01-481 4100. Reg. as a newspaper at the P.O. No. 5,756. Class is 21p, France 7fr, Greece 100dr, Italy 1300L, Port. 100esc, Spain 150pts, Malta 16c, Yugoslavia 650din.

The back page of the London Sun, 12 May 1988

lads were certain it was another one of my stunts. In fact, Ronnie Moran said that he'd bet his wage packet that I'd be back next season. On the night before the big game I fronted Kenny and the coaching staff to explain exactly what had happened and to assure them it wasn't a stunt. They were sympathetic and their advice was that I should put it out of my mind until after the match. Until the story broke I was convinced that I was in the starting line-up for Wembley. I'd played well in the lead-up games and was confident of my chances. Come the team selection meeting in the dressing room at Wembley and I was named as substitute.

By retiring, I was turning my back on much more than a Liverpool first-team shirt. The bottom line was that, at twenty-seven years of age, I was forsaking a glamorous and lucrative career. Another two seasons at Anfield would have brought up my testimonial year which might have yielded a small fortune on top of my wage. I'd already discussed with the club the possibility of a testimonial game in Sydney, possibly against Australia. I did take into account what I stood to lose by prematurely pulling the plug.

On the day the story appeared, Peter Robinson predictably called me in for a chat. At the end of our meeting he told the media that as I had another year to run on my club contract, I would be in breach of the agreement if I did not return to pre-season training in July. Ultimately, Liverpool would call in the lawyers and threaten to sue me. It was the only stance they could have taken. My decision had put them between a rock and a hard place. It wouldn't have been so bad if I'd wanted to leave Anfield for another club — Liverpool could have recouped some cash on the deal. Instead, I was dropping out of the game in my prime. It was the equivalent of valuable livestock dying uninsured on the hoof. There was no way Liverpool would realise a penny. Rather, they would have to dive back into the transfer market to buy a player to replace me.

As far as the legal aspects were concerned, I was of the opinion that I was well within my rights. Before making my announcement I had phoned the Professional Footballers Association secretary, Gordon Taylor, who said that he could envisage no problems. There were problems, however. The management called me in and what ensued was one almighty slanging match. They threatened to freeze all my assets and sue for compensation on the half million quid they felt was walking out the door. However, in consultation with a Queen's Counsel, it was illustrated that I was only worth, say, half a million *providing I wanted to play football.* A footballer who chooses not to play is worth nothing, the QC advised. My case, with the exception of a Wolverhampton player who quit the game to become a Jehovah's Witness, was all but unprecedented.

Although the decision had been sneaking up on me for some time, I can clearly recall the precise moment when I committed myself to footballing retirement. It was on Bank Holiday, 2 May 1988. We were at home to Southampton and before the match the fans were treated to the sight of our skipper Alan Hansen being presented with the League Championship trophy. That was the only celebrating we did that afternoon as our lads played their worst soccer of the season to be lucky to escape with a 1-all draw. Primed for a party, the fans became increasingly agitated. Sitting there on the bench in the role of substitute, I would normally have been super alert and straining at the bit to get into the action. Instead my mind was elsewhere.

With a quiet word, Kenny Dalglish told me to start warming up. It was late in the piece but the Boss was banking on a change of personnel to snap the Reds out of their lethargy. On I went, bearing the expectations of 35 000 fans, spoiled by success, that the substitution would swing the course of the game. The Kop expects. The game was virtually in its last gasp, when I found myself arriving at speed inside the area to meet a ball that had evaded the Southampton defence. With the goal seemingly at my mercy and unable to change stride, I lunged at the chance only to slice it wide. The Kop, that vociferous yet sometimes most critical of galleries, groaned its disappointment. The boos and hisses were like a knife in the back. Then came the criticism from isolated sections of the crowd; 'Wanker, wanker!'

During the postmortems to that match I analysed my own shortcomings. The player who had trotted

The job I was leaving

out as substitute for Liverpool wasn't the same hungry, self-motivated character of two seasons before. What had been on my mind? Certainly not the match at hand. I'd been sitting on the bench contemplating anything except the task before me. Instead of thinking 'I'm too good to be on the bench, give me a go at this', I'd had other concerns on my mind. How was my latest record performing? I have to get home and process some film. Would I get a run at Wembley? Would my back injury return? How was Faye? . . .

For the first time in my career it became patently obvious to me that I'd let outside pressures encroach into the ninety minutes of the match. Football was secondary. No wonder I'd missed the chance. From just 8 metres I'd missed and let everyone down. I'd looked up at the Kop and sampled the full weight of their frustration. I knew then that I had to quit.

Later that evening Jenny and I left Anfield and passed through the Mersey tunnel on our way home. With spring upon the land the first signs of twilight were offering the promise of warmer days and balmy nights. But not for the Johnstons. With season's end we would be heading south, into another winter. It seemed my football career had been one long winter, whether in the Northern or Southern Hemisphere. Thirteen years, twenty-six winters back-to-back. I had no idea what Jenny was thinking as we drove. We were both downcast, deep in thought. Then I spoke:

'Do you want to go home?'

She looked at me sideways. 'We are going home.'

'I mean home to Australia?'

'Yeah,' she answered in an even voice. There was no fuss, no emotion. The decision had been made. It was over.

I could write an entire book about my reasons for pulling the plug while still in my prime. The story goes back to Kenny's words in the lift at the Mountbatten Hotel on Cup Final night 1986. He was right, it never did get any better than that magical moment. Perhaps I should have retired then. Instead, I launched into a demanding program of extraneous activities that made the years 1986 to 1988 too crowded for comfort. There was the tension of the Double season, the Sport Aid campaign, television commitments in Australia, fatherhood, the back injury, Faye's tragedy, photography, recording projects and a major renovation job on a stately home we'd purchased in the Wirral countryside. And the thought of my family back home in Australia contemplating the day-to-day struggle of Faye's long and uncertain rehabilitation made kicking a ball around English football fields seem rather frivolous by comparison. As far as my football was concerned, I'd given all that I could give on the field. I'd always tried my best but I never totally satisfied my critics. Under the circumstances, I had nothing more to give. The welfare of our daughters also influenced my thinking. Had I played on for, say, five more years, Chelsea and Cassie would have been well into their schooling and our ultimate return to Australia would have meant wrenching them away from friends and the only place they considered home. For the kids' sake, sooner would be preferable to later.

I didn't need too much incentive to return home. For almost thirteen years, and in spite of the great friendships and hospitality we'd encountered in Britain, I'd never really mastered the chronic homesickness that had dogged me since my arrival. To make matters worse, every time we switched on the television during the northern winter of 1987–88 there was yet another idyllic image of Australia during its Bicentennial celebrations to torture us. To anyone trapped in frigid Britain the Bicentenary seemed like one endless, sun-drenched carnival unfolding under clear blue skies in that magical Down Under land. We were more homesick than ever.

One of the problems for Australians in Britain is winter. The first winter is a novelty, the second a sentence. The torment stems not so much from the cold and grey but the image of your mates on the other side of the world. You know that they're sitting bare-chested in the sun, fresh out of the surf, feet up on the verandah rail, sipping cold beers . . . That image tormented me for years. The realisation that Jenny was equally homesick helped push me towards that fateful decision.

Had things been different I could have taken the specialist's advice and booked into hospital for an operation to rectify my back problem. The warning, however, was that should the operation prove unsuccessful, I could be left with a permanent disability. Nonetheless, the prospect of a season away from the game to cure my ills and allow me to put my life back into some semblance of order was tempting. It occurs to me now that had I decided to have the operation instead of retiring, I might have presented myself at Liverpool in July 1989 for pre-season training.

While I still played my heart out on the park during my appearances throughout 1987–88, it must have been glaringly obvious to those who run Liverpool FC that I was mentally tired and monumentally distracted. All the signs were evident: football was no longer my obsession. Unless you have been exposed to that level of achievement, it is hard to understand how people can so totally devote themselves to one pursuit. Take Peter Beardsley, England international and indisputably one of the finest players of the 1980s. Peter is a Geordie boy and steeped in the footballing traditions of the North-East. On the England squad's trip to Yugoslavia I took the opportunity to ask Pete what he did in his spare time. 'Watch football on telly,' he said. Yes, but what about the rest of the time? 'Read.' Read what? *Shoot, Match Weekly* and other football magazines.' Anything else? 'Yeah, the football annuals.' The more I probed the more I learned that Peter Beardsley ate, drank and slept football. When he wasn't training, he was resting in preparation for the next time a game or training session would place demands on his strength and resources. He was totally focused and committed to the disciplines of his job. I can remember thinking at the time: 'What a boring existence.' I was dumbfounded and I told him as much. He turned to me and said:

'It's my life, and I live it with a passion. For me, there is nothing else.'

I felt both happy and sad for him at the same time. It was his profession, religion, science and hobby. It was him. It was part of the equation that made Pete an exceptional footballer. That level of single-mindedness is not exclusive to sport. There are many professionals in other disciplines who devote themselves totally to their jobs. Earlier in my career my strength had been a similar Spartan-like approach to my work. In more recent times my focus had waivered.

However, my personal problems were of little importance to LFC during 1987–88, a season in which Liverpool surpassed its own awesome standards. On the way to winning the League Championship by nine points the Reds equalled Leeds United's all-time record of twenty-nine consecutive games without loss. I'll be able to tell my grandchildren that I scored the goal that enabled Liverpool to match Leeds' feat. In a total of fifty matches in three competitions we were beaten a mere four times. Everton, who finished twenty points adrift in fourth place, would claim solace from knocking us out of the Littlewood's Cup 1–0 and ending our unbeaten run in the league by the same margin.

Our fourth loss of the season, however, was more disappointing than the other three combined. History will record Wimbledon as not just winners of the 1988 FA Cup but the team that denied Liverpool the honour of becoming the first side in the history of the game to win the Double twice.

In discussing the FA Cup in the context of one of Liverpool's most memorable seasons it seems trite to say that the ball didn't bounce our way on the day. Peter Beardsley definitely didn't hear the refs whistle in the thirty-fourth minute when he went on to pop the ball into the net after unravelling himself from a foul challenge. Judging by Dave Beasant's attempt to save the shot, he hadn't heard the whistle either. So, instead of a goal, all Liverpool received was a free kick. Two minutes later, Wimbledon scored the winning goal off a free kick decision which certainly should have gone the other way. I've no doubt whatsoever that if Pete's 'goal' had stood we would have won comfortably against an extremely defensive side facing the prospect of having to come out and attack us. Fair dues to Wimbledon — they battled hard, rode their luck and scored one of Wembley's great upsets.

FA Cup Final disappointments aside, my own contribution to that memorable season was a total of thirty-five appearances, many of them as substitute, and a goal tally of six. After being in the side from the outset of our pre-season tour spanning five different countries, and the start to the season proper, I suffered a groin injury and returned at a time when the lads were on their way to reaching twenty-nine games without loss. A knee injury later in the season further limited my appearances.

The groundwork to Liverpool's extraordinary success that year was laid well before the season kicked off in August. If recent seasons had provided slim transfer market pickings for Anfield managers, Dalglish more than made up for it in preparing for the 1987–88 season. With midfielder Kevin MacDonald and left back Jim Beglin both sidelined with broken legs, Mark Lawrenson suffering a ruptured Achilles tendon, and Rushie grappling with the phrase book in Italy, Liverpool surfaced with a cast of expensive new faces. Into the side came England internationals John Barnes and Peter Beardsley from Watford and Newcastle United respectively, while John Aldridge, who had stood on the Kop as a youngster, was joined by ex-Oxford team-mate Ray Houghton at Anfield.

Competition for selection was hotter than ever. At any one time the reserves line-up included Spackman, Walsh, Molby, Whelan, Wark and Johnston. With only eleven first-team shirts to be filled, there were bound to be a few disappointed souls when it came to naming the side. And with the Reds on a record-equalling unbeaten run, Kenny was placed in the happy position of being able to stick with the same formula.

Despite the obvious disappointment of those not in the all-conquering starting line-up, morale was still running high. In fact, the fringe squad became a modest clique in itself, jokingly referred to by its members as the Sour Grapes Gang, or SGG. We were a determinedly good-humoured bunch out to make the most of the fact that it was damned hard to crack a side that simply refused to lose. Like any boys club, we had our own code. For example: At AGM at HQ after AV away in the FA a motion was passed that BG be accepted to SGG; which means that we held an annual general meeting at the Old Victoria pub soon after playing Aston Villa at Villa Park in the Cup and Bruce Grobbelaar wanted in on the gang. After much deliberation, bearing in mind that he was a first-teamer, he was accepted largely on the basis that his registration fee be used to buy established members beers all night. John Barnes wasn't a fully-fledged SGG member but gained affiliate rights. When SGG founder-member Paul Walsh was transferred to Tottenham, his mates gave him an emotional and very liquid farewell party. It was only when I caught Walshie brushing away what just might have been a tear that I realised how much those friendships meant to us all. Nobody blamed Walshie for upping stakes. He had arrived at Anfield as a fully-fledged England squad member but after a long spell out of Liverpool firsts had disappeared from Bobby Robson's calculations. Maybe he could work his way back as a regular in Spurs' all-star attacking line-up.

My rotation in and out of the Liverpool side didn't prevent the England boss naming me on 3 November 1987 in the squad to meet Yugoslavia in a European Championship qualifier in Belgrade. I watched England's resounding win realising that Bobby Robson wouldn't be making any adjustments to his side. I knew, however, that Robson was keen that Craig Johnston collect his first England cap to wipe out any doubts once and for all about what national side he was tied to. The chance presented itself when England were to play Israel in February. A week later a newspaper reported that Kenny had refused to release me for the game preferring to play me in reserves instead. The Boss vehemently denied the tale explaining that he had been advised that Bobby Robson would be contacting Liverpool to ask for my services. Kenny left his home number with the England management but the call never came. The upshot was that Craig Johnston, despite numerous invitations, would

finish his career without a run at full international level for any country.

Back on the club front, Kenny knew exactly what was needed to keep Liverpool in perfect tune. As the season unfolded, nobody could dispute the wisdom of Dalglish's purchases nor his team selections. If winning the league wasn't enough, Liverpool supplied the first three place-getters in the Professional Footballers Association Player of the Year Awards. John Barnes topped the poll from Steve McMahon and Peter Beardsley, with Alan Hansen also being included in the top six. After that glorious result there was no doubt about who would be named Manager of the Year. At the awards dinner in May, Kenny Dalglish stepped up to receive the prize for the second time in his three seasons as manager.

From that season there were games that will long survive in my greatest memories of Liverpool. I participated in many of them and there were others in which I sat on the bench spellbound while the lads tore the hearts out of Britain's finest teams. Who knows what sort of season the Kop might have enjoyed if that side had been allowed to play in Europe. I'll never forget twelve days in April when we were drawn to meet Nottingham Forest three times and Manchester United once. On 2 April we went down 2–1 in the league to Forest at the City Ground. On the Easter Monday, just two days later, we were back at Anfield drawing 3–all with Manchester United in an absolute thriller. Determined to dispose of a side destined to finish second in the league, Liverpool were rocked by an early goal from England skipper Brian Robson. The lads regrouped and, in a passage of football of the highest quality, jumped to a 3–1 lead courtesy of goals by Beardsley, Gillespie and McMahon. It was a match we dominated for much of the ninety minutes so it was still a surprise the next day to read that United had grabbed a draw after having a man sent off.

The two tough outings in as many days put the side in the perfect frame of mind for the trip to neutral terrain in Sheffield where we were to meet Forest again, this time in the FA Cup semi-final at Hillsborough. Exactly a year later the same two great clubs would keep another fateful appointment at Hillsborough.

The most exhilarating point along the road to Wembley comes when the referee blows his whistle to signal the end of the semi-final and you know your side has made it. You're there! We sampled that sensation at Hillsborough simply by outplaying Brian Clough's lads 2–1. John Barnes was absolutely magnificent. Britain's finest attacking player doubled up on defensive duties to produce a totally unselfish all-round performance. I was bitterly disappointed to be named number twelve and not given a chance to play a part.

As substitute I played no more than twelve minutes of the return league match against Forest at Anfield on 13 April. Yet it was a privilege simply to be there that night as Liverpool rewrote their own code of excellence with an awe-inspiring 5–0 victory. The conduct of that match defies superlatives, but there are two salient comments worth making. One is that far from being disgraced, Nottingham left Anfield with their heads high having approached the match with an attacking zeal that might have dismembered lesser opponents. The other concerns an incident in the thirty-seventh minute that characterised the sheer potency and precision of that Liverpool side. After surviving a period of intense Forest pressure, our defence cleared the ball towards Beardsley who was lurking in the inside left position on his own side of halfway. With a defender arriving, Peter simply allowed the ball to run past him, an intuitive ploy that left the Forest player floundering. Then, the Liverpool man turned and, with his first touch, struck a 30-metre diagonal pass towards the far corner of the Forest penalty area. Aldridge arrived on cue and clipped the ball neatly over the advancing keeper into the net. You may see more spectacular goals but few could be as brilliant in their simplicity and efficiency of execution. If you wished to grab an incident from that season as a souvenir of all that was fine about the 1987–88 Reds, you couldn't go past the golden moments surrounding that goal. No sooner was the match over than I was heading for London where I had booked studio time for a recording project. I arrived as the game was being replayed on television and sat back and enjoyed it all over again. I worked all night on the record and made it back to Merseyside to put in a bleary-eyed training session with the reserves the following morning.

Within a few days of the Forest massacre I was back in the starting line-up as a result of Barnesy suffering a groin injury. It was bad luck for the Player of the Year because it put him out of the action, though not the celebrations, when we beat Tottenham 1-0 on April 23 in a result that clinched the League Championship trophy for a record seventeenth time.

On the Saturday before the Cup Final John Aldridge was obliged to rest a foot injury giving me the opportunity to have a run in a central striking role against Sheffield Wednesday at Hillsborough. By then, I'd made my decision to quit and, for all I knew, it might well have been my last game of football. I stood there before the kick-off knowing that I was the only one in the ground who knew. I felt sad but, at the same time, I was desperately determined to turn in a blinder. My reasoning was that if I played well enough I'd earn a start in the Wembley line-up. Peter Beardsley struck twice in the space of a minute with two neat goals and Barnesy provided another. When it comes to finishing, I'm no Ian Rush or John Aldridge, but I played out of my skin that day scoring twice as we routed Wednesday 5-1. Judging by the number of times we hit the woodwork or came close to scoring, Wednesday got off lightly. And their fans knew it. The home club's supporters gave us a standing ovation which showed that quality football and good sportsmanship are alive and well within the professional soccer scene. Speaking of good sports, Liverpool proved that footballing excellence does not have to be achieved at the expense of fair play. With the lowest number of penalty points for foul play, we were rated the fairest as well as the finest.

If the old adage 'Winners can laugh' still carries any weight, then we were also the fun side of the Football League, as illustrated by the lads' efforts in the recording studio. Undeterred by my previous tilt at the music business, I sat down and penned a tune called 'Anfield Rap'. The subject? Liverpool FC, of course, or more pertinently, the lads themselves. I started with the premise that the Liverpool dressing room was a United Nations of footballers, a real mix of accents from Glaswegian to Zimbabwean, Jamaican to Irish. The only true Scousers in the squad were Steve 'Macca' McMahon and John Aldridge. As the song went, it was their job to teach the rest of us to talk like proper Scousers. The lads knew I'd invested an awful lot of time and money and got right into the act. Kenny Dalglish really came to the party for which I was very grateful. It was pretty difficult, however, to upstage those two natural performers, Barnesy and Bruce, who could have stolen the show at any moment.

Unlike my first recording attempt, 'Anfield Rap' was a success, thanks largely to the fact that we were flying high on top of the league. The song raced to number three in the British charts and everybody was tipping that it would vault straight to number one as soon as we completed the formality of blitzing Wimbledon in the Cup. Well, things didn't quite work out that way. As with the previous recording effort, it ended up costing me money. I've not received so much as a whiff of a royalty cheque. Virgin Records must be laughing all the way to the bank!

I bade farewell to the Kop on Monday, 16 May, just two days after the disappointment of the Cup Final. It was Jocky Hansen's testimonial match and goodwill and emotion were running sky high. However, I wished I wasn't there. Among the Liverpool supporters there were those who, because of the newspaper debacle, blamed me for what went wrong at Wembley. In spite of my misgivings, I couldn't miss this event. I knew for sure that this was my last game of football.

In light of the occasion, the anticipated return of Ian Rush to Merseyside and the drawing of the curtain on a glorious season, Anfield was gripped by a carnival atmosphere. My over-riding emotion, however, was one of unbridled sadness. When Kenny pulled me off at half-time I wept inwardly. The fact that we beat an England XI 3–2 that night seemed incidental. How does a player say farewell to those fans and friends who stuck by him throughout seven testing years? I never afforded myself a wave to the fans. Words and gestures are inadequate. Goodbye and good luck. In no time at all your memories of a battling Aussie who briefly wore a red shirt will be

blown away by the deeds of those to follow. But I'll never forget.

The farewell parties seemed to go on forever. It was an emotional few weeks. Who knows, we might never see some of these friends again. Saying goodbye to the lads took some doing. There were so many 'Remember whens . . .' — a thousand images that will continually drift in and out of my thoughts. I'll never forget 1984 when we won the treble and it seemed like all of Liverpool had turned out to welcome us home, like soldiers returning with the spoils of war. As we rode on an open bus through the packed streets, we spotted two scruffy lads running alongside, just two young boys chasing a glimpse of the dream. As soon as the bus slowed to a crawl we hurled them aboard and gave them pride of place up on the top deck with the Anfield stars. The youngsters stood there, brandished the trophies and waved to their mates. For a while that afternoon their dreams also had come true. Then there were the low points, especially Brussels. Even out of that tragedy sprang the hope that the dignity of the human spirit can prevail. Among the homecoming celebrations at Liverpool after we won the Double, the players found themselves in a crush of well-wishers outside the Liverpool Town Hall as we alighted from the bus. Moving through the throng, I felt something draped around my shoulders. I was surprised to see that it was the black and white flag of Juventus. Almost a year after the disaster and in the midst of our own euphoria, it was a moving reminder that the true Liverpool fan still retained a sense of proportion.

Most of the reminiscing that went on during our protracted farewells evoked the spirit of camaraderie that had seen the Liverpool lads at their best, and worst. Like the night before the last match of the season when, with the championship already sewn up, we had gone out on the town. Returning to our hotel near dawn after a marathon drinking session, I had started thumping on the door to wake Bruce up. He'd agreed to leave the key out for me. Instead of Bruce, a very bleary-eyed senior coach, Ronnie Moran, answered the door to be confronted by an extremely drunk midfielder who had broken curfew by a good eight hours. Whoops, sorry Ronnie, wrong floor! My punishment was to play the next day nursing a force ten hangover. Then there was the time in Lisbon when Bruce's curiosity to learn what was happening in another room got the better of him. With a few drinks aboard he clambered out the window and ledge-hopped up and down the facade of the building many storeys above ground level. My stomach still turns at the thought of him leaping around on those narrow ledges. But that was Jungle Man. When he was awake he was so hyperactive he'd be swinging from the light fitting. But the minute he decided to sleep, he was off in a twinkling leaving me wide awake and grinding my teeth. He was the most infuriating, talented, courageous and endearing roommate anyone could ask for. Sure, there was that time when he asked for a change of partner but it was only a short break. In no time at all the two colonials were back together driving each other crazy. Yes, I would miss Bruce a lot.

Returning to Australia, in some respects, would not be easy. As a nation of sporting nuts, Aussies had taken particular pride in the fact that one of their own had made it in the toughest act of them all: the English top drawer. Now, he was quitting. Why? I knew the question would be asked the minute I stepped off the jet in Sydney and I privately pondered how to explain my motives. What were they?

I had arrived in England more than a dozen years ago, a wide-eyed boy chasing a dream. That dream had been realised and my immediate desire was to return to Australia. Football had been just one chapter of my life and it would provide a million memories, but the reality was that I had fallen out of love with the game. The romance was gone. Without that spark, I knew I could no longer achieve the standards I had set for myself. For those reasons, I had made my decision with a clear conscience. When I told my mother of my plans to quit she said in her usual calm, matter-of-fact way: 'I'm not surprised. You must be sick of winter.' My father didn't say a word.

There were those in England who refused to believe it. As far as they were concerned it was a ruse to get out of my Liverpool contract, transfer to another club and pick up some cash along the way. One London club had heard that I was interested in the music business. Convinced that all I wanted was a transfer, the club's agent had said to me, 'One of our directors owns a recording studio. We'll give you unlimited access to the studio if you sign with us!' Then there were approaches from agents said to be representing European clubs. No doubt some of them were genuine but one or two left me with the sneaking impression that they were operating on behalf of English interests anxious to find out if I was really retiring or, simply seeking the most lucrative transfer offer. Ironically, I had long entertained the idea of playing for a Continental club and at one stage my name had been linked with a few such as Monaco and several Italian outfits including Juventus. The speculation was that the Turin club had wanted Johnston to keep Rushie company. Ah well, the only continent I'd be seeing would be the wide brown one Down Under.

I knew that there would be a few in Australia who wouldn't need an explanation about why I retired. One would be Peter Tredinnick, my old Booragul mate who had joined me at Middlesbrough when we were wide-eyed kids. Pete had gone to England for a determined shot at making it as a professional. For one frustrating week after another he had sat out that winter awaiting his chance. By the time they gave him a trial he was fed up. Peter had already made up his mind to return to his studies. He scored a hat-trick in the triallists' 3–0 victory, declined the proffered contract and promptly boarded the next flight to Australia without ever looking back. Unlike Craig Johnston, Peter Tredinnick went on to represent his country and even won a national league club championship medal. He has since graduated with degrees in arts and law and is a practising solicitor with a large city firm. Throughout my career and more especially since I retired, I've been approached by parents and players anxious to know the secret to carving out a successful professional career overseas. There is no simple answer. Maybe I should tell them the story of Peter Tredinnick, a player who should and could have had a fine career in England but who weighed this up against what he would have to sacrifice by doing so. Usually, I tell them to think seriously before attempting to follow in my footsteps. In 1975 I was motivated by the desire to play full-time football. Back then, there was no such thing as the Australian Institute of Sport where talented players can now live and learn in a total football environment. Perhaps if the AIS had been founded when I was fifteen, I wouldn't have set foot outside Australia. While I was in England I met at least a hundred hopeful Australian teenagers who were trying their luck with pro clubs. Almost all went back home sooner rather than later. Some were better for the experience, many were bruised by it. It is not something I'd ever prescribe for my children.

Believe it or not, there is life after football. News of my retirement statement triggered an interesting sequence of events in Australia. Among the first to react was Ian Chappell who called on behalf of Channel Nine's 'Wide World of Sports'. Chappelli advised that I should consider knocking on Nine's door the minute I landed in Sydney. Within a few hours his boss, Nine's executive producer of sport, David Hill, was on the phone to friends asking if that 'curly haired bastard was fair dinkum' about quitting. Assured that the curly haired bastard was fair dinkum, Hilly said. 'Then tell him to come and see us first!' This was all great news considering that I was out of work as of May 1988. As a human resource, retired footballers are not necessarily the most sought after commodity. Yet, I was being offered a chance to get my foot in the door of a sportscasting career. Could mullet still be jumping into my boat?

Perhaps the toughest part about going home was that Faye's story, which had stayed under wraps until now, was almost certain to break. Quite a few English journalists were aware of the story and were anxious to run with it, particularly in the wake of a series of gassing accidents involving British tourists in Mediterranean countries. To compound the problem, Liverpool had put me under considerable pressure to reverse my retirement decision and return to see out the final year of my contract. In this atmosphere of strained negotiations I had been at pains to outline the exact situation in Australia where my parents' lives had been turned upside down since they had taken on the awesome responsibility of Faye's rehabilitation plus the parenting of their grandchild Jamillah. With that much flak around the story was bound to get out, and it did, with the result that the news organisations beat a path to my parents' door in bushy Cooranbong, one of the quietest backwaters in the Lake Macquarie area. The glare of publicity placed my family under pressure they could well have done without, and I regret that. But at least it gave us the opportunity to publicise the plight of the many brain-damage victims whose care and rehabilitation have been taken on by their loved ones without recognition or support from governments or the medical establishment.

Our homecoming meant that we would have to find a place to live. Unsure of what the future would hold as far as my career prospects were concerned, Jenny and I bought a home on top of the hill overlooking the lake where we used to walk together as childhood sweethearts sharing each other's dreams. It was only a short drive to Jenny's parents' home and not far at all from Cooranbong. It looked a great place to sit down for a while and watch the kids grow. Meanwhile, I kept in touch with Liverpool FC via Bruce and Barnesy. At first, it distressed me to read that my departure had strained my relationship with Kenny Dalglish, as this was never so. Later, I ceased to worry about it, especially after resuming contact with Kenny and discovering that our mutual respect was as strong as ever.

Liverpool will always be a part of me although my role these days is little more glorious than that of the long distance fan. Few extracted more delight from LFC's courageous revival in 1988–89 than an ex-Anfield midfielder watching from the other side of the world.

If cracking it as a pro footballer looked a tough hurdle, becoming a proficient sportscaster was every bit as daunting. Like that ignorant teenager who went to Middlesbrough, I suddenly found myself the artless newcomer in a challenging world peopled by talented individuals. I figured, however, that if I could muster that same walk-through-walls commitment that helped me come to grips with the pro soccer scene, I just might establish a solid future in the next phase of my working life.

Regrets? Yes, I have loads of regrets. I've no doubt that I never realised my full potential as a footballer. And that's possibly the biggest. I've made a ton of mistakes and I've learned from them, too. But, by the same token, I've had more than my share of blessings. If Liverpool had sued me and I'd lost all my financial gains, I'd still be a millionaire by virtue of the wealth of memories and experiences harvested from a fortunate

Working for Channel Nine's 'Wide World of Sport'

Skateboarding with a friend

career. I walked away comfortable in the knowledge that I don't owe anybody a thing. My allegiance now is to my family and on that score I've been lucky to have the best any man could wish for. As I finish writing this chapter of my life I think that maybe some other kid might extract some value from what I've learned. Whether the book sells or not is not important to me. What does matter is that a boy from Lake Macquarie scored at Wembley. That, in itself, might inspire others with seemingly unattainable dreams to reach their own goals.

GOING BACK CHAPTER 12

erseyside called me back sooner than expected. On Sunday, 16 April 1989, Australia awoke to the news of a tragedy in England. The story led all bulletins. More than ninety fans — Liverpool fans — had died in a crowd crush at Hillsborough within minutes of the kick-off to the FA Cup semi-final against Nottingham Forest. On call for the Nine Network, I was in Sydney when Jenny phoned to wake me with the news. For some reason I'd felt nervous and edgy all through the night and hadn't slept well. Something was gnawing at me. Trouble in the family? I didn't know.

Jenny's first words were; 'Something terrible has happened!' I immediately thought of our own kids. 'Craig, there's been crowd trouble at the football in Sheffield,' Jenny continued. 'The reports are saying that more than ninety Liverpool fans are dead and the toll is expected to rise!'

The radio reports confirmed the news. Still, I couldn't believe it. I phoned my old mate Colin Bridge in Liverpool. Bridgey came on the phone, his voice breaking with emotion. No, it wasn't hooliganism, he said. It was a crowd crush. Bridgey sobbed uncontrollably as he told me how his former business partner had taken his two teenage sons and daughter to the game. One of the boys had died in the crush. Neither Colin nor his family had gone to the game but, like almost everybody in Liverpool, they knew of somebody directly involved in the disaster. The magnitude of the tragedy had cast its shadow over every street and home on Merseyside.

On the other side of the world, the news seemed unreal, too awful, too momentous to grasp. I couldn't comprehend it. Not even when my boss at the Nine Network phoned to say that I'd have to comment on the disaster. Still unable to absorb what had happened, I told him I couldn't do it. Instead, I went to the studio and watched transfixed as the satellite feeds from the numerous news sources transmitted footage of the horror and its aftermath onto the banks of monitors.

As the unofficial Australian ambassador for all things relating to Liverpool, I was targeted by the media for comment. Still unable to fathom exactly why and what had happened, I spent time on the phone to John Barnes and Bruce Grobbelaar, piecing together the tragic minutes on either side of 3 p.m. on 15 April. Now it was clear to me; I could see it all and I was rocked to the core. Nine demanded that I make a comment, pointing out that if it had been a motor sport disaster either Barry Sheene or Alan Jones would be required to file. As it was soccer, they said, it was my duty. That's what they were paying me for. So, I fulfilled my professional duty then jumped in the car and headed up the coast for a surf — anything to get away from the television monitors and telephones, away from the horror.

Out there in the surf, alone with my thoughts, I tried to shut out the horrifying images I'd seen on the monitors. What had gone wrong at Sheffield? Looking down at my surfboard with the water sluicing gently over the deck, my eyes fell on the logo that set it apart from every other board. It was the red and gold crest of Liverpool Football Club. I knew then that I had to return to England.

Bridgey collected me from Manchester airport at 6 a.m. on Wednesday, 19 April. My departure from Australia had been hasty but I'd managed to fulfil three important tasks before boarding the jet. I'd received at least five calls from Scousers, both Liverpudlians and Evertonians, all feeling as I did — far away and helpless. So, at their suggestion, we rounded up my collection of football gear and memorabilia plus my surfboard with the liver bird logo and passed it on to the Australian branch of the Liverpool Supporters Club to aid the Hillsborough Disaster Fund. When I returned to Australia I would learn that the Aussie fund had poured tens of thousands of dollars into the appeal. They had raised some $60 000 at a charity auction in Sydney. The surfboard alone fetched more than $5000 and the purchasers promptly donated it back for forwarding on to Anfield.

The second task was to grab a copy of a book called *The catastrophe of coma — a way back* by Ted Freeman, a pioneering authority on the rehabilitation of the victims of brain damage. I knew that the dead were not the only casualties, that there would be coma victims as well. Because of the nature of the incident, I knew that there would be an awful lot who would have suffered neurological damage as a result of almost suffocating in the crush. From my own family's experience with Faye's accident and with the help of Ted Freeman's book, I felt I could offer the one thing that the families of the brain damaged casualties would need most: hope.

My last act before grabbing a cab to Sydney airport was to phone Kenny Dalglish and tell him I was on my way. Whatever differences I'd had with the Anfield management over my untimely retirement no longer mattered. During that week, nothing else mattered.

When I arrived at Anfield, I headed straight for Kenny's office. His reception was one of warmth and gratitude. He was genuinely glad to see me. 'Thanks for coming,' he said. 'So many people in this town need so much help.'

'By the way,' he continued, reaching into his drawer, 'this is for you.' In his hand was my 1987–88 League Championship medal from my final season. 'You forgot to take it when you left.'

My next call was to the home of Les Steele, Bridgey's former business partner. The sense of grief and loss within that house was palpable. My heart almost broke on meeting the surviving son who couldn't understand why fate had chosen him to survive while his brother had died. They had both been altar boys at their local church and were as close as brothers could be. Yet, as I'd witnessed before in times of tragedy, the attitude of the bereaved alternated from despair to determined good humour. Even in the midst of their terrible loss they could still share a few jokes at Everton's expense. Such is the nature and character of these people I had grown to so admire. They struck me as a religious family and I could see that they had the strength to carry each other through the crisis.

Borrowing Bridgey's car, I made the journey alone to Sheffield. In light of what had happened just four days before, access to the ground was not permitted. But an official recognised me and I was waved through. My previous visit to Hillsborough had been under happier circumstances almost exactly a year before. We'd beaten Sheffield Wednesday 5–1 and I'd scored twice. The ground had been nearly full and the Wednesday fans had stood to applaud our performance. Now Hillsborough, draped in floral tributes and red scarves, was a silent and eerie reminder of the carnage of the previous Saturday. On the terraces where many of the Koppites had died, barriers and fencing designed to withstand tonnes of pressure were bent and twisted like copper wire. I looked at the devastation and thought of the fans trapped in that awful crush.

The Hillsborough players' lounge had been set up as a counselling room for the families of victims arriving from Liverpool. As I entered, I was immediately enveloped by the grief of those left to mourn. Some I recognised as Anfield regulars, others were strangers, but they greeted me as one and we wept together.

In the company of a social worker I went to nearby Hallamshire Hospital where some of the injured had been taken. Again, I witnessed remarkable spirit and courage. The families had nothing but praise for the players who, I was told, had visited earlier in the week and had spent so much time delivering words of encouragement to the injured, comforting the families and talking to the coma victims. Since the players' visit, three or four of those suspected of suffering brain damage had emerged from their comas. One victim had miraculously come to on hearing Kenny Dalglish speak to him. Another, on regaining consciousness, had immediately asked, 'How did Everton get on?'

'Cozza' was one of the teenagers whose face had appeared on page one of newspapers the world over. He was right against the fence when the crush started and must have experienced literally tonnes of pressure as he was sandwiched between the steel mesh and the terrible weight pressing against him. Cozza didn't die but when I saw him in Hallamshire he was still in a coma. His dad, sitting by the bedside, held up a newspaper and there, in full colour amid the horror, was Cozza, his face shockingly contorted and turning blue through lack of oxygen.

'That's our Cozza,' said the father, pointing at the page, 'the one with the blue face.' Then, turning to the inert figure on the bed, he said; 'Look, Cozza, Craig Johnston's come all the way from Australia to see you. C'mon lad, open your eyes and look at him!'

The same newspaper photo showed two teenage girls trapped helplessly, their faces masks of agony and resignation as the life was crushed from their bodies. What had happened to them?

'They're both dead,' somebody said.

At this news, I broke down and wept. I had known those two kids, yet I had not known them. Every day after training they had been familiar faces at Anfield, just two polite, bright teenagers, ever present but never intrusive. Each day I'd sweep past them without much more than a smile and a cursory nod, never taking the time to really say 'hello' or find out their names. Now they were gone. I felt angry with myself and consumed with guilt that I had taken their faith and support so much for granted.

My mind was reeling when I left that hospital. Tired and confused I returned to my parking spot at Hillsborough but couldn't find my car. After searching fruitlessly, I reported it to the police giving them a description of a white Ford Falcon sedan. Two hours later, I realised why they had looked at me sideways. No such model exists in England. So stupefied was I by the flight and the day's events, I'd given them the description

A tribute to the dead – the Anfield pitch transformed into a sea of scarves and flowers

of my car back home in Australia! Late that night, after locating Bridgey's car, I attempted to drive back to Liverpool. Emotionally drained and with my body clock dangerously out of synch, I found it impossible to keep my eyes open. I pulled into a lay-by and almost instantly fell asleep.

All that week people instinctively made a pilgrimage to Anfield and queued for up to five hours to lay their most prized footballing and personal mementos on the Kop and the field itself. Bill Shankly's widow, Nessie, queued for three hours and was near the head of the line when ground staff were compelled to close the gates for the night. Rather than step forward and identify herself, this lovely lady — the widow of Liverpool's greatest servant — quietly went home and returned the next day to queue for another two hours.

The players' lounge, one of Anfield's inner sanctums, became a refuge for the families of the victims. Rather than stay at home, in between funerals the players joined them there. The magnitude of the tragedy became apparent as we met bewildered kids who had lost their fathers, grieving mothers clutching photos of dead sons, and youngsters mourning the loss of a brother or sister. It was touching to witness the gratitude of the families. A woman who had lost her husband remarked that she felt warm and close to him when she was at Anfield. A little tot, not old enough to comprehend that her dad was gone for good, lifted up her sweater to show me the brand new Liverpool shirt she was wearing underneath. Looking around the lounge at the sight of the lads sharing the heartache with the families, a grieving relative said wistfully, 'I just wish our lad could have been here to see this!' By this, she meant the love and the care the players displayed for the families in their hour of need.

No one did more than Kenny and Marina Dalglish. In his inimitable style the Liverpool boss displayed the perfect touch for each occasion. To many, he seems devoid of emotion, yet, deep down, Kenny is a man of compassion and wit and these two traits shone through as he moved among the bereaved. I saw people who had cause to believe that they would never smile again actually laughing in response to the Boss's optimistic good humour.

Perhaps the most remarkable impression from that scene in the players' lounge was the concern of the families for the welfare of the players and their wives. Many of the latter had sat helplessly in the stands only a few feet above the terraces while the tragedy had unfolded before their eyes. As John Barnes pointed out to us, out of those players' lounge sessions emerged a new realisation of the relationship between footballer and fan. Until the players spoke to the bereaved, they hadn't realised the huge stakes they'd been playing for. In Liverpool, football is the one thing that so many people have clung to as the source of communal pride. That devotion would claim ninety-six lives. It would be a normal human reaction for the bereaved families to be repelled by the very thought of football, yet instead the game was the one thing that gave them hope and inspiration for the future. The footballer was the focus and embodiment of that hope. It was a shock to the players to be so embraced by the supporters.

Not for the first time did I hear how important it was to the bereaved and the injured that the team rally to do Liverpool proud. The few remaining matches for that season would stand as a memorial to those who died at Hillsborough. The record shows that the players, mindful of who and what they represented, did their bit. With a mixture of sadness and respect I thought of Shankly's famous words in response to the question of whether football was a matter of life and death. How prophetic they had been.

In the players' lounge one day, a hand on my arm drew me aside and I turned to see one of the churchmen who had brought comfort to the mourners. 'There are two kids I'd like you to talk to,' he said. 'I think they need it.'

He led me to a small lounge, and I knelt on the floor to be on the same level as the two forlorn figures seated on the couch. I was transfixed by the sight that met my eyes. I was looking straight at the face of one of the girls who had appeared on the front page and who just about everybody assumed was dead. And there beside her was her mate.

'You're not dead, you're not dead!' I shouted and immediately shed tears of joy.

Embarrassed at the sight of a footballer weeping at their expense, Debbie and Lisa (I now knew their names) told how their families had received condolence calls from friends who had assumed the girls had not survived. The pair had reluctantly agreed to an interview with the Liverpool Echo to assure friends and relatives they were alive. To their profound embarrassment, the world's press seized on the story, dubbing their escape 'The Miracle of Hillsborough'.

The girls begged me to take them back to Sheffield. Although carrying their own injuries, they wanted to help people worse off than themselves. Just the sight of them walking into the hospital ward instantly boosted morale. To me, Debbie and Lisa represented not only the spirit of the Kop, but the humanity of Merseysiders.

Drawing on advice from Ted Freeman's book, the lads had got together to make some tapes to play to the coma victims. The techniques differ according to the extent of the brain damage. Some require almost gentle persuasion while others call for something sterner. For example, we had hard man Steve McMahon barking in his strong Scouse accent, 'C'mon ya great lump; ya can't stay in bed all day. Get off ya back and come out with us for a pint!' Or John Aldridge saying, 'C'mon lad, out of bed. Put your boots on and 'ave a game with the lads!' In contrast there was Jocky Hansen pleading in his soft Scots accent, 'C'mon, son. For God's sake, give us a sign. Try and open your eyes or move your fingers for us. We're all with you.' Knowing how much the team meant to the injured fans, our theory was that the sound of the players' voices just might help break the spell of the coma. The tapes were very well received by the doctors at Hallamshire and Sheffield General hospitals. A week after the disaster there were still eight people in intensive care suffering the after-effects of near-suffocation. I'd like to think that maybe the tapes helped people like Gillian Edwards, a teenager who reminded me so much of Faye and who, like my sister, was fighting the battle to beat her injuries.

It was a week of funerals, a week of overwhelming emotion, and it was a week that united Merseyside as never before. The barrier of rivalry that for so long had existed between Liverpool and Everton fell away as the supporters of both clubs joined hearts and hands to mark the terrible loss that had befallen the city. As an outsider, I felt intensely proud to have been part of that community, never more so than during the emotion-charged memorial service at Anfield on the Saturday when I joined my former team-mates on the field. Peter Robinson, the Liverpool chief executive, had sought me out and asked me specifically if I would like to go on the field with the official Liverpool party. I felt honoured.

At 3.06 a minute's silence was observed in respect for those who hadn't made it home from Hillsborough the week before. Merseyside came to a halt as did the cities of Sheffield and Nottingham. Inside Anfield, where the stands customarily reverberate to the chants of the Kop, I could hear nothing save the quiet sobbing of the players either side of me. It was raining. Standing there in the middle of the pitch, now a sea of flowers, contemplating an empty Kop draped in the scarves of fans, the sadness was overpowering. As the brass band broke into the opening strain of 'You'll Never Walk Alone', I looked up into the rain. The sun was doing its best to break through the cloud cover. Needing a reason to believe, I felt sure that the ninety-six were shining down on the scene below. Summer was on the way and the most remarkable season in the history of football's most remarkable club was nearing its end.

After scrutinising all the televised reports, including footage too horrific to go to air, after speaking to no less than a hundred people who were on the spot, policemen and stewards who were on duty that day, I have my thoughts about what went wrong on Saturday, 15 April 1989. Footballers are professionals paid to turn up at 3 p.m. on Saturday and do their best. The fan's role is to scrape up enough money to be able to afford to support his team, home or away, as often as possible. The administrator's job is to make sure that the organisational side runs to plan. The police, too, have a role to perform at football matches. At times it is exceedingly difficult, but they're professionals and they understand that that's what they're paid to do. With the aid of the stewards, they're on hand to ensure that 40 000 people enjoy the match in an orderly fashion.

I'm not saying that there weren't fans there without tickets and that some supporters didn't stop off for a beer on the way. After having watched almost all the available television footage, including plenty that newspaper reporters haven't seen, I'm convinced that what took place at Hillsborough wasn't due to drunkenness or hooliganism. Nobody should lose sight of the fact that at exactly the same time that people were dying at the Liverpool versus Nottingham Forest match, not two hours away at Villa Park the same size crowd of the same Merseyside stock was enjoying the other semi-final between Everton and Norwich. What was the difference?

No words can say more about the irrepressible resilience and character of Liverpool Football Club than the fact that between 15 April and 26 May it emerged from the devastation of Hillsborough to win the FA Cup Final and be dramatically pipped by Arsenal for the League Championship. In going so close to collecting the

'Hey mate, did I ever tell you about when I scored the winner at Highbury in 1980...?'

elusive Double again, LFC provided a fitting tribute to the memory of the fans who died while supporting their team.

As a studio commentator back home in Australia, I watched that dramatic Cup Final between the two great Merseyside clubs, suspecting then that the events of the past few weeks had left an indelible stamp on my attitudes. Whatever I've done in my life, I've always tried to live by a basic set of rules because that's the way my parents raised me. I said my prayers and went to church on Sunday. For a while there I was even reading the sermon but I thought that was a bit hypocritical because, after all, I'm no saint. Before every game I'd deliver up a prayer asking that I not hurt anyone and not suffer an injury myself. My philosophy was that if I ever came a cropper in football or life it was because I hadn't lived righteously enough. I'd have no cause for complaint.

Whatever my actions, I've genuinely cared about the society in which we live and what we plan to leave behind for our kids. One of the lessons of that post-Hillsborough week was that, while football is a glamorous business, this world is full of self-effacing people, anonymous types who do what they can for others, and nobody stands up at three o'clock on a Saturday afternoon and gives them a round of applause. They're humble folk but heroes in their own right. Those of us who've spent our lives in the limelight have lots to learn from them.

One day during the week after the Hillsborough tragedy, I was driving to Anfield when I found myself near Joe Fagan's house. I had an overwhelming urge to knock on his door and say, 'Joe, I'm truly sorry about all the aggravation that existed between us. You were right, the game is not about me.' But I didn't stop and say it. Instead, I'm saying it in this book.

Football has provided me with a life and a persona, but now that chapter is finished. If I can apply the lessons of that experience for the betterment of my family and those around me, then it will have been worth the struggle. There's another chapter just beginning, and I'm looking forward to it.

Nowadays, instead of playing football, I go surfing. It's a return to one of my great boyhood loves and the perfect physical outlet for a former pro sportsman who might easily turn to flab if he didn't find something to keep him in shape. I surf in summer when the waves are gentle and the water warm. And I surf in winter when the water is colder but the waves are more powerful and have better shape. Sometimes, when driving home from an early Saturday morning surf, I'll spot a junior soccer game in progress at a neighbourhood ground. Pulling over, I'll sit and watch for a while, looking for the talented player, appreciating the joy with which the youngsters approach the game oblivious to parents, coaches or other external pressures. But I never stay too long. The scene is too likely to stir memories best left dormant. Before those feelings have a chance to surface, I slip the car back into gear and quietly drive away.

POST SCRIPT

A good many years have passed since the preceding account of Walk Alone first appeared on book shelves. Since then fish have continued to jump in and out of my boat. Today, I am the father of four girls – Chelsea, Cassie, Harley and Bonnie. Sadly, my marriage to their mum Jenny didn't survive yet we remain on the very best of terms.

As for the rest of the Johnston clan, we lost my elder sister Charmaine to cancer at 40 years of age. Faye survived her ordeal but unfortunately there would be no miracle cure to her profound brain injury. In November 2012 my Dad and greatest fan, Colin 'Bruno' Johnston retired to the great goalmouth in the sky leaving Mum to continue in her indomitable way.

At times, I regretted my decision to retire from football at 27 years of age, to help look after Faye, yet I resisted any urge to make a comeback. My television career was brief, overtaken by an idea to develop a better football boot. The result was the Craig Johnston-patented and adidas-built Predator. To this day, it is the world's best selling football boot.

Australia's grand return to the World Cup stage for the 2006 finals in Germany was the cause for tremendous pride in this ex-footballer's heart but also caused me to ponder the circumstances that meant I was never destined to wear the green and gold of my country. I was truly sad that I could never be a member of that proud club of ex-Socceroos. But, in 2009, that wound was healed in part by a beautiful gesture courtesy of the Australian Professional Footballers Association in naming me as the third recipient of the Alex Tobin Medal for services to the game. On hand were some of Australia's golden generation including Mark Schwarzer, Tim Cahill and Harry Kewell who spoke of how I had inspired their own ambitions. It was a truly humbling occasion.

Today, I spend much of the year in the UK and Florida with my partner Vivienne Lewis but return to Australia on a regular basis to remind myself of the path that took me from gumtree-lined parks to the hallowed turf of Anfield.

My burning passion has always been youth development –a quest to unlock the secrets of the great game for all those bright-eyed kids with mud on their knees and stars in their eyes. Kids who remind me of me, all those years ago.

I dream that one day Australia will win the World Cup with a generation of players who learned as I learned. After all, the secrets and methodologies are still the same.

Maybe Neil Jameson and I should have called the book Walk Alone - Part 1. Watch this space.

Lightning Source UK Ltd.
Milton Keynes UK
UKHW051052230621
386021UK00007B/1073